Journey of the Heart

Journey of the Heart
A true story of A Southern Belle in the "Wild West"

ISBN-0-9735467-0-0
Printed in Canada, July, 2004

Books Available From:

SINGING WINDS BOOKSHOP
Box 2197
Benson, Arizona
85602
(520) 586-2425

or the publisher:

GRAYTWEST BOOKS
Box 835
Markerville, Alberta
T0M 1M0
janegray@telus.net

Cover photo: Mamie and Epifanio Aguirre.
Background: Aguirre Peak, Arizona, named for Epifanio Aguirre.

Journey of the Heart

The true story of Mamie Aguirre (1844-1906)
A Southern Belle in the "Wild West"

Annette

Annette Gray

Those girlish footprints in the sands of time
Erase the cruelty of man and beast,
Cradle the gentleness of southern winds
Turn desert harshness into modern feast.
                              (annette gray)

Table of Contents

Foreword

Some of my earliest childhood recollections are the stories my father, Pedro Joab Aguirre, told me about my great-grandmother, Mamie Bernard Aguirre. He told of her travels on the Santa Fe Trail and her adventures in the Southwest. Even as a child these adventures made history come alive for me. In my travels, from childhood to adulthood, Mamie and her stories have always been with me, and perhaps they seemed even more real to me because we were fortunate enough to have an old trunk filled with her treasured memories. Like Mamie, her journals and loving remembrances have traveled many miles over the last six generation of our Aguirre family.

Among the treasures she saved for us was a christening gown that was made for her first born, my grandfather, who was also named Pedro Joab Aguirre. This wonderful gown was first worn in Mesilla, New Mexico, in 1864, and was recently worn in Mesa, Arizona, by Mamie's great-great-great-granddaughter when she was baptized.

Over the years I have enjoyed sharing Mamie's adventures with family and friends. It pleased me whenever I found articles about Mamie in newspapers, books and historical reviews. Yet none of these bits and pieces had been put together to tell Mamie's full story until *Journey of The Heart* was written.

In Mamie's journal she tells us, "I have been a traveler all of my life." How appropriate it is that author Annette Gray, another traveler, should find these bits and pieces of Mamie's story and, with much research added, weave them together to make history come alive for the reader.

Rowene Medina Aguirre

Explanations and Acknowledgments

In the aftermath of September 11, 2001, we look back at what we, in the twenty-first century, perceive to be one of America's greatest tragedies. And so it is! Our heart bleeds for the families who lost loved ones—for those whose lives were changed forever in the blink of an eye. We are shaken, appalled, grieved! And for many of us, September eleventh has triggered a new understanding of American history. It has made us realize the devastating effect an earlier national tragedy had on the American people; it has put the Civil War into perspective, so to speak.

On September eleventh less than three thousand souls were lost. Yet, during the Civil War, there were six-hundred and twenty-thousand casualties. The South lost one quarter of her men of military age. Statistics such as these boggle the mind as we try to imagine the magnitude of that dreadful civil uprising and how it touched the lives of so many Americans. Our ancestors were not merely watching an event on television, they were living day by day with the terrible consequences of distrust and hate.

The book you are about to read is not a figment of imagination. It is the story of a real woman, a prim and proper Southern Belle. Her family was wealthy enough to send her to a young ladies' finishing school in Maryland. At sixteen, she returned home to Missouri—finely groomed—and no doubt expecting to become the wife of a prestigious Southern gentleman. Then the Civil War broke out, inciting waves of terrorism along the Kansas-Missouri border and, similar to 9-11, the lives of civilians caught up in these hideous events were changed forever.

Admittedly I never intended to write about any aspect of the Civil War, nor those who fled from it to the untamed West. However, I stumbled across a picture of Mary (Mamie) Aguirre in *Echoes of the Conquistadors*, a family history written by Yginio Aguirre. There was something about the young woman in the photograph that I found intriguing. "Here is a woman with character," I told myself. Anxious to learn more about her, I searched for "her book," only to find Mamie's complete biography had never been written. As I visited archives, read journals and listened to stories told by Mamie's family, it struck me that her story must be told in book form. We who live in this century need to know there were Americans like Mamie who experienced tragedies yet never abandoned hope. We need to know that mule trains, stage coaches and ambushes were not invented by Hollywood or television—that folks actually lived through very difficult times. We need to understand that love, hope and forgiveness are as important today as when Mamie first practiced these virtues over a hundred years ago.

Her name was linked with many legendary heroes and heroines; she taught the daughter of Larcena Pennington Page and played a part in the well-known Pennington-Page history. She was acquainted with Jesse James, Cole Younger, Wyatt Earp and Geronimo. These now famous men were her contemporaries, and her story sheds new light on their exploits as well as lending credence to Mamie as an historic figure.

Mamie's natural optimism was an inspiration to her family, friends, neighbors and the students she taught. This same cheerful philosophy enabled her to successfully bridge the gap between the Mexican and Anglo-American people of her day. As a victim of Apache raids, she bore no grudges, but learned all she could about the native culture and took a delight in collecting baskets made by Apache people. Her non-prejudicial outlook also won the affection of a former slave, an Afro-American, who spent his final days with Mamie and her family in Arizona.

I would like to thank all those who helped me collect the data for this book. Among the many helpful folks, I would like to give specific thanks to the staff at the Arizona Historical Society, Tucson; Peggy Smith and the Westport Historical Society, Missouri; Jennifer Parker of the WHMC-Kansas City, the Rio Grande Historic Collection, New Mexico, and the great folks at the Enoch Pratt Free Library Periodicals Dept., City of Baltimore. Special thanks go to members of Mamie's family: Rowene Aguirre Medina and Andra Aguirre, her great-granddaughters, and her grand-nephew, Yginio Aguirre. Thanks also to my editor, Karla French; proofreaders, Joan Beaudin,Elaine Rutschke and Kathleen Raines; photo designer, Shirley Dye; historians, Mary Kasulaitis; helpers, Delores Cannon, Bruce and Karen Buchanan, Caco Elias, Eleanor Bernard and Mary Aguirre-Vogler. Other Arizona contributors include Winifred Bundy of the Singing Wind Bookshop, Benson, and the staff of the Buenos Aires National Wildlife Refuge, Sasabe, Arizona. Without their help, and the tremendous support from my friends and husband, Dennis, *Journey of the Heart* could not have been written.

In compiling Mamie's story, I have included excerpts from actual conversations—precious stories passed down from one generation to the next. The dialogue has been carefully chosen to enhance the realism of the story without deviating from the truth, or as near the truth as records and memories allow. It is not my intention to critique the American Civil War, but capture pictures of the times as seen through Mamie's eyes.

Where possible, I have traveled in Mamie's footsteps and lingered in the spots which held special meaning for her. On a warm, but windy day, I stood (as Mamie had done), in the parade area of Fort Union, New Mexico. The actual barracks are long gone; the once homey fireplaces, which over a century ago held family pictures on their mantels, are fast crumbling away. Yet, I fancied I could hear the wheels of don Epifanio Aguirre's huge freight wagons creaking up to the fort's warehouse, could hear the women of the fort welcoming Mamie into their parlors for a cup of tea.

Later, I toured rural areas where Mamie taught school. I also visited the beautiful Tucson home she shared with her brother, and spent a month at her favorite haunt, the old Las Ruinas Ranch in Arivaca. As a result I am hopeful the reader will see, not only a dedicated teacher, mother and friend in this story, but the changing face of the American west. Yes, all that has shaped the grand states we admire today.

Introduction

Mrs. Gray has had to dig deep in history to uncover the life story of Mrs. Mary (Bernard) Aguirre.

As a young belle of eighteen, Mary Bernard married don Epifanio Aguirre in 1862, a freighter who conducted an extensive freighting business in the West. Later, she made various trips with her husband on the Santa Fe Trail to Las Cruces, New Mexico.

After a heavy loss, due to Indian attacks in New Mexico, don Epifanio decided to visit his brother, don Pedro, in Altar, Sonora, Mexico, where both had a store.

While making a trip to Tucson by stage coach in 1870, the stage was attacked by Apaches and don Epifanio was killed, leaving his wife, Mary, and three young sons. In the years that followed, Mary suffered many setbacks and had many interesting adventures.

Readers who enjoy history, will enjoy this book.

Yginio Aguirre
(grandnephew of don Epifanio Aguirre)

MAMIE'S FAMILY TREE
****

1st generation in America: John Bernard emigrated from Gascony, France about 1720

2nd generation: John Bernard II (Nov. 16, 1736 - Jan. 15, 1824)

3rd generation: Allen Bernard (Jan. 29, 1763 - April 1, 1851)

4th generation: Joab Bernard and wife, Arabella Mather Bier (descendent of John Cunningham Scottish Earl)
(Born: July 12,1800) (Born: Dec. 18, 1816)
(Died: April 30, 1879) (Died: Nov. 12, 1899)

1	2	3	4	5	6	7	8
Margaret Jane	Catherine Comfort	Mary (MAMIE) Bier	Annie Marcella	Jesse Gliencairn	Arabella Wilson	Noah Worthington	Allan Cunningham
(Andrew Johnson)	(Rezin Worthington)	(Epifanio Aguirre)	(Phidelah Rice)	(Thadeus Byrne)	(unmarried)	(Amy Price)	(Min Chouteau)
(Nov. 14, 1840)	(.....1842)	(June 23,1844)	(June 17, 1848)	(June 5, 1850)	(Dec. 17, 1851)	(Jan. 4, 1854)	(Feb 11,1859)
(Mar. 30, 1920)	(Sept. 28, 1863)	(May 24, 1906)	(Dec. 26, 1931)	(July 29, 1902)	(Jan. 27, 1868)	(Mar. 23,1907)	(July 4, 1930)

1	2	3
Pedro Joab Aguirre	Epifanio (Jr.) Aguirre	Stephen B Aguirre
(Wife: Lucy)		(Wife: Willie Sneed)
(June 26, 1863)	(May 12, 1865)	(Feb. 4, 1867)
(Aug 2, 1907)	(Aug 27, 1878)	(July 21, 1926)

Pedro Joab Aguirre

1	2	3
Jean	Andra	Rowene

1	2	3	4
Stephen Epifanio	Benjamin Sneed	Helen Bernard	William Monroe

Westport relatives (relevant to Mamie Bernard's biography)

Thomas Bernard (brother of Mamie's father, Joab)
(July 15, 1792 - Aug. 28, 1866)

1	2	3	4	5	6	7
Anne	Emily	Cornelia (Hamilton) (1822 - 1912) ....(Cornelia married James Hamilton)	Cousin William R. Bernard (1823-1907) Cousin William married Susan Simpson Harris	James	Ellen	Cousin Joab (Joe) (1832 - 1889)

James Hamilton's sister married Albert Boone, grandson of Daniel Boone)
Albert's daughter Eliza Boone was the second wife of Henry Jones
Dory Jones (Henry's son by a first wife)

****

John Harris (1798 - 1874) wife Harriet Simpson (sister of Duke Simpson, who lived next door to Mamie)

1	2	3	4	5	6	7	8
Sarah Harris (wife of Peter Behan) Mother of Johnny Behan	Susan (wife of Wm. Bernard)	Josephine (wife of Charles Kearney)					

don Epifanio's Family Tree
****

In the 1600s a number of Aguirres moved to America, "New Spain."
Some became miners, lawyers, presidio soldiers, land owners and governors of Chihuahua.
The following chart depicts Epifanio Aguirre's new world ancestry
1st generation: Captain Joseph de Aguirre (Came to New Spain in 1699)

2nd: don Juan Miguel de Aguirre (Born in Sonora, Mexico, in 1715)

3rd: don Barolome de Aguirre (wife, doña Andrea Colomo)

4th: don Juan Antonio Aguirre (wife doña Valle)

5th: *don Pedro Jose Ygnacio Aguirre* (1805-1865) (first wife doña Ana Maria Redondo)

6th generation: 1	2	3	4	5	6	7
Felicita	**Epifanio,**	Pedro,	Conrado,	Beatris,	Guadalupe,	Yjinio
(born 1832)	(1834-1870)	(1835-1907)	(1836-1889)	(born 1838)	(born 1842)	(1844-1907)

don Pedro Jose Ygnacio Aguirre's children (second wife, doña Narcisa *Ornelas*)

1	2	3	4	5
Dolores	Patrosinia	Emilia	Feliberto	Mariano
(born 1851)	(born 1853)	(born 1855)	(born 1858)	(born 1861)

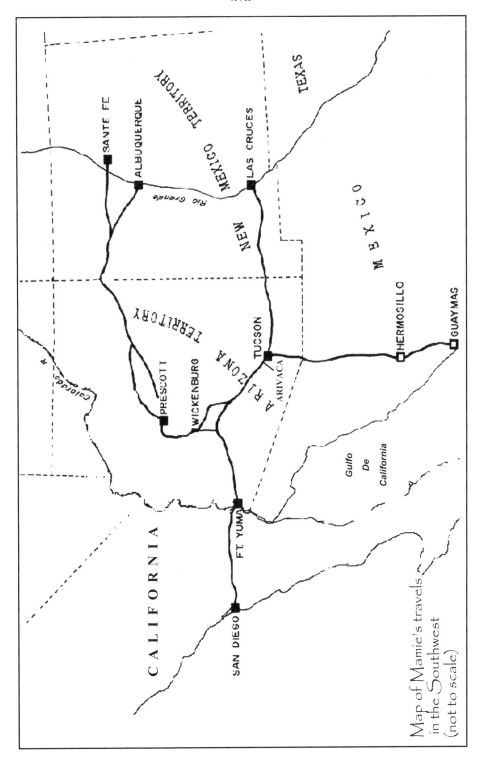

Map of Mamie's travels in the Southwest (not to scale)

Chapter One—In The Beginning

> "I was born in St. Louis, Missouri, in 1844, which year was made famous by the greatest overflow ever known before or since. I have heard my mother say the river at St. Louis was ten miles across and no end of people were left homeless by the floods..."
> Mary (Mamie) Bier Aguirre

That was how Mamie's life began, with pelting rain and muddy water surging across the countryside, destroying everything in its path, drowning livestock and sweeping away homes which had previously sat in blissful serenity along the banks of the Missouri River. It was a disaster of unimaginable proportions, and one which Mamie believed influenced her own stormy life.

When Mamie was born on June 23, 1844, her parents, Joab and Arabella Bernard, were living in St. Louis, Missouri, which was then a very small town; the streets were narrow and muddy and there was no gas or city water.[1] Yet the Bernards were reasonably well-off by the standards of the day. Joab was working in the mercantile business with a longtime friend, John Roe, and Arabella had servants to help care for the children: four-year-old Margaret, two-year-old Catherine and the baby, Mamie.

Joab's initial reaction to Mamie's birth was one of disappointment. At forty-four years old, he had three small daughters and no male heir to carry his name, and, being a gentleman of significant social stature, the continuation of lineage was extremely important.

All the same, Joab was thankful Arabella and this rather fragile looking infant had survived the birth. His first two wives and daughter had not been so lucky, and the mere thought of losing another wife and child was more than he could bear.

Joab lovingly called his third wife "Bell," a rather frivolous nickname for a pious woman who "adorned herself in modest apparel," as the Good Book decreed. With wire-rimmed glasses and hair severely combed into a bun, she was not a raving beauty, but a woman with common sense and an air of refinement, qualities Joab appreciated. She was accustomed to having servants, knew how to direct their activity and kept her large home in order. She was also a no-nonsense mother who demanded total obedience from her children—a tenacious idealist—who firmly believed her earthly duty was to ensure her family was physically and spiritually nourished and her offspring did nothing to blemish the family's good name.

Having found so capable a partner in Arabella, Joab was free to pursue a variety of interests. He loved to wander and was often away from home for long periods of time, looking for promising businesses to invest in, dabbling in politics, and when called upon he preached in the Methodist Church. With a full head of dark, wavy hair, steady brown eyes and a neatly-trimmed mustache, he could be described as handsome, even debonair when he strode down the street, swinging his gold-topped cane. The cane, a gift from Governor Culpepper of Virginia, was made from the wood of Old Ironsides (the Constitution, a battleship used against Britain in the War of 1812), and it served as a constant reminder to Arabella that her husband may have achieved great things in the world of politics had he set his mind to it.

Soon after Mamie's entrance into the world, Joab and Arabella dutifully made their way to church to christen the new baby "Mary Bier Bernard." From the very beginning she was known as "Mamie," a nickname spelled "Mame" by both friends and family. (For the purpose of this book, we use the familiar spelling to insure correct pronunciation.)

Arabella was not cut out for frontier life. She had been used to more civilized conditions and yearned to go back East, so when Mamie was six months old, the Bernard family moved to Baltimore, Maryland, traveling as far as Wheeling, Virginia, by steamboat, then by stage over the Allegheny Mountains. This was a long arduous journey for a mother with three small children, but Arabella had help. With the family were two black women, which Mamie referred to as "family servants who were part of my mother's wedding gifts from her mother and father."

Arriving in Baltimore in 1845, the Bernards lived on the family estate, sixteen miles from the city of Baltimore at Locust

Grove, on Reisterstown Road in Baltimore County. The estate was landscaped in the style of a Scottish manor and was a real show place with lush green lawns and huge oak trees. This was Arabella's birthplace and she was delighted to return with her three small daughters.

While in Baltimore, Mamie flourished under the doting eyes of her grandparents. She was a tiny child with a sweet disposition, two characteristics she retained throughout her life. In due time the stork brought three more sisters, Ann, Jesse and Arabella. "We were six girls in all," Mamie said, "before the long-awaited brother made his appearance."

Mamie's first brother, Noah, was born January 4, 1854, and needless to say Joab was a very proud man. A son, at last! Similar to Mamie, the little fellow was given a nickname, "None," which family and friends pronounced "Nonie." From the first day Mamie set eyes on her baby brother she loved him and, when he was grown to manhood, he became her dearest confidant and friend.

The new baby was christened "Noah Worthington Bernard," the name "Worthington" given in memory of Joab's first wife, Ann Marcella Worthington. Joab had been particularly fond of Ann, and named three of his and Arabella's children after his late wife. He also maintained a lifelong friendship with Ann's family. However, this link to Joab's past appeared to hold some type of curse, and later we will see how it resulted in another family tragedy.

The next few years, spent in Baltimore, were happy years for Mamie and, from her own telling, represented her "age of innocence," a time when her ultimate pleasure was romping on neatly trimmed grass with her sisters: Margaret, Catherine (Kate), Ann (Nan), Jesse (Sis) and Arabella (Bell). What lovely, summer hours they spent in the garden—six happy little girls—enjoying a game of hide-and-seek or weaving daisy chains and giggling when the sweet-smelling pollen turned their noses yellow. Often the little girls were engrossed in capturing fuzzy caterpillars and collecting stones to drop in a pinafore pocket. Sometimes the girls sprawled contentedly on the lawn, watching clouds and laughing with childish glee when they spotted an imaginary rabbit or kitten in a bright blue sky. Yet, Mamie's favorite activity was swinging on a queer looking swing that hung by two long wooden poles from the branches of an oak tree. Here she would swing for hours, sailing as high as a tiny person could go, her long dark ringlets flying out behind. What wonderful carefree days!

Far too soon it was time to go to school, but for Mamie there was no mathematics, social studies or science. Such challenging subjects were thought to be injurious to the delicate female brain, so Mamie's lessons dealt with reading, writing, memorizing Bible verses and studying music and, at home, she learned to master various kinds of needlework. Every Sunday, Mamie accompanied her family to church, and it was there she was exposed to the Methodist doctrine of "assurance, conversion and holiness." The church stressed that "no wrong temper should be displayed contrary to love; pure love should remain within the soul, and all thoughts, words and deeds must be governed by love."

Joab and Arabella were from affluent Southern stock, and although Joab's family owned no slaves, Arabella's family did. Arabella firmly believed that having servants, black or otherwise, was a God given right. Had not the Bible given instructions on how to manage servants? This being the case, Arabella taught her daughters how to "give orders to the family servants."

Mamie was often reminded of her parents' "blue blood" and encouraged to be proud of her heritage. Arabella was the great-granddaughter of John Cunningham, the last Scottish Earl of Glencairn, while Joab was a descendant of a French nobleman who arrived in America in 1652. In 1812, Joab's people fought against Britain in the War of Independence and, as victors, gained a substantial amount of political recognition. Consequently, Joab, himself, had many prestigious friends, among them fellow Virginian, US President John Tyler. [2]

The first dramatic change in Mamie's young life took place in early 1856 when her father decided to move west, to greener pastures. His elder brother, Tom, had settled on a farm called "Rose Glen" in Callaway County, Missouri, in 1839. The name, "Rose Glen," had an appealing ring to Joab's ears, as did the jingle of gold coins in his brother's pockets.

However, Kansas territory had just begun to open up, so it was Kansas, rather than Missouri, that was drawing new settlers. So, in 1855, Joab joined the throng heading west and staked a claim in Kansas with the intention of opening a trading center. Later, when he returned to his wife and children in Baltimore, he was full of stories of the land of plenty and was determined to move Arabella and the children west. [3]

In retrospect, Mamie envisioned her father in their Baltimore parlor, his shiny boots pacing back and forth, him stopping only long enough to argue with her mother. "Now see here Bell, there's a fortune to be made in the Kansas territory. Trust me! I know what I'm doing. It's perfectly safe for you and the children to accompany me."

Of course Mamie's mother objected to moving. Her roots were buried deep in Baltimore's soil, and she was not about to be pried loose to go into some "ungodly wilderness," but being a good Christian woman, she took it as her duty to obey her husband—most of the time. So, when scolding and cajoling failed, she grudgingly packed her bags and set off to pursue her husband's dream.

Describing their trip, Mamie said, "In April we started our long journey 'out west.' I can well remember hearing Westport being called the 'jumping off place,' having in my mind's eye an immense bank from which one could look down and down into space. Our route was from Baltimore to Wheeling by cars on the B. & O. Railroad. We were then seven children, so moving was no light matter."

Servants went with the family, two black slaves and a white housekeeper and "no end of luggage." There was even a piano included in the household furnishings. If not the first, it was one of the first pianos ever to reach the new frontier. Huge lunch baskets were filled with all sorts of goodies. What fun Mamie had on the train with her small nose pressed against a window, her dark eyes full of wonder as they fixed themselves on an ever-changing scene. There were no sleepers on the train in those days, not even upholstered seats. Falling asleep on a hard wooden seat, then toppling onto an even harder floor was something Mamie never forgot.

Within a day or two, Mamie and her family transferred their belongings from the train to a riverboat. With water frothing and churning around them, Mamie's fear of swift, running water came to the fore, and she held her breath as the boat lifted and heaved above the falls on the Ohio River at Louisville and

Cairo, hung precariously in the swirling foam, then plunged over the rocky edges. By comparison, the rest of the trip seemed tame, and the children settled down to visit with fellow passengers. Later on, Mamie began to enjoy the trip and helped one of the lady passengers. "I had an immense doll," she recalled, " It was as large as a three-month-old baby and a cradle to match. And in this, a woman—a tired mother—rocked her baby to sleep. It was like living at home almost, for it took so long that we became accustomed to the boat and felt at home. Finally we reached Westport Landing. I suppose nearly all the passengers came on the same boat for my cradle was used right along. I remember such lovely rocks on the banks of the Missouri, and how the water looked where the Mississippi and Missouri Rivers met. At last we had reached our journey's end, the end of April 1856. We arrived in the very heat of the pro-slavery war in Kansas, of which my only recollection is seeing people marching at night through the streets with drum and fife and being told they were going to Kansas to fight."

Mamie was only a child, so naturally did not appreciate the significance of people going to fight in Kansas, but the fact remained: the Bernards had come west at a very bad time and were about to witness the worst kind of terrorism.

Oblivious of danger, Joab began working on the project initiated the previous year, that of building a town from the ground up, his very own town, named St. Bernard—after himself. St. Bernard would be a grand town, a major trading center—or so he thought.

He had been appointed postmaster of St. Bernard on March 3, 1855,[4] and by way of promoting his town, he enlisted the help of James Hamilton (Tom Bernard's son-in-law), and two friends, Dr. Herriford and C. Spalding. Designating them as trustees, Joab ran this ad in the March 22 and April 5, 1856, edition of the *Westport Border Times*.

"Notice To All Settlers, St. Bernard, Kansas Territory. The undersigned Trustees for the town company of St. Bernard are authorized to donate lots to anyone, or all persons who may desire to settle in the town, the only conditions imposed being occupancy and improvement. For further information apply to J. M. Bernard, of St. Bernard or J. G. Hamilton or Dr. H. G. Herriford, Westport, Mo. or C.C. Spalding, Kansas City."

Joab's town-building scheme was not without merit. There was a large number of natives in the area, as well as hundreds of new settlers, and they all needed the store and postal service Joab was offering. Another favorable condition was the fact that supplies for the store could be freighted in from the relatives in Westport.

All things being equal, the project may have been a huge success, had it not been for the fact Joab had unwittingly built his new town a scant thirty miles from Osawatomie where John Brown, the famous abolitionist, had recently joined five of his sons. Brown was poised to drive Confederate slave-holders out of Kansas. [5] In other words, Joab was a made-to-order target, for not only was he a Confederate, but his wife was a slave-holder.

Unaware of the threat, Joab hung up his shingle as store-keeper and postmaster, and within a month's time was doing a lively trade with the Sacs, Fox and other native tribes. Business surpassed everyone's expectations. The town was literally a gold mine, and Joab was sure he'd struck it rich.

Then came the dreadful event—the Pottawatomie massacre—the killing, in cold blood, of five Kansas settlers on May 25, 1856, by John Brown's men. News traveled slowly in those days, and Mamie's father was not to learn of the massacre until two days later when a messenger burst into his store with a chilling warning.

"Brown's men are on their way to St. Bernard!"

Chapter Two—A Narrow Escape

Joab's face paled as the messenger relayed the gory details of the Pottawatomie massacre. Armed with broad swords, John Brown's vigilantes had hacked to death five settlers. Considering the settlers were unarmed and had no personal grievance with Brown, the massacre was especially chilling. As Joab soon realized, the victims were Southerners, like himself. They had come west, hoping to make an honest living in the Kansas territory, but now they were dead, their innards spilled on their own newly worked fields. Numbed by the news, Joab could only ask, "Who is John Brown, and how could he conceive such gross acts?"

In response, Joab was told that Brown had recently come from New York. He had successfully solicited financial backing for his raids from eastern financiers: Parker, Stearns, Higginson and Sanborn, all of Boston, and Smith of New York. Believing that he had been directed by God to eradicate slavery, Brown was attempting to wipe out slavery by killing Southern slaveowners.

"And Brown's men...you say they are on their way to St. Bernard?"

"Yes!"

Joab knew beyond a doubt that if Brown or any of his followers were on their way to St. Bernard he and his family were in real danger. As quickly as he could, Joab locked his store and fled to Westport. None too soon either, for John Brown's sons, Frederick and Oliver, and three members of the Stubbs family arrived in St. Bernard on the morning of June 3, 1856. Kicking in the door, the raiders ransacked Joab's store before burning it to the ground. The raid left no doubt in anyone's mind: this was only the beginning of John Brown's antislavery campaign; more atrocities would follow. Yet, when asked the reason for the attack, Sandi, one of Brown's henchmen, merely shrugged and said, "We wanted to improve our exterior." [1]

"Improving their exterior," was partly true. Brown's men were certainly a ragged lot. That is, they *were* ragged until they availed themselves of Joab's merchandise: palm-leaf hats, check shirts, linen coats, even a few linen and bandanna handkerchiefs. All told, the raid on Joab's new establishment netted them four thousand dollars worth of goods and two thousand dollars in cash. It was a staggering loss for Joab. [2] Worse yet, he feared for the lives of Arabella and the children. Having already lost two wives and a daughter, he was not about to risk losing this family too. As quickly as he could (and perhaps at Arabella's insistence), he loaded his family aboard an east-bound steamer destined for Baltimore.

Not understanding the reason for their sudden departure, twelve-year-old Mamie pouted. She didn't want to go back to Baltimore. She loved her new home and wanted to stay in Missouri, grumbling that "We left Westport, much to my disgust, for I liked the 'jumping off place' very well. Back we traveled to Baltimore…the trip back was over the same route and left no lasting memories except that I left many of my treasures behind, among them the cradle, but the doll went along and arrived with a broken head from falling out of an upper berth on account of having no cradle to sleep in."

Family life was not nearly as pleasant as it had been before the Kansas business failure. For one thing Mamie missed her father. He had remained in Missouri, while Arabella and the children lived in Maryland.

Many of Joab's relatives were living in Missouri at the time, and the most affluent of these were residents of a small, but aggressive trading center called Westport. In the early 1800s, Westport was a rowdy little town standing on the edge of Indian territory, or as the saying went, "it was the first watering place for the red man and the last for his white brethren."

Yet it was this town—Westport—situated in the picturesque bluffs, four miles from its port on the Missouri River, that captured a very special place in Mamie's heart.

It seems Joab had been offered a partnership in a Westport trading store, an offer he gladly accepted. The store in question was being operated by Joab's thirty-three-year-old nephew, Tom Bernard's son, William. This, of course was Mamie's cousin, so from this point on he will be referred to as "Cousin William."

The partnership was just too good a proposal for Joab to refuse, considering Cousin William's previous business partner, Charles Kearney, made enough money in the store in three years to retire and travel abroad. [3] Could Joab do as well and, perhaps win back his wife's respect and affection? He hoped so!

Two years went by, and life on the Kansas-Missouri border appeared to be settling down. Joab and Cousin William's trading store was thriving. Greater numbers of freighters were trading exclusively at the store and the two men had captured much of the lucrative Mexican trade. So, believing conditions had improved, Arabella brought the children back to Westport in 1858. Mamie recalled how the family returned over the same route they had previously taken, except at Louisville they went by boat through a freshly cut canal, sparing passengers the trauma of traveling over the falls. It was a long, tiring trip, but eventually they came to Westport Landing.

Much to Mamie's delight, her father met the family at the boat dock and escorted them back to the town of Westport. The village had been established in 1833 and was so named because John McCoy, who platted Westport, considered it a portal to the West. Previous to this Independence, Missouri, had been the preferred port for transferring supplies from boats on the Missouri River to freighters traveling inland. However, when McCoy discovered a huge rocky ledge in a farmer's field, several miles west of Independence, he named it Westport Landing. It was an ideal docking area for riverboats. Thus, by 1845 the town of Westport had successfully replaced Independence as the major shipping point for wagons heading west. [4]

The area's first permanent residents, the Chouteau brothers, were French-Canadian fur traders who established a trading post on the Missouri River in 1821. (Mamie's brother, Allan, married a descendant.) The Chouteaus were victims of two major floods, one in 1826 and a second in 1844, the year of Mamie's birth. In 1844, their entire settlement was destroyed, including two large warehouses. Consequently, the family rebuilt on higher ground in the vicinity of Westport Landing, and the settlement which sprang up around the docking area was known as Frenchtown, Kawsmouth and Chouteau's and formed the embryo of a better known center—Kansas City. This original section of Kansas City was platted in 1838, five years after the town of Westport. At first the town was named "Kanzas" before officially adopting the name "Kansas City." But the actual boat dock has retained the name "Westport Landing" to the present day.

Amazing developments had taken place in Westport while Arabella and the children were in Baltimore. The town was now a hive of activity with shops carrying everything from fancy carriages to Sunday bonnets. From a town of less than five hundred residents in 1856, Westport had grown to a metropolis of nearly two thousand by 1858.[5]

What an exciting town! They called her the "Queen of the West," the place where everything happened. Creaking ox carts, fringed shays and freight wagons; jingling harnesses, clip-clopping horses and men's voices—these were the sights and sounds of the busy center. The town was now the most important trading center on the Missouri River—a bartering center which linked eastern cities with the western frontier. Three major trails, the California, the Oregon and the Santa Fe branched out from Westport and, for travelers leaving the waterway to take any one of the trails, Westport was the final outfitting post. Hundreds of heavily-laden wagons lurched through the middle of town every day, some carrying raw produce to the boat dock; others carried manufactured goods in the opposite direction. On one particular occasion, a single caravan was observed which consisted of sixty-three wagons, each wagon carrying 6,000 pounds of merchandise, and each drawn by six yoke of oxen. [6]

Westport's busiest east-west street was appropriately called "Main Street." [7] Harris House Hotel, a sprawling three-story brick building, sat on the northeast corner of Main and Main Cross and was the most prestigious establishment in town. It often played host to English lords, Mexican Civil War heroes, wagon masters and visiting dignitaries. Somewhere behind the hotel, away from the eyes of women and children, was the auction block where slaves were bought and sold.

In front of the hotel lay the town square with its flagpole and public well. Very often the little square was as peaceful as a monk's sanctuary, but it was also known to stage some rousing fist fights and equally stormy secessionist rallies.

As the Bernard family approached the Harris Hotel, Joab

pointed proudly to a smaller structure abutting the hotel's east wall. This was the Metropolitan Building where he and Cousin William operated their trading store.

Soon they arrived at the house the Bernard family would call "home." This was situated approximately one block east of the store and sat beside the large colonial home of Duke Simpson. [8] Constructed of logs and sided with weather board, it had an outer fort-like appearance, but inside it was warm and cozy with ample room for family, servants and overnight guests. Certainly the house was not as grand as the Baltimore manor the children had grown accustomed to, but they loved it and chattered happily as they unpacked their belongings.

Fourteen-year-old Mamie was elated; living in Westport was going to be fun. Best of all, her father was living with them, so they were one big, happy family again. As might be expected, no new babies had arrived in the Bernard household since 1854, but soon the children were told that a new sister or brother was on its way, and the news was greeted with a great deal of excitement.

Moving back to Westport held another attraction for Mamie. Now she could play with children she had met on her first trip west—her old friends. And since the town swarmed with her father's kinfolk, most of these friends were her relatives. Residents with surnames such as Harris, Hamilton, Behan, Jones, Simpson and Boone were all related, either by blood or marriage: Cousin William married Susan *Harris*; his sister, Cornelia (*Bernard*) married James *Hamilton*; Sarah *Harris* married Peter *Behan*—and so it went. To simplify matters, Mamie referred to the children of these relatives as "my cousins."

Johnny Behan, one of these shirttail cousins, stood out among the rest. A year younger than Mamie, he was a good-looking kid, short in stature, but as agile as a cat. Remarkably, this dark-eyed youngster was destined to become a sheriff of considerable renown—the one involved in the Wyatt Earp shoot-out in Tombstone, Arizona.

There had been a huge family rift when Johnny's parents were married. His grandfather, John Harris (the owner of the stylish hotel), strongly disapproved of his eldest daughter marrying Peter Behan. Among other shortfalls, Peter was a laborer with very little money and, to top it off, was an Irish-Catholic—

not exactly the credentials John Harris was looking for in a son-in-law. Harris went to great lengths to put a stop to the courtship. However, truelove prevailed; Sarah Ann Harris married Peter Behan and, in due time, little Johnny arrived. Attempting to appease her father, Sarah named her first-born, "John Harris Behan." It was a ploy which obviously had no effect on the stubborn old man because, when he died, Harris left his other children's inheritances free and clear, while poor Sarah was forced to wrestle her share of the estate from trustees, in a series of ugly court battles.

Besides owning the Harris House Hotel, John Harris probably had a stake in the Metropolitan Building, too, since his favorite sons-in-law, Cousin William and Charles Kearny, [9] operated their store from the confines of the "Met building." After Kearny retired, Cousin William partnered with Colonel Boone,[10] before striking a partnership with Mamie's father.

Harris was a slave owner who was known to keep at least sixteen slaves. A family of slaves catered to guests at the thirty-two room hotel. The hotel cooks, Aunt Minerva and her husband, Mark, endeared themselves to all comers with bright smiles and delectable cuisine. Mark was said to "roach up his hair, put on a white apron and soft slippers and fly into the dining room, where he turned from head cook to head waiter." He would carve wild turkey, venison, home-cured ham or whole roast pig with a finesse that won him fame throughout Missouri. [11]

Other slaves worked in Harris's home, the elegant mansion he built in 1854. This massive two-story brick home sat on a ridge just east of town and, as Mamie fondly recalled, it was a grand place to visit—an almost magical place where she drank from lovely china cups and nibbled on tea biscuits. Its graceful black walnut staircase was the product of trees cut in the nearby woods and the thousands of bricks used to build the outer walls were fired locally. [12]

There were no dances given in Harris's large home, or the Harris Hotel for that matter. John's wife, Henrietta, didn't approve of dances. She raised her seven daughters and one son the same way Arabella Bernard raised hers—with a firm hand. Like Mamie, each of the Harris girls learned to hem fine cambric and be discreet and modest after the fashion of a well-bred gentlewoman. [13] However, son John caused the family no end of embarrassment by marrying a young woman of his parent's choice, then divorcing her.

The Westport Harris-Bernard clan were strict Methodists from powerful Southern families. They were the generation not in line to inherit estates in the old South and, figuratively speaking, were forced out of the nest. As they moved into the Midwest, they came en masse. Bound together in marriage, business, religion and politics, these displaced Southerners formed a tightly knit society. History would repeat itself when Mamie and her cousins made their exodus into Arizona. In both Missouri and Arizona, the ancient bonds held fast as the extended family converged on new frontiers. They helped each other secure capital to set up homes and ranches and, more importantly, they banded together to fight each other's enemies.

Spring of 1859 came to Westport like the proverbial lamb, bringing the sweet taste of prosperity to the Bernards. Business boomed as Mexican freight wagons rumbled into the family owned trading store, and of course there was quite a celebration when another baby boy, Allan Cunningham Bernard, made his appearance on February eleventh of that year.

1859 was also the year "Westport's Wonderful Windwagon," made its debut, a momentous occasion, providing Mamie and her family with no end of laughter.

The windwagon was a four wheeled vehicle designed to catch the wind and propel itself forward across the prairie. Twenty-five feet in length, it had twelve foot wheels, and its masts held twenty foot sails. [14] Cousin William told the following story:

> "...the windwagon was invented by a man known as 'Windwagon Thomas.' If he had any other name no one knew it. He had been a sailor. He rigged up a small wagon as a trial model and sailed out on the prairie as far as Council Grove, Kansas. With this success the Westport and Santa Fe Overland Navigation Company was formed, to build a fleet of wind-wagons, the company having six other members besides 'Windwagon Thomas.'
>
> "In due time a second wind-wagon was completed and a mammoth vehicle it was! Two yoke of oxen

towed it out about three miles to open pasture. All the stock holders but one, and a number of prominent citizens embarked when its trial run was made. It was an even greater success than the first one, and the way the cumbersome looking rig scooted over gullies and small hillocks was surprising!

"Thomas, intoxicated by success, began a series of fancy navigating not in the catalogue of prairie sailing. A sudden veering of the wind, while Thomas was tacking, brought catastrophe. The wagon halted and then started backward at a speed never before attained, and the steering mechanism became deranged. Faster and faster went the wind-wagon propelled by a freshening breeze and guided by whimsical fancy.

"Dr. Parker, the only stockholder not aboard, followed on a riding mule as fast as possible, fearing his professional services would be needed. The steering mechanism became locked, and the vehicle started in a circle about one mile in diameter. As the vehicle gathered momentum in its circular flight, the terror-stricken stockholders started to abandon ship, which strewed prominent citizens in its wake. All except Thomas who, remaining at the helm, sent the outfit careening into a stake-and-rider fence near Turkey Creek, collapsing the wagon. We fished Thomas out of the wreckage, virtually uninjured."

Dr. Parker (the Bernards' family doctor and a Southern sympathizer who was deported from Westport during the Civil War) was quoted as saying, "It was the most laughable thing I'd ever seen. Oh how that wagon could go. I had one of the best saddle mules in the country and he couldn't hold a candle to it." [15]

The June 1859 edition of Westport's *Border Star* spared readers the grim details, reporting that, "It is generally conceded the Westport Windwagon has proven a failure." [16] Failure or not, it furnished the town with some much needed amusement in the wake of the Civil War.

That year, Mamie was enrolled in a boarding school, twelve miles away in Independence. Here she spent her school days, as she says, "…having a girl's usual experiences of joys and sorrows—very few of the latter, that I can I remember, for I was a happy girl."

However, at age fifteen, she was sent back east to Baltimore's Female Academy. Once again there were tears as she left Westport and as she sadly reported: "My father took me (to boarding school) and we went to St. Louis by steamboat and from there by rail to Cincinnati, where we laid over one day, it being Sunday. People did not travel then on Sundays. We went over to Covington, Kentucky to visit relatives, but all I can remember is a deathly homesickness that blotted out all pleasure for me."

For the next ten months Mamie remained in Baltimore. While there, Dr. Kane of Arctic fame was brought through for burial; the Duke of Wales came through for a royal visit to the Americas and the "Great Eastern" made her first trip. Who was to know these events, experienced by a fifteen year-old, would have such historic significance in the years to come? Mamie also recalled hearing the gunfire, announcing the death of her father's old enemy, John Brown.

The slavery issue had not yet gained political momentum and, given the violent nature of Brown's activities, it was inevitable that he would run afoul of the law. His downfall came in October 1859, when he and about twenty followers stormed an artillery station at Harper's Ferry, Virginia, killing four federal troops, wounding nine and stealing millions of dollars worth of Federal arms and ammunition. Later, in a barrage of gunfire, Brown's sons, Watson and Owen, were mortally wounded and Brown himself was taken prisoner. [17] A short time later the white-bearded zealot was convicted of treason, and at eleven o'clock on the warm, sunny morning of December 2, 1859, he climbed the steps of a newly constructed scaffold. His manner was calm and, after shaking hands with the jailer, a hood and noose were slipped over his head and the trap dropped.

The execution evoked horror in those watching. Many took Brown's composure in the face of death as a sign the abolitionist had been a righteous man. Thus, amid the pealing of bells and the firing of cannons, it was an emotional mob that hit the streets that day, chanting messages of sympathy for Brown.

No doubt, Mamie and her family welcomed the news of Brown's death, but if they breathed a sigh of relief, it was not a long one. Brown had become a martyr. Larger in death than in life, he was soon eulogized in song: "John Brown's body lies a-moldering in the grave, but his soul goes marching on." Indeed, his fiery spirit appeared to "march on," as radicals on both sides—North and South—adopted his vicious tactics. It would soon become apparent that Brown's death was by no means the end of violence, but the beginning, and before 1860 was out the Bernards would find themselves surrounded by vicious bands of terrorists.

When the school term ended in June of 1860, Mamie joined friends in Philadelphia and traveled with them to St. Louis where she was met by her sister. [18] Then what a great time the young ladies had, laughing and joking and being entertained in grand style by the John J. Roe family, the old friends who had launched Joab in business many years before. Now they played host to his daughters, introducing Mamie anew to the city of her birth.

The girls stayed in St. Louis for a month, until it was time to board a steamboat for Westport, perhaps the *Polar Star*, the luxury craft with a large glassed-in pilot house, deck chairs cushioned in leather and huge windows trimmed with brightly colored drapes.

Standing on deck, their floor-length gowns and long hair billowing in the wind, the Bernard sisters listened to the mighty thud-thud of engines and the shrill toot of the boat's whistle. They were homeward bound and wildly excited, never once suspecting the horrific problems that lay ahead.

Chapter Three—Trouble On The Border

Leaves were beginning to turn from green to shimmering gold, in August of 1860 when Mamie Bernard came home to Westport. True to its reputation, the Baltimore Female Academy had turned the bubbly little girl into a refined young lady. She was sixteen, arriving home with all the "poise and polish" the distinguished school could instill in her. Surely the young men of Westport noticed her and turned to gaze appreciatively as she walked by, and women folk, too, would crane their necks and whisper to one another, "There goes little Mary Bernard. She'll make some Southern gentleman a fine wife!"

Yet, even as "Miss Mamie" smiled and curtsied in true Scarlett O'Hara fashion, there were certain political events taking shape that would change the course of her life in ways she could never imagine.

Nothing in and around Westport seemed particularly out of place in the autumn of 1860. As always, the town throbbed with vitality, and the feeling of prosperity rippled through Westport like a warm breeze. Downtown businessmen were smiling as they rang up sales. Among the happiest were Cousin William and Joab Bernard whose store grossed $260,000 that year from trading with 2,113 wagons.

Ironically, the very factor responsible for Westport's good fortune would later lead to her ruin—and that was the town's location. Perched on the Missouri-Kansas border, with the navigable Missouri River at her door, Westport was ideally situated for business in peacetime, but during times of unrest it was possibly the most dangerous spot in Missouri. This was in part due to Kansas and Missouri having some major differences. Missouri had gained her statehood in 1821, while Kansas did not become a state until 1861. Missouri was a slave state, whereas the official policy regarding slavery was in limbo in the territory of Kansas, and while it can be said that slavery issues caused a good deal of animosity between Missouri and Kansas, it is also true that many of the grievances arose over land claims. [1]

Typical of the friction between the two states was the friction between the townspeople of Westport, Missouri, and those of Lawrence, Kansas. Before the Kansas-Nebraska Bill of 1854 opened up Kansas to settlers, the residents of Westport roamed freely over the territory to the west. Men who warmed themselves in front of Westport fireplaces by night, trapped, farmed and traded in Kansas by day. Many had gone so far as to establish permanent campsites, complete with cabins, along the Wakarusa River. Grass grew green on both sides of the border and cattle grazed wherever. This unwritten herd law, giving cattle free range, had been practiced since livestock were first introduced to Missouri, but all that changed when immigrants began pouring in from the east.

A company called the "New England Emigrant Aid Company," outfitted hundreds of settlers and sent them west to take up claims in Kansas. The first party of immigrants arrived August 1, 1854. They pitched their tents on a ridge overlooking the Kansas and Wakarusa Rivers and christened the site "Lawrence" after Amos Lawrence the founder of the aforementioned emigration company. [2] Lawrence was an eastern investor who had never set foot in Kansas, but he told his wards the land in Kansas was free for the taking, so they happily staked claim to the best looking real estate.

That was all very well, but some choice property had already been claimed. One particular piece belonged to a man named Baldwin. Eighteen men on horseback accompanied Baldwin from Westport to inform the New Englanders of their mistake. Rifles in hand, the eighteen stood guard while Baldwin's sister tore down the newcomer's tent and replaced it with her brother's. This in turn prompted thirty New Englanders to draw their guns. Outnumbered, the Baldwin party backed down, threw their tent in a wagon and departed, but from that time on, Baldwin and his Westport friends actively sought revenge.

During the early months of 1855, more eastern immigrants poured into Kansas—a thousand at a time—and Missourians perceived this mass emigration to be a deliberate ploy by their political enemies to take over Kansas and implement trade and anti-slavery legislation unfavorable to Missouri.

Of course there were further land disputes between the old-timers in Westport and the tent dwellers of Lawrence. Although the people of Westport had given up tearing down tents, reclaiming what they perceived to be their land in Kansas was never far from their minds. Various schemes were bantered back and forth, then on March 30, 1855, an election was called to establish the first territorial legislature in Kansas. Opportunity knocked, and the men of Missouri sprang into action.

One of Lawrence's new residents had this to say: "The evening before, and the day of the election, about a thousand men arrived in Lawrence. They came in wagons (of which there was over one hundred), or on horseback, under the command of Colonel Samuel Young of Boone County, Missouri, and Claiborne Jackson of Missouri. They were armed with guns, rifles, pistols and bowie knives and had tents and flags with them. They brought with them two pieces of artillery, loaded with musket balls." [3]

Gun wielding residents of Missouri had come to Kansas to vote—one way or another they planned to regain control of the land which they considered had been stolen from them, as well as elect legislators who supported their own pro-slavery legislation. Reportedly, hundreds of nonresident voters cast their ballots from one end of the Kansas territory to the other. In spite of this outside interference, the resulting government actually had anti-slavery representation, however Lawrence constituents still believed it favored Missouri interests. Consequently the people of Lawrence (citizens of Kansas for less than a year) decided to repudiate all laws enacted by the new legislature. As a further act of defiance, they ordered and received a large shipment of Sharpes rifles—which included a howitzer. Their intention was to take the "law unto themselves." [4]

Owning this arsenal strengthened Lawrence's resolve, and they began to boast that their newly acquired rifles could fire ten times a minute and kill a man a mile away. Of course this was an exaggeration of the rifle's capabilities, designed to put fear in the hearts of their enemies—and it did. In fact it created such panic, the new territorial government was forced to take action, and declared the Sharpes rifle to be an illegal weapon. As a result, a posse headed by Sheriff Samuel Jones (Postmaster of Westport and friend of Joab Bernard), was sent to Kansas on May 21, 1856, to confiscate Lawrence's arsenal, cannon and all. [5] This event was known as the "Sacking of Lawrence," the word "sacking" referring to upending a gunny sack and shaking out its contents. And that is what the sheriff did; he and his men hunted through buildings. (No guns were fired; no lives were lost.) Jones literally turned the town upside down until the weapons were found and confiscated.

Years later, the phrase "Sacking of Lawrence" became associated with Quantrill's attack on Lawrence, but William Quantrill's raid in 1863 was an entirely different event; it was no mere "sacking," but a massacre carried out with savage brutality. Which is yet another example of how dissension on the Kansas-Missouri border gained momentum. It began with insignificant bouts of haggling, then pushing-matches which led to gunfights, each incident more violent than the one before, until the beautiful border towns were literally washed in blood.

Another hotbed of contention between 1855 and 1865 was the Shawnee Methodist Mission. Located in Kansas (one half mile from the Missouri border), the mission was closely tied to Westport. Three or four stages a day made the nine mile trip from Westport to the Shawnee Mission. [6] Established in 1831 as an industrial school for the Shawnee Indians, the mission had been built by the Methodist Missionary Society, so the Westport Methodists considered it their property.

Tom Johnson (later related to Mamie by marriage), had been put in charge of the mission in 1834. Referred to as "Shawnee's misguided missionary," Johnson brought slaves into Kansas in the early 1800s, kept slaves himself and sold slaves to the Shawnee Chiefs. [7] Receipts, registered in St. Louis, prove transactions of this nature occurred. For instance, on May 31, 1853, Johnson purchased two black girls for the sum of five hundred and fifty dollars from N. H. Scruggs. He paid seven hundred dollars to B.M. Lynch for fourteen-year-old Harriet on June 7, 1855, and on May 24, 1856, he purchased fifteen-year-old Martha from David Burge for eight hundred dollars. All girls were recorded as being "of black complexion, sound in body and mind, slaves for life and free from all claims. "[8]

Under slave labor, the Shawnee farms flourished, the tall, brick mission buildings multiplied and, after the controversial elections of 1855, the Shawnee Mission became the headquarters of the first Kansas state legislature. [9] From the very beginning the mission, under Reverend Johnson's jurisdiction, seemed unsuited to hosting government officials, and by 1855, relationships between Johnson and the legislators were tense.

Despite the fact some of the Kansas voters were unhappy with the recent election, the first territorial governor, Governor Reeder, was a man after their own heart. He was a staunch abolitionist and, similar to the people of Lawrence, he regarded the Westport Southerners with suspicion and contempt.

An event which took place August 15, 1855, as told by Colonel Eldridge, describes not only the enmity between Governor Reeder and Reverend Johnson, but the growing distrust among the various factions on the border.

"During the session of the bogus legislature the governor (Reeder), being alone among a crowd of Pro-slavery men, spent the nights at the American house in Kansas City. He was in constant fear of assault and, one morning, asked Colonel Coates and myself to accompany him to the Shawnee Mission. In preparation for an emergency, we went well armed. The forenoon passed with only a display of studied reserve in his presence. When dinner was called the governor took the head of the long table and Coates and myself took a seat on either side of him, while the Rev. Mr. Johnson occupied the further end. Reeder, while adjusting himself in his seat, loosened his revolvers and brought them to the front, concealed by the table cloth. Observing this, Coates and I did likewise. When the table was filled by the guests, who gave us only the recognition of a vacant stare, his reverence raised a large carving knife and brought it down with such force as to startle us. When we had recovered our nerves it was seen that the startling rap was not a signal for assassins, but a call for attention while he (Johnson) invoked the divine blessing." [10]

By the end of 1860, the atmosphere along the Missouri-Kansas border was explosive. The two states had not yet resorted to open warfare, but isolated murders were cropping up with disconcerting regularity. To say that federal legislation, declaring Kansas a free state in January 1861, did not impact Southerners would be untrue. Pro-slavery advocates were extremely uncomfortable with the legislation. Although the universal freeing of slaves was not, as yet, on the national agenda, slaveholders could see the writing on the wall. More and more Americans, including many Southerners, were crying out against the practice. Yet the Southern economy depended on produce from plantations, and plantations depended on slave labor. If slavery was to be abolished, then the Southerners wanted to take charge of the transition and from this grew the desire to govern themselves.

In February of 1861, the Southern States announced their separation from the Union. The new country, the Confederate States of America, was made up of South Carolina, Mississippi, Florida, Alabama, Georgia, Louisiana and Texas. Soon the state-territorial legislatures of North Carolina, Virginia, Tennessee, Arkansas and Missouri drafted bills to allow their constituencies to join the Confederacy. [11]

Mamie's father took particular interest in these latest developments, as his old friend, John Tyler, was a central figure in Virginia's decision to join the Confederacy. As former president, Tyler had gone to great lengths to keep the discontented Southerners in the Union. Later, as chairman of the Richmond Peace Conference held February 13, 1861, he pleaded for a peaceful settlement in order to keep the states united. However, in March, when negotiations collapsed, Tyler threw up his hands and advocated the immediate secession of Virginia. [12] Shortly after this conference, Tyler died and, although his demise was attributed to natural causes, friends were suspicious, particularly since Tyler's stamp of approval on Confederacy had drawn such deadly hate from the Unionist sector.

Amid speculations of foul play, Joab mourned the death of his old friend and, with added fervor, renewed his loyalty to Virginia, the state of his birth. Unfortunately this political stand would have devastating effects on the Bernard family, when the Union troops took Missouri.

Lincoln, who had just been elected as President of the Union, responded to the Southern states' secession by sending troops to blockade Atlantic seaports, the idea being to choke off southern trade and bring the rebels to heel. The struggle to keep the South in the Union was paramount in Lincoln's mind; the abolition of slavery was not, or as he so eloquently declared, "My paramount object in this struggle is to save the Union, and it is not either to save or to destroy slavery. If I could save the Union without freeing any slave, I would do it; and if I could save it by freeing all slaves, I would do it." [13]

Perhaps Lincoln's main reason for not wanting to be drawn into the slavery issue was that (similar to Joab Bernard), Lincoln's Kentucky born wife, Mary, kept "black servants" who besides performing household duties, "washed, dressed and combed the first lady's hair each morning." [14]

Although Lincoln often spoke of his personal desire for freedom, slavery might not have become a Civil War issue had it not been for outside forces. France and Britain were strongly opposed to the war, and Britain, whose initial sympathies lay with the South, was poised to intervene. At this time, Lincoln was compelled to embrace a moral issue to keep the foreigners at bay, for he could ill afford to fight more than one enemy at a time.

Since Westport was a major trading center, the very mention of Lincoln's trade restriction caused a great deal of concern for local merchants—especially William and Joab Bernard who relied on free trade.

The next news came on April 12,1861: Confederate troops, attempting to seize Fort Sumter, had fired shots at Union troops—the nation was now in a state of civil war.

By mid-April, Missouri was recruiting troops to send south, which set the Westport lads to polishing their guns with even more fervor than they had the year before. Southern blood ran through their veins and they were quick to come to the defense of their kinfolk. Once again, the "all for one and one for all" brand of Southern loyalty was repeating itself. Westport's able-bodied men felt they had no choice but to leave fiancées, wives and families and march south to fight.

Chapter Four—A Confederate Flag

The scent of lilac blossoms, the caw of crows, the clip-clopping of horses—all gave a sense of normalcy to Westport's main street, where the editor of *The Border Star* sat in his office, cranking out another weekly paper. Joab Bernard was a regular subscriber to the paper and liked nothing better than to sit in his easy chair and read the news as seen through the eyes of the radically Secessionist newsman. Mamie was also an avid reader and, after browsing the Star from cover to cover, she would listen as her father discussed the latest news with his Southern cronies. Every aspect of the Civil War was of interest to her, from the most recent battles in Virginia to the local recruitment of troops.

She reasoned that if Westport's young men were joining the Missouri State Guard in defense of the South, then she, too, should help with the war effort. Her opportunity arrived when her father's friend, Tom Rosser, requested volunteers to help make a Confederate flag. When finished the flag would be the first Confederate flag to be raised in Missouri and, to a teenager, that sounded exciting. Even more exciting was the discovery that Westport's newly-formed army would carry the flag into battle.

It was a beautiful spring day when Mamie and sister Margaret hurried from the house, long gowns sweeping the wooden sidewalk and sewing baskets tucked under their arms. They were on their way to their first flag making session, which would take place in Rosser's store, located on the second floor of the Boone Building. [1]

It was a day which spoke of adventure rather than espionage. They could hear the cheerful gurgle of water in Mill Creek with its alluring scent of spring run-off. On the south side of the street, the sun danced on the windows of Peter Smith's three-story hotel, where swallows swooped to half-built nests under the hotel's overhanging eaves. The Spalding Building sat on the north side of the street. Here the girls dodged horse and carriage traffic, for this building was a hive of activity, housing a market in front, the town clerk's office upstairs and the town jail in back. [2]

After passing the family trading store and the Harris Hotel, the young ladies crossed an intersection to reach the Boone Building. Gathering their skirts, they climbed the stairs to Rosser's store. At the top of the stairs, they were confronted by a glass-sided counter filled with bottles of various shapes and sizes: liniments, smelling salts and elixirs. Above this, arranged like a regiment of toy soldiers, were pipes, blocks of tobacco and boxes of cigars.

The heady aroma of Virginian tobacco filled the air as Colonel Tom Rosser lifted his pipe to speak. "Miss Margaret, Miss Mamie. Do come in!" With that, he motioned the sisters to a table where sunlight streamed through a window onto a mound of colored cloth. Seated at the table were two friends, Mrs. Baker and Florence Price. [3] This was the entire cast of flag makers—just four women and a shopkeeper. It scarcely looked like a history making event—but it was.

The Colonel's eyes shone as the four women set to work under his direction. This was a gratifying moment for Tom Rosser, a Virginian who held a commission with the Virginia Militia. In his gray frock coat and high-topped boots, he looked every bit as efficient as the commanding officer he would soon become.

Throughout the afternoon the thumping of heavy boots on the stairs signaled Rosser's return to his counter. Most customers ordered tobacco, prompting him to take a large plug from the shelf, mentally calculate the amount ordered, whack off a slice and wrap it in brown paper, all the while carrying on a lively conversation. The outbreak of war was on everyone's mind and, as Mamie worked, she listened to the men's interpretation of political events. As they spoke, she became aware that Richmond, Virginia, her father's birthplace, had just been declared the capital of the Confederacy.

Tom Rosser made his views clear: He may not have supported slave labor in principal, but he felt that Southerners should have the right to govern themselves. Under Union jurisdiction the South had been treated unfairly—so Rosser thought—and with Lincoln barricading the ports to halt Confederate trade, the economy of the South would surely be ruined. [4] For Rosser, there was only one solution: Missouri must join the Confederacy. The fact of the matter was, members of the Missouri's General Assembly were already in the process of drafting an ordinance of secession.

Much of the political debate taking place was too complex for a sixteen-year old to understand, but when the men turned their attention to local happenings, Mamie quickly grasped the gist of the conversation.

It seemed Reverend Tom Johnson, the Shawnee missionary, had recently changed his political affiliation and was now championing the Union—and Rosser and his patrons thought this was incredible. Here was Johnson, a man who had owned slaves for years and preached secession from the pulpit, turning his back on his Southern friends.

"There's method in his madness," Rosser declared.

Apparently the Shawnee School was closing its doors due to poor student attendance, and Reverend Johnson intended to take ownership of the land and buildings. However, the members of the Methodist Missionary Society, founders of the mission, were not about to give the property up—at least not without a court battle. Rosser and his friends had heard that the Reverend predicted the Confederates would be defeated and, by throwing his support behind the Union, Johnson expected to get the mission—free for the asking.

Such talk was bound to upset Margaret, for she had grown quite fond of Andrew Johnson, the Reverend's son, and felt certain this latest state of affairs would ruin her life. *Why, her father would never allow her to marry a Unionist!*

Having no such problems, Mamie concentrated on her needlework and, at the end of the day, when the flag was held up for inspection, it was truly a beautiful thing with red, white and blue stripes, stars at each corner and a palmetto tree in the middle.

A few days later, the whole town turned out for the flag raising. Once again Mrs. Baker, Florence Price, Margaret and Mamie met in Colonel Rosser's shop. But this time they flung open an upstairs window, unfurled the flag and, as it took the breeze, patriotic speeches sprung from the lips of the town fathers gathered below. Spectators clapped, stamped, chanted. More people arrived and men gave speeches. As the crowd grew, voices took on a note of hysteria, hundreds of voices, soaring together in waves akin to frenzy. "Long live the South!"

From the crowd's outer rim, several young men pushed their way forward, their eyes glossy, their faces flushed with patriotic fervor, and seeing a pretty sixteen-year-old girl under a billowing flag caused their Southern blood to swell in already heated veins. She had ivory skin and dark ringlets, a Southern belle—the image of something worth fighting for.

At this point in the rally a most unfortunate incident occurred. Several young German immigrants appeared on the scene. Having heard the commotion in the square, they had come to investigate. They were feisty young men, fresh from the German revolution, and they were currently living in Kansas City. One of them, Frederick Daab, later reported seeing a brand new flag, fluttering from an upstairs window of the Boone Building. Being newcomers, he and his buddies may not have been fully aware of what the flag stood for. At any rate they decided to join the celebration by raising the Stars and Stripes.

Needless to say, a Union flag at a Confederate rally was as dangerous as a keg of dynamite. With fists doubled and ready for action, the young Southerners tore down the Union flag and put the run on Daab and his companions. Anticipating a return of their uninvited guests, the defenders blockaded the street with wagons. Sure enough the young Germans reappeared, this time bearing clubs and ready to face off. Then a man shot twice into the crowd, "thereby persuading the combatants to disperse." [5] For the time being violence had been averted. But as everyone returned to their homes a sense of uneasiness settled over Westport, and the feeling would only grow stronger in the days to come.

The first company of Confederate soldiers to leave Westport proudly carried the flag sewn by Mamie and her friends. Even Mamie's sister, Kate, felt obliged to join the war effort by making a miniature Confederate flag out of red and white silk. (Some years later, Mamie lovingly pasted the little flag in her scrap book—in memory of Kate.)

After the first flag departed, Mamie helped make a second. It had red and white stripes, with stars on a blue square, and once again, this flag was taken south and went through the war, but what happened next was more than anyone could have predicted.

Having been publicly humiliated on the day of the rally, the German youths sought out Union troops who were patrolling in the area, and lodged complaints. They accused the citizens of Westport of waving strange flags and shooting at new citizens.

Mamie concluded the story by saying: "...soon afterwards a storm came down. Some United States soldiers came through Westport from Kansas City on a sort of exploring expedition and they were stoned and hooted at by boys in the streets. Very foolish this, and not approved of by the elders. It brought down upon our devoted heads the storms of war, and troubles followed thick and fast. Everything changed. Able bodied men had marched off to the South, Colonel Rosser among them, and his drug store was burned and his family persecuted until life was a burden for them. You see, he had some half-grown boys and they were first and foremost in the mob that stoned the soldiers. No one was left (in Westport) but old men and half-grown boys."

Other than the Rosser boys, there were several hot-blooded teens from Southern families living nearby, such as fourteen-year-old Jesse James and sixteen-year-old Cole Younger who frequently visited Westport, and it is quite possible that either one, or both of these notorious characters may have been present when the soldiers were stoned.

Unfortunately the Union soldiers took a very dim view of rock throwing, even if it was done by "half grown boys." Orders were immediately issued; there would be no more rock throwing, no more Secessionist rallies and definitely no more Confederate flags flying over Westport. Reinforcements were sent in from Kansas; the people in Westport must be punished for their transgressions. With all the hale and hardy men gone to war, the town lay unprotected. And so it was that Lawrence's most unforgiving citizenry came to grind their ax, swaggering into town, happy to lay a licking on their old enemies.

In the German camp a great celebration got underway; the immigrants had shown those Westport folks a thing or two, or as Frederick Daab happily remarked, "There are 2,500 (armed) men here (in Westport). The stars and stripes fly. The Secessionists are now as tame as a lamb." [6]

Some of Westport's old men wanted to stand up to the intruders, but it was hopeless. There were too many troops. Those who put up any kind of resistance were quickly subdued—made an example of—dragged out on to the street and shot in front of their families. And then the Kansas Cavalry emptied the Harris

Hotel and set up headquarters there. The once proud hotel no longer hosted elegant visitors, but lodged ruthless men, such as Captain Walley and Captain Jennison, both of whom wore cruelty like a badge. [7]

As previously mentioned, Colonel Rosser had joined the Confederate army prior to Westport's occupation by the Union and was leading the James Rains 8th Division of the Missouri State Guards under General Sterling Price. In his absence, Rosser had left his wife in charge of the store, so it was she and the children who would bear the brunt of Kansas' wrath. Yet Mrs. Rosser wasn't alone in their grief. The sound of crying could be heard in every Westport household as the air thickened with smoke from burning buildings.

"Men were shot down in the streets," Mamie said. "Stores and houses of Southern sympathizers were robbed. Soldiers were billeted upon us by the dozens to be fed when there was scarcely enough to eat. Our house was very large and afterwards was called "Fort Bell" (because my mother's nickname was Bell). The women and children always took refuge there when there was rumor of a battle or skirmish. We were persecuted in turn by the Bushwhackers (South) and Jayhawkers (North). My father was too old to go to the army, so looked out for those destitute and was threatened from time to time by both sides."

Mamie was terrified. Would their house be the next one razed? Realizing how serious the situation had become, Joab called his family together for prayers. Always the practical one, Arabella's prayers were followed by action: long, full dresses could conceal many things, so coins, jewelry and other small valuables were put in bags and tied around the girls' waists. If the house burned, hopefully the family would still have enough resources to keep body and soul together.

The outspoken editor of *The Border Star*, a Southern sympathizer, fared only a little better than his Westport neighbors. Having written a series of articles, blistering the Union, he fled town and set up shop in Independence. But he barely had time to run off a few copies of the Star before the Missouri Militia caught up with him, ransacked his office and tossed his type to the four winds.

Another family deeply affected by the war was the Philip Elkins family. They owned a farm just outside Westport and were old friends of the Bernard family. Having been born in Virginia, both Philip and his wife had much in common with Joab. As to be expected, Philip's sympathies lay with his home state, and he and his eldest son were among the first Missouri Confederates to go to war.

When war broke out in 1861, Stephen Elkins, who later played a significant part in Mamie's life, had only just graduated from the University of Missouri, in Columbia. The guest speaker at his graduation ceremonies was none other than the Confederate leader, Sterling Price. Eighteen year-old Stephen Elkins could well have been another of Price's recruits, but his mother insisted he stay home. It was difficult enough for Mrs. Elkins to have her husband and eldest son march south; Stephen must help her manage the farm.

Stephen was a sensitive, fair-minded young man. Standing six feet in his sock feet, he had broad shoulders, a winning smile and kindly blue eyes. [8] Having earned a degree in education, he began teaching at Nathan Scarrett's School in Westport as an assistant teacher. Before and after school, he busied himself with farm chores.

No sooner had he completed his apprenticeship under an experienced teacher, than he was transferred to a school on Big Creek, near the family farm. This was a one-room, rural school, so he was on his own to manage his neighbors' rambunctious children. The boys, all from Southern stock, were especially rebellious. Their main object in life was to shake the confines of school and join the Confederate army as quickly as possible. So primed were they to fight, that instead of playing ball at recess, like ordinary youngsters, they played war, North against the South. [9] Of course the South always won! No one wanted to be a Northerner, so straws were drawn—then, pity the lads drawing the shortest straws. Seen as real Northerners, the unlucky boys were whipped soundly at recesses and, if they failed to step lively at home time, were treated to another thrashing.

In this rough and tumble environment, young Elkins began his teaching career, the success of which hinged on whether or not he could break up fist fights among lads close to his own age and muscular ability. [10]

Perhaps the best behaved student Stephen taught, was Cole Younger (the same Cole Younger who rode with Jesse

James). [11] Although Cole participated in the Big Creek war games, records show that he was a quiet and studious scholar. Cole was born to affluent parents who lived a few miles east of Westport on a 3,500 acre farm in Cass County. Similar to Mamie's father, Cole Younger's father, Henry, was actively engaged in politics and often made business trips to Washington. Henry Younger had been elected three times to the Missouri State Legislature, was a Jackson County judge and became the mayor of Harrisonville, Missouri, in 1859. These were unusually high credentials for someone about to meet a lowly fate.

Joab Bernard and Henry Younger traveled in the same social and political circles; both were Southerners; both favored a peaceful settlement to the civil unrest. Neither man endorsed slavery, yet each kept two black servants, arguing these were not slaves but indispensable members of their family.

For seventeen year-old Cole Younger, the winter of 1861 was indeed the year of his undoing. [12] It all began when he and his sister were invited to a fancy dress ball. Cole's sister was a charming young woman with a gown that billowed around her like a crystal bell as she stepped onto the dance floor. Her beauty drew the unwanted attention of Irvin Walley, the captain of the Union troops stationed in Westport. When he asked the young lady for a dance, the haughty Southern Belle refused to dance with him, and the rejection angered the captain. Bitter words were exchanged and Cole sprang to his sister's defense. A shoving match ensued in which Cole knocked the captain down. As the captain fell, he drew his pistol and may well have killed the young lad, had it not been for a fast acting bystander who seized the pistol.

The well publicized incident embarrassed Captain Walley, and the very next day, he and six of his men arrived at the Younger home, intending to take Cole into custody. Acting on his father's advice, the teenager "took to the bush." By necessity, other young Southerners escaped to the bush, formed packs and became militant—and from this came a new word, "Bushwhacker," synonymous with "Southern rebel." Life as a Bushwhacker was full of challenges, hiding in barn lofts, or in makeshift shelters in secluded ravines, or, when the coast was clear, Cole would sneak home for food and a change of clothes.

Yet, if the Younger family felt life was hard in 1861, the

following year was far more difficult. In July 1862, Cole's father was driving home from town in a buggy when Captain Walley and his men overtook the elderly gentleman. After robbing him, the Captain shot and left Henry Younger to die at the side of the road. [13] For Cole things would never return to normal; his father was dead and he was an outlaw, destined to spend the next fifteen years on the run.

Members of the Elkins family were also under duress. The provisional State Government of Missouri, newly set up by Abraham Lincoln, ordered "all able-bodied men in the state (regardless of sympathies), to enlist in the Missouri Militia." In short, Missouri residents were given a choice: either swear allegiance to the Union, or face a firing squad. Mrs. Elkins, whose husband and eldest son were already in the Confederate army, stood helplessly by as Stephen was forced to join the Pro-Union Westport Home Guard. [14] The one redeeming feature of Stephen's joining the Missouri Militia was that he did not have to take up arms, but was assigned to railway maintenance by the militia commander. When not on active duty, recruits of the EMM were allowed to pursue their civilian lives, thus Stephen could still teach school part-time.

The Bernards attempted to keep their trading store open, but it was scarcely worth the effort. Customers who risked traveling to Westport were promptly enlisted in the Union army and, by the second half of 1861, active traders had dwindled to a few Mexican freighters who could not be conscripted unless they were citizens of America.

The Civil War was certainly taking its toll. During the last half of 1861, nine major battles had been fought in Missouri and, in them, over 7,000 lives were lost. Still, these battles were overshadowed by the monumental confrontations in Virginia. For instance, when Confederates drove the Union back from Richmond over five thousand men died in one seven-day battle. By comparison, Missouri's losses seemed pale, and were not reported with equal fervor.

If war was perilous for the armed forces, civilians encountered an added menace. There was no way of knowing a Jayhawker from a Bushwhacker, for they often disguised themselves in each others' uniforms. A stranger, dressed in either blue or gray might appear on one's doorstep at any hour of the day or night, ask what the homeowner's sympathies were, "Union or Secesh," and the wrong answer often brought instant death. [15]

Joab worried continually about his family's safety. He was a sixty-one year-old Southerner, surrounded by Union troops and northern Jayhawkers—men armed to the teeth—who might shoot him, burn his home, rape and murder his daughters. Crimes such as these were being perpetrated on a daily basis and none of his six daughters were married. None had the protection of a husband. What was he to do? On December 3, 1861 a knock came on his door which helped to make up his mind.

Opening the door, Joab found himself face to face with Colonel Jennison, organizer of the Independent Mounted Kansas Jayhawkers. [16] Jennison was now a commanding officer of Union troops—a man described as a "thief and murderer" and blamed in part for the border conflict becoming a bloodbath instead of what the army termed "a nice clean war." [17] Certainly Jennison's manner was threatening as he thrust papers into Joab's hand and told him to sign, or else.

With only a moment's hesitation, Joab took up his Bible and pledged allegiance to the United States Government. What else could he do in order to prevent his family from attack by Union troops? The declaration of immunity read:

"TO ALL WHOM IT MAY CONCERN: Know, that being assured of the loyalty of Mr. Joab Bernard to the Government of the United States, I have this day granted to him and his family and property full protection, and hereby warn and forbid all persons from any interference with him and his possessions. UNDER PENALTY OF DEATH. This order shall be good so long as the said Joab Bernard shall remain a good and loyal citizen, and NO LONGER. Dec. 3rd, 1861. C.R. Jennison Colonel, Commanding 1st Kansas Cavalry, Kansas City, Missouri." [18]

It was a demoralizing thing for Joab to have to do—to renounce his Southern loyalties. And he knew his worries were far from over. Reverend Tom Johnson was already receiving death threats for severing his ties with the South. Would Joab's friends consider him a traitor, too? If so, perhaps he was further jeopardizing his family's safety by declaring allegiance to the Union.

Never had the future looked so bleak.

Chapter Five—Romance

Once again winter passed and temperatures warmed, but what a contrast the spring of 1862 was to the previous year, when Mamie had helped make Missouri's first Confederate flag. An insidious gloom hung over the town. Fire blackened timbers marked the sites of once proud homes. Flower beds which, in past years, overflowed with tulips and crocuses now held only a few scraggily volunteers. Similarly, vegetable plots, normally alive with new green sprouts, were nothing more than a tangle of last season's dried chickweed. Mamie longed for former days when black servants attended to chores, when life had some sense of order. Gone were the days of fancy-topped carriages, chauffeured by men with skin as dark and shiny as the horses they drove. Gone, too, were the days when she could stroll downtown in her cashmere gown with its lovely silk ruche. Westport's era of pomp and prosperity was a thing of the past, and Mamie felt a tremendous sense of loss.

What with Union troops occupying the town, she was seldom allowed to venture outdoors. Yet a teenager who was naturally inquisitive was bound to wonder what was happening around town, and Mamie quickly discovered that an ideal spot to view the surrounding area was from an upstairs window. Hidden behind lace curtains, she could amuse herself for hours, sometimes knitting, sometimes embroidering, but always watching, the activity below.

Today, as she looked down on Main Street, she saw it was empty, except for an area flanking the town square where blue-clad soldiers loitered in front of the Harris Hotel. Nothing else moved, other than a configuration of flicking tails, which is all Mamie could see of cavalry horses tied at the hitching rail between Yoacham's Tavern and Roby's Indian Store.

Raising her head, Mamie focused on the steep, crescent-shaped bluffs to the southeast, which were covered with a growth of young timber so dense that a bird could scarcely fly through it. In certain areas, the trees appeared almost black, pinpointing the gullies that fanned out in all directions. Somewhere in this maze, Cole Younger, Jesse James and other teenagers hid from the Kansas Cavalry. Mamie knew most of the young men by name and sympathized with them, knowing they could never go home. Some of the neighbors left food and ammunition at selected spots for the young rebels to pick up. She wished she could do the same, but penalties for aiding Bushwhackers were harsh and inflicted on whole families, and she knew she could never do anything to harm her family.

As Mamie mulled over the situation, she became aware of a large cloud of dust on the horizon. It looked like a convoy of wagons coming down Wornall's hill. *But it can't possibly be freight wagons. Freight wagons seldom come to Westport anymore. Not now! Not since the Union troops have taken over the town!*

Mamie watched for several minutes before deciding the objects were indeed freight wagons. From this distance they looked like thin wooden beads threading their way through the trees. The hill was steep and the wagons descended slowly, cautiously. First one, then another reached Brush Creek and began zigzagging through the willows on their way into town. She counted ten enormous wagons, towering to the height of a one-story house, each wagon pulled by ten mules and flanked by men on horseback wearing wide-brimmed sombreros.

Why, it's the Mexicans! She recognized the wagons. They belonged to Epifanio Aguirre. Only don Epifanio had such tall mules and so many riders. There were well over one hundred, road-weary animals approaching Westport.[1] Plumes of dust swirled in huge brown loops over the heads of long-eared mules and bronze-skinned vaqueros. These men had been traveling for eighty or ninety days and were anxious to enjoy all the pleasures of civilization—all the town had to offer. Little did they know how the town had been robbed of the comforts they enjoyed when they last visited Westport.

The rumble of wheels grew louder. Dogs barked. Teamster's whips popped above the "Hooch! Houch! Who-hahs!" of the vaqueros. Union soldiers appeared like flies from cracks and began lining the street. They were anxious to see don Epifanio, the famed wagon master, the man who was riding ahead of the freight wagons in a carriage drawn by two white horses. [2]

"The Mexicans are here! The Mexicans are here!" Suddenly a thundering of feet pounded upstairs and seven year-old Noah appeared at the bedroom door. "We're safe now 'cause the Mexicans are here!" As Noah roared from one bedroom to another, telling his siblings the good news, Mamie smiled to herself. *Noah and his childish dreams! Poor little waif, believing such foolishness! How can Mexicans keep the family safe? Most likely Captain Jennison will stop the Mexican wagons from going to the boat dock. Oh, dear, he might even confiscate the Mexican trading goods and shoot don Epifanio!*

But none of Mamie's worries materialized. The soldiers simply watched as the Mexicans continued down the street. Below the window, a door opened and Mamie saw her father leave the house. The stress of living in a war zone was evident in his sagging shoulders. His hair looked grayer than it had a short while ago, and Mamie noticed that he was leaning heavily on his cane as he made his way toward the incoming wagons.

Obviously, don Epifanio spotted her father and instead of turning north, the trader drove down the street to meet the older man. Mamie craned her neck in order to see all that was possible to see: the sunlight dancing on the silver trappings of the horses' harnesses; the man's black tailored suit; the glint of silver pistols, one on each side. He was a fine specimen of a man with hair the finest shade of brown, and wavy too.

For many years, don Epifanio and his wagons had arrived in Westport, usually once in the spring and again in the fall. Mamie recalled her encounters with don Epifanio in her father's store, how he smiled and greeted her with a few Spanish words. She remembered his voice as musical as a harp plucked ever so gently. And much to her surprise, she discovered his eyes were blue, not black like his companions. At times she had caught him gazing at her, his eyes flashing with a look that made her feel most strange. *What did it mean?*

Years later she knew when she pasted the following poem in her scrap book. Entitled *Fate*, it was written by Susan Marr Spalding.

"Two shall be born the whole wide world apart,
And speak in different tongues and have no thought
Each of the other's being, and no heed.
And these o'er unknown seas to unknown lands
Shall cross, escaping wreck, defying death;
And, all unconsciously, shape every act
And bend each wondering step to this one end—
That one day out of darkness they shall meet
And read life's meaning in each other's eyes."

Mamie watched as the white horses came to a full stop and don Epifanio offered her father a hand up. And then the carriage turned north, and Joab and don Epifanio disappeared on the wagon route to Westport Landing where the Mexican trading goods would be stored in warehouses, until they could be shipped east by steamboat.

Down the hall, Mamie could hear Noah still chanting his song to anyone who would listen. "The Mexicans are here! We're safe, now! Nobody can trifle with the Mexicans, 'cause they come from a different country, and nobody can make them fight in the army, and nobody can kill 'em...not Jayhawkers, or Bushwhackers or anybody."

The things Noah said had some credibility. Neither the North or South wanted trouble with Mexico and, since the Aguirres claimed to be Mexican citizens, they were exempt from having to serve in the American armed forces. [3]

And so it was that two guests appeared at the Bernard's dinner table that evening. One was Jesse Polk, the Spanish interpreter, the other Epifanio Aguirre. Since the hotel was closed for customers, don Epifanio was invited to stay with the Bernard family as a house guest.

For the first time since Union troops arrived in Westport, Joab's eyes twinkled as he introduced each of his children to the honored guest. When it came Mamie's turn to be presented to Señor Aguirre, she curtsied as she had been taught to do.

Sadly, the meal was very plain. There was little to eat

besides potatoes, hominy pork and tea biscuits, glazed with the preserves Arabella had hidden away for special occasions. Similar to other townspeople, the Bernards had to feed Union troops on a regular basis, and more often than not the pantry was bare.

Fortunately, don Epifanio was not one to complain. His manner was pleasant and confident, his words (translated by Jesse Polk) were well chosen and showed appreciation. Yet, when Mamie's sisters were out of hearing range, they broke into fits of girlish giggles, for they couldn't help noticing how often don Epifanio's eyes came to rest on Mamie.

As soon as dinner was over, the men retired to the sitting room. At first the talk touched on insignificant matters: the weather and condition of the trail to Santa Fe. The fact that Jesse Polk interpreted much of the conversation had little effect on the men, for they were used to conversing in this manner.

Somewhere along the line, Joab broached the subject of don Epifanio providing his family with protection from the vigilantes who lurked in and around Westport. The conversation went something like this:

"Señor Aguirre, we have been friends for many years and, as a friend, I am asking…no, begging you to help me. As you can see, Westport lies in ruins. I have been forced to pledge allegiance to the Union, and now men from both North and South are threatening to kill me. The lives of my wife and children are in danger. Please, I beg of you, help me protect my family and I will give you what money I have."

It was something new for Joab to beg. No longer a rich man, he had only the jewelry and coins hidden in his family's clothing to barter with. *How on earth could he pay for the protection he needed?*

There was a long, thoughtful silence, while the trader considered Joab's request. In don Epifanio's heart he knew what he wanted, but he was a shrewd man and knew that a good trade takes time to negotiate.

Finally, Spanish flowed in an oration that seemed both wordy and emotional—a proposal which Jesse Polk translated to Joab. "Señor Aguirre says he has given your request a great deal of thought, and is willing to protect the Bernard family with Mexican gunmen. Although Señor Aguirre will never accept money from such a highly esteemed friend, there is something of much value Señor Aguirre wishes in return."

"Tell Señor Aguirre to name anything I possess…anything at all…and I will give it to him. Just as long as my wife and children are safe."

The translation was shorter this time. "Señor Aguirre requests the hand of your daughter, Mamie."

Chapter Six—The Handsome Mexican

With the coming of the Mexicans to Westport, the atmosphere in the Bernard home was much more relaxed. Mamie could feel the difference and was pleasantly surprised when she was allowed to accept visits from don Epifanio. She was seventeen and completely captivated by this Spanish-speaking man— he was very handsome. It is said that when they were together, Jesse Polk sat nearby, translating Epifanio's Spanish to English and vice versa. Naturally the inquisitive teenager asked many questions about this intriguing man.

He came from a land the Spanish called the Northern Mystery, the vast territory of New Mexico which was said to abound in sagebrush, rattlesnakes and hostile Apaches. Many visitors, such as the famed General Sherman, were repulsed by the territory's rough landscape and seemingly barbaric citizens. With as much disdain as a high-ranking military man could muster, he was quoted as saying, "United States ought to force Mexico to take the territory back, it is that troublesome."

Yet others who returned from New Mexico described it as a place of wonder with endless plains and pristine mountain wilderness. Undoubtedly, the second description suited don Epifanio, for he often spoke of his love of the southwest.

Epifanio was acclimatized to the rugged country as well as attuned to managing the family's vast properties. He bore an air of confidence, for he was "don Epifanio," the eldest son of an upper-class Mexican family, the heir of the Aguirre hacienda. And, just as Mamie's family kept "black slaves," so Epifanio's family relied on Mexican peons to do the manual labor.

Born March 24, 1834, in Aldame Chihuahua, Mexico, don Epifanio's parents were don Pedro Aguirre and doña Maria de Refugio Aguirre. Their ancestry reached back to high-ranking aristocrats who had come from Spain during the time of Cortez. Sometime later, the Aguirre family had received large land grants in Mexico from the Spanish Crown and, on this gifted land, they raised livestock, mined silver and gold, owned flour mills and developed gardens and huertos grandes (large orchards). The King of Spain also bestowed on the Aguirres the honorary title of "don" for male members of the family and "doña" for female members.

At an early age Epifanio learned to ride burros, mules, horses and galloped at breakneck speed as he took part in "pulling the gallo." This is a Mexican game in which a live gallo (rooster) is buried with only its head and neck showing above ground. Horsemen race toward the buried rooster and, when abreast of it, reach down, hoping to grab the bird by the neck. The lucky contestant, the one who pulls the bird out of the sand, is the winner. As such, he is allowed to lambaste fellow players with his prize, until nothing remains of the hapless bird but a few blood-soaked feathers.

When Epifanio was a teenager, he regularly won such games. Friends claimed he possessed the strength of a bull and the courage of a mountain lion. He could track and bring down wild game as well as any native hunter. In this way he furnished meat for the table, so that those living on the family's hacienda never went hungry.

With a Catholic upbringing he was morally as well as physically strong, enduring bodily pain without flinching. Yet, in 1849, at age fifteen, there were tears in his eyes as he bent over his mother's bed. Cholera had spread through the town of San Peblo de Meoqui, Chihuahua.[1] Many of the villagers had already died, and his mother, Refugio, had contracted the disease. The telltale beads of perspiration were cold on her forehead as her fingers moved weakly among the beads of her rosary.

Mamma, don't die! Surely the plea formed on his lips, but couldn't be uttered in a room weighted so heavily with the smell of death. From the dampened dirt floor to the slatted ocotillo-rib ceiling, the room held a sense of finality, and Refugio had made her peace with God.

The following days were filled with sadness as the family gathered at his mother's newly dug grave. Women wailed and strong men sobbed, for the placid, long-suffering Refugio had been loved by everyone in the hacienda. It was a time of great mourning made bearable only by the kindness of friends, such as the Ornelas family. Earlier, don Narciso de la Ornelas had been honored to be a padrino (godfather) when Refugio de Aguirre had taken Guadalupe, Epifanio's baby sister, to church to be baptized. Now it was the Ornelas women, Narcisa and Andrea, who came to live with Pedro Aguirre and care for his motherless children.

This meant fifteen year-old Epifanio had to share his living quarters with several other youngsters, for it appeared twenty-six year-old Andrea Ornelas had children slightly younger than Epifanio. Although church records show Andrea to be a single woman, census and church records indicate she was the mother of five children bearing the Aguirre surname: Nabor Aguirre, born in 1844; Albina Aguirre, born in 1848; Indalecio Aguirre, born in 1849; Guadalupe (Santitos) Aguirre, born in 1853 and Jose Aguirre, born in 1856.[2]

It is not known what part Andrea played in the Aguirre household, but shortly after Refugio's death, Epifanio's father took Andrea's younger sister, Narcisa Ornelas, as his wife. Later, on July 11, 1851, a daughter, Dolores (Lola), was born to the couple. Half sister to Epifanio, this tiny dark-eyed girl would one day become the wife of Mariano Samaniego, one of Tucson's most prominent citizens and, when Mamie joined the family, Lola and Santitos Aguirre shared in many of Mamie's activities.

Early in 1852 another event occurred: The Aguirres were visited by a company of American troops who crossed the Rio Grande and came to the Aguirre hacienda. The commander requested food and lodging for his men and horses, so the Americans were treated by the Aguirres with the same hospitality afforded any other guests; both the Americans and their horses were fed. It was an act of frontier courtesy, nothing more. However, a few days after the Americans departed, the Aguirres were surprised to find Mexican troops on their doorstep. [3] And the Mexicans were not there for a pleasant visit.

"You are under arrest for disloyalty to Mexico," the "capitán" told Epifanio's father. "You are guilty of harboring enemies of Mexico."

"Feeding hungry men? How can that be construed as disloyalty to Mexico?" The idea seemed preposterous to don Pedro

Aguirre. "Surely the Mexican soldiers are wrong!"

Yet, the Mexican capitán insisted that helping Americans was treason and ordered the Aguirre patriarch to face a firing squad. Had it not been for a shred of luck, the elder Aguirre would surely have been killed. However, as the capitán was tying a scarf over don Pedro's eyes, he noticed his prisoner was wearing a Masonic ring and said, "I see that we are brothers of the same order. You are a Mason, and for me to shoot you would not be right. Therefore, I give you a chance to live, but you must leave the country."

This was quite a turn of events. The Aguirres never intended to leave Mexico, but they had no choice. As quickly as they could, they packed their belongings into wagons and set off in a northerly direction, taking with them one hundred and thirty families from the Aguirre properties (the Hacienda de Chorrera). Indeed, it was a very long line of covered wagons which arrived in New Mexico in 1852.

At that time Mesilla was still in Mexico because the Gadsden Purchase had not yet been negotiated. [4] So the American-Mexican border lay between Mesilla and Las Cruces. Once the Aguirres crossed the border, they lost no time in getting settled in Las Cruces. Over the next few years they purchased land near Las Cruces, established a ranch, a flour mill and developed a mine.

To fully comprehend what the Aguirres' new home was like, one must first understand the society from which they evolved. Men like Pedro Aguirre and his sons considered themselves Spanish aristocrats—not mere Mexicans. They were the masters of the haciendas and, like all masters of their time, they expected working class Mexicans to know their place. Their lifestyle did not change by moving to a new country. Life simply went on much as it had in Mexico. The climate in New Mexico was similar to that in Chihuahua; they continued to speak Spanish and their way of life evolved much as it had before with exactly the same customs—and caste system.

Epifanio appeared to channel all his energy into his work and, in a short time, built a very impressive freight business. Originally in partnership with his father and younger brothers, Pedro and Conrado, he was sole owner of the company after the partnership dissolved by mutual consent on November 20,

1865.[5] His freight route lay between Westport, Missouri, and Chihuahua, Mexico. The journey between these two posts took approximately ten to twelve weeks (depending on the weather and load) and included a multitude of hazards, such as a ninety mile waterless desert between Las Cruces and Santa Fe, and 750 miles of rugged terrain where men and beasts were forced to scale the outer slopes of the Sangre De Cristo range. The untamed waters of the Arkansas River had to be crossed, and always there was a possibility of being attacked by native raiding parties.

Epifanio soon became known as one of the bravest overland freighters in the territories. Scorning danger, he established a solid freight business. Fellow travelers had the highest regard for him, as did the men who worked for him, and, it was said, he employed over three hundred workers at one time on his ranch and freight wagons. He was honest and compassionate, yet represented a force to be reckoned with when he saw others treated unfairly.

Once, when his brothers were unjustly taken into custody in Magdalena, Mexico, it needed only Epifanio's appearance at the jailhouse to gain their release. [6] His ability to be a firm negotiator was again demonstrated when, at the age of twenty-six, he was sent as a delegate to the 1860 conference of the National Government in Tucson. Here he assisted in drafting legislation whereby the New Mexican territory could be cut in two, thus forming the territories of New Mexico and Arizona in 1863. As a delegate, Epifanio was also instrumental in electing territorial officials.

Epifanio was well-known across the developing states, from Missouri to Mexico. Charles Raber, a Westport trader, wrote of encountering Epifanio and his mule train on the Santa Fe Trail and selling him a wagon train including forty yoke of oxen. Traveling constantly up and down the Santa Fe Trail (then called the Road to Santa Fe), don Epifanio was known as a tireless worker, never stopping to consider his own happiness, nor a permanent relationship—until he met Mamie.

It was little wonder Epifanio chose Mamie over all the other women he had encountered. Tiny in stature, she had an infectious laugh which was never more than a heartbeat away. She marveled at a cloud's silver lining, the song of a bird, a dew-laden cobweb—it was her childlike inquisitiveness that Epifanio found invigorating. What did it matter that neither spoke the other's language! More than anything else in the world, don Epifanio longed to have Mamie by his side.

As for Mamie's father, during seven years of business dealings, he had had ample time to acquaint himself with his prospective son-in-law. Joab knew don Epifanio to be a wealthy man with a reputation for bravery, a handsome man who had the ability to win his daughter's heart. Most certainly there were times when Joab had misgivings. To begin with, there was the question of Mamie's age. She was only seventeen—far too young to be sent off to live among foreigners. Yet, the Civil War was upon them, and if Joab must sacrifice one daughter to save the family, then he must approve the marriage.

Mamie was ecstatic when Epifanio invited her go riding in his carriage. He owned a stylish carriage and a team of snow-white horses which made an impressive sight when driving the streets of Westport. [7] Proudly, Mamie sat beside her gallant suitor. He was in every way the answer to a young woman's dreams: her Romeo, her fearless knight. Sometimes, when she saw him on horseback, it seemed he had ridden out of the pages of a fairy tale. The following poem (title and author unknown) speaks of the love which placed this verse among Mamie's most precious belongings.

> "From the desert I come to thee on a stallion shod with fire;
> And the winds are left behind in the speed of my desire.
> Under the window I stand and the midnight hears my cry:
> I love thee, I love thee, a love that shall not die."

Mamie never gave a detailed account of her marriage during the war years, but simply wrote:

> "We picked lint, tore bandages to send South and studied and played the piano, when the soldiers would let us, and in fact a year went by insensibly until 1862, when I was married just in the midst of all these war troubles. My husband was a freighter, a native of Chihuahua (Mexico) and was not available as a soldier, so was not molested."

The wedding of Mamie and Epifanio took place in Westport, Missouri, on August 21, 1862. She had just turned eighteen;

Epifanio was twenty-eight. Florence Price, the young woman who helped make the controversial flag, was Mamie's bridesmaid. Years later, the couple's whirlwind courtship and dazzling wedding were still remembered as the romance of the century. Many young women sighed as they watched the happy event. To the younger set, Mamie and Epifanio made the perfect couple; he was the rich, handsome groom; she was the pretty Southern Belle.

Yet, rumor has it there were some misgivings: the town gossips "tut-tutting" over the perceived language barrier, the idea of a Catholic marrying a Methodist. And what about future children who would be Mexican, Scottish and French, and perhaps ostracized because of their mixed blood? "Not exactly a recipe for wedded bliss," said the skeptics.

Years later, columnist Robert Pearman published an account of Mamie and Epifanio's wedding in *The Kansas City Times*. Although not entirely accurate, Pearman captures the romance of the day by saying:

"The oppressive heat of mid-August had settled like a furred robe over the town of Westport. Chickens dug dust-holes beneath the burnished bushes. Dogs no longer chased the creaking wagons the first hundred yards toward Santa Fe, but lay with their tongues extended, panting in the meager shade of buildings.

"Only the people ignored the discomfort and engaged in bustling activity. For here on August 21, 1862, the day of the wedding was at hand.

"Westport belle, Mary (Mamie) Bernard, was to be married to a dashing Spanish trader who had traveled across the rolling sea of prairie from another land to claim his bride. There was no doubt that Señor don Epifanio Aguirre, 28, from far away Chihauhua, Mexico, was a rich man—an attribute much admired here on the Missouri border in the throes of economic depression brought on by the Civil War. Señor Aguirre's bridle and saddle glittered with silver. He was a partner in a wagon train and his villa in Chihuahua was said to be of fabulous dimensions. His clothing was cut from rich fabrics, but his handsome Latin features bore the marks of exposure to the sun and the wind and the rain from his many days on the trail."

Another writer for *The Kansas City Star* published the following report some years later. [8]

"As you stroll today through what was once the town of Westport, centering around Westport Road and Pennsylvania Avenue, it does not seem possible that anything very romantic ever could have happened there. It is a placid, drowsy region of retail business houses in no way pretentious. Collarless men are much in evidence and never in a hurry.

"If anyone were to tell you that a young Mexican don, immensely rich, his saddle and bridle glittering with silver, came there to woo and win a pretty American girl—well, you might be pardoned for supposing your informant was suffering from a touch of the sun, or perhaps too many movies.

"Yet, that is what happened in Westport. The bride was young Mamie Bernard and the bridegroom don Epifanio Aguirre of the state of Sonora, Mexico.

"Don Epifanio had come to trade with the Bernards. He was a young man who knew exactly what he wanted. He desired ardently and at once the love of young Mamie Bernard and he wanted to marry her. He spoke no English and she knew no Spanish. But they both knew a young man named Jesse Polk in Westport. He could speak fluently in both languages. You can picture, if you will, the amiable Polk sitting on a side porch with Mamie and don Epifanio, acting as Cupid's interpreter. You can imagine how delicate a degree of perception was required for Polk to know the exact moment when it was polite and kind for him to withdraw, leaving the glamour-struck young couple to say it with eyes and hands in universal language. That it is not so very difficult when there is cooperation on both sides.

"The town of Westport must have buzzed indeed as this romance progressed. Why, it was like something out of Shakespeare, only more exciting. It was like Othello and the fair Desdemona, except, of course, that Señor Aguirre was not jealous, like Othello. He was courteous, so thoughtful, so good looking. Lucky Mamie! Ah, do you think so? She will have to go far away, to a country where she will hear no language except Spanish. Pretty daring, pretty difficult. Thus the matrons and maids of old Westport prattled on their verandahs, shaded by honeysuckle, bright with morning glories..."

Undoubtedly the wedding was the happiest event to be staged in Westport in the summer of 1862, especially since it followed hot on the heels of two major Civil War conflicts. Both were fought a short distance from Westport. One battle took place at Independence, twelve miles away, on August 11,1862, and the other was the Battle of Lone Jack, a few miles further south on August 15th and 16th, 1862. Both battles were won by Confederate armies, but it was a hollow victory when measured against the six hundred new graves on the outskirts of Westport.

Food was still in short supply. However, by careful rationing, Arabella was able to save enough choice baking ingredients to make her daughter's wedding cake, and since Arabella specialized in decorating cakes, Mamie's wedding cake was decorated to perfection.

The groom, too, added finesse to the occasion when he presented Mamie with an exquisite silver tea and coffee service, consisting of a tea pot, cream jug, sugar bowl and coffee urn. Each piece was beautifully engraved with the intertwining initials, "EMA," signifying the union of Epifanio and Mamie (Aguirre). A set of silver cutlery, also a gift from the groom, was similarly engraved. The unique gifts are still in existence today—family heirlooms—reminding descendants of a romantic past.

From Mamie's journal entries we learn that after the wedding don Epifanio took her only as far as Leavenworth, Kansas. Why did he not take her home to Las Cruces? Perhaps an explanation can be found in this excerpt from *Arizona Days* by Rosco Wilson of Tucson:

"...shortly after his marriage to Mary Bernard, he (Epifanio) loaded up a train and started it out on the Santa Fe Trail, intending to follow it in a carriage with his bride the next day. Fortunately for the newlyweds, business came up that detained them for a couple of days. When the business was transacted they joined a company of soldiers headed for Arizona by way of the Santa Fe, expecting to join Aguirre's train within four days. Three days out they came upon the smoldering remains of the wagons. In the wreckage lay the bodies of the teamsters. The wagons had been plundered and burned by the Indians and the stock driven off.

"While they were looking over the scene of the attack, a scarecrow of a man approached them from a nearby clump of willows. It was the major dominio, or "Capataz" of the train who, while wounded in the neck by an arrow, had managed to escape and conceal himself in a shallow coulee among the willows. He was the sole survivor of twenty-one men who had been in the train. Had don Epifanio and his bride not been detained they would undoubtedly have met the fate of the twenty teamsters.

"With a detachment of ten soldiers as guards, Aguirre and his bride then turned back to Independence, where two weeks were spent in getting together another outfit and goods to replace those destroyed by the Comanches."

The same article reports that,

"Don Epifanio made and lost several fortunes... but, with the backing of his father, don Pedro, as well as credit extended to him by wealthy merchants with whom he dealt, and by drawing on the resources of ranches he had established in Sonora and on the border, southwest of Tucson, he was always able to start over and recoup his losses."

Much as Mamie may have wanted to accompany her new husband over the Santa Fe Trail in the fall of 1862, she was unable to do so. Instead, more than a year would elapse before she found her way to Las Cruces. With the Cinderella wedding over, Mamie went back to live with her parents until her first born was old enough to travel, setting a precedent for Mamie's sister, Nan, to follow eight years later.

While Mamie's thoughts were taken up with her wedding, radical political changes were taking place in Washington: Abraham Lincoln had changed the character of the war, by changing the platform on which it had previously been fought. Now, instead of focusing on saving the Union, Lincoln began to speak about freeing slaves. Prior to this a former slave and eloquent abolitionist, Frederick Douglas, had frequently urged Lincoln to change his platform from "anti-secession" to "antislavery," but the Union President had steadfastly refused to interfere with slavery.

Years before Lincoln devised a plan to send Afro-Americans (born in America) to Africa, saying he would "restore a captive people to their long-lost fatherland." [9] This proposed legislation, which called for the deportation of all slaves and compensation for former slave holders on a per capita basis, had been extremely unpopular and almost cost Lincoln his political career. As far as the president was concerned, the Civil War was about saving the union, not freeing slaves. "I will not see my country broken," he stated. In 1861 he had no intention of taking a political stand on slavery, however, by the summer of 1862, Lincoln was beginning to waver. The Civil War was claiming far too many lives, and there was no end in sight. Surprisingly, the Southerners were not only holding their own, but chalking up an impressive list of victories.

Each day the war dragged on, the president could feel himself losing popularity with his electorate. Furthermore, it was evident that England was preparing to aid the Confederate army and that was something the Union could ill afford. "We must change tactics or lose the war," he told his cabinet. So, on September 22, 1862, the Emancipation Proclamation to free slaves was issued and was permanently endorsed on January 1, 1863.

Mamie had been quite accustomed to seeing slaves going about their various tasks in Westport. According to the Jackson County Census of 1860, eighty-five Westport families owned 421 slaves. Black hands worked the fields, washed clothes, cooked meals, scrubbed floors and tended children. Mamie never witnessed slaves beaten by ruthless masters, nor ever attended a slave auction where black arms and legs were shackled to iron stakes. Mamie saw only "black servants," as she called them, such as her beloved nanny who she regarded as family.

The identity of Bernard's black servants have not yet been proven, but two are thought to have been nicknamed "Roe" and "Inie." Possibly they were the parents of Angeline, the thirteen year-old girl who accompanied Mamie to New Mexico. However, we do know that Arabella's black servants were always treated fairly. After Joab died and Arabella moved to Tucson, she was accompanied by a former slave (presumably Roe). This man was free, but chose to live out his life in Arizona as an important member of the Bernard family.

Among other things, the fall of 1862 saw major changes in the Civil War. Previously the Confederates had had the upper hand, but the tide was turning, and Southern troops were defeated in battles fought in Springfield, Fredericktown and Belmont, Missouri. Jesse James and Cole Younger were involved in some of the battles that sprang up along the Kansas and Missouri border. At first Cole merely ran errands for Sterling Price, but in August of 1862, he enlisted as a first lieutenant in General Shelby's brigade. Later, in October of that same year, Cole was in charge of a dozen men camped just outside Westport, on Big Creek, about five miles from his parents' farm.

One day, while Cole was in camp, a soldier by the name of Hays came galloping up to the tents with news that Quantrill had captured Stephen Elkins and was planning to have Elkins shot as a Union spy. As quickly as he could, Cole rode to Quantrill's camp where, sure enough, Quantrill's men were preparing to shoot Cole's former teacher.

"We shoot all spies," Quantrill said, as Cole hurried to Stephen Elkin's defense.

"I know this man to be a Southerner," Cole explained. "His brother and father are Confederate soldiers, and he would be in uniform himself, had he not been staying at home to care for his mother." [10]

Apparently, Cole's plea was convincing: Quantrill turned his prisoner over to eighteen-year-old Cole who took his former teacher to the Harrisonville-Kansas crossroads, where the two struck out in opposite directions—Stephen, on the road to success—Cole, on the road to becoming a notorious outlaw.

Chapter Seven—Parting

After Epifanio and Mamie's wedding there was a brief spell when border fighting slowed to a halt. The Confederate army appeared to be winning the war, and many people believed the conflict would soon be over. During this lull, the people of Westport resumed normal activities and, after purchasing another mule train, Epifanio decided to return to New Mexico—without Mamie.

His wagons were loaded, ready to begin the long overland journey. Once again whips cracked and the dust rose in gray swirls as the wheels of the huge freight wagons took up their melancholy creaking down main street. Taking the lead, Epifanio escorted the train out of town. Then, after checking to see that all was as it should be, he swung back to the Bernard residence. Preparing to say goodbye, he tied his horse in the shade of Duke Simpson's woodshed where the scent of currants and wild plums lay heavy in the autumn air. Leaves fluttered to the ground, crunched under his feet, reminding him of a summer which had passed too quickly.

Suddenly the door opened and his eighteen year-old bride rushed out, her hair streaming down in dark ringlets, her long gown billowing out like the delicate petals of a windblown flower.

How can she bear to part with him, she wonders. How can she remain in Westport while her new husband makes a long dangerous trip without her? As Epifanio walked toward her, she heard the nervous pawing of his horse. Anxious to join fellow travelers, the horse whinnied, a high pitched sound that gave a sense of urgency to the solemn occasion. Tears, more tears than Mamie had ever shed, flowed freely as her husband embraced and kissed her, then promised to return early in the New Year.

The following poem, found in Mamie's poetry collection, unveils the unhappiness of that long ago day:

"The saddest tears that human eyes can weep
Are clustered round that pregnant word, Farewell!
Oh, tender heart, may all thy memories keep
Our happy love, untouched by time's sere spell!"

(title and author unknown)

Four and a half months is an eternity for young lovers to be separated, but true to his promise, Epifanio returned in January. After a long, tedious haul to New Mexico with heavily laden freight wagons, his return trip on horseback took much less time and was probably made in the company of a fast moving stage.

Once again the young couple were reunited. Picture the pretty brown-eyed Mamie in a long full gown, covering all but the tips of her toes, her dashing hero beside her in the family parlor in Westport. Together, they had made plans to go "East." Although the Civil War was still problematic for travellers, and Jayhawkers and Bushwhackers posed a major threat, Mamie and her mother had coaxed Epifanio to take them to Baltimore. Mamie's sister, Kate, was marrying Rezin Worthington, a young man from one of the wealthiest families in Baltimore, and no amount of persuasion could deter the two women from their objective. Both mother and daughter could be stubborn when they set their minds to a plan of action—and both planned to go to Kate's wedding, on February 9th.

Arabella was confident that young Aguirre could protect them from any villains they might encounter along the way. That was a legitimate assumption, for her Mexican son-in-law successfully faced multiple hazards on a daily basis.

"In January 1863, we took a trip to Baltimore," Mamie wrote. "We went from Kansas City, Missouri, to Leavenworth (Kansas) by stage and from there across the Missouri River on a ferry to Weston, where we took the Hannibal and St. Joe Railroad to the 'East' going through Chicago. Here we laid over a day to see the city. While in the 'East' I went to New York and Philadelphia."

Although Kate's wedding was the highlight of the trip, it also gave Arabella a chance to visit her kinfolk, and Mamie an opportunity to visit old friends. As for Epifanio, the trip enabled him to meet some of his eastern suppliers and buy much needed equipment for his freight line. All told, the excursion took the best part of three months and, when the travelers arrived home, they had exciting news: Mamie was expecting her first child.

"We returned to Westport in March 1863 by the same route we took going," Mamie explained. "When we came to Weston there was no ferry running, as the soldiers had taken it, so we had to cross in an open boat with the wind blowing a gale and the water coming in at every dip of the oars. Our feet were soaking wet and we were nearly frozen. When we reached the landing place, the boat would not touch the shore, so the passengers had to wade it or be carried out. There were three ladies, my mother, a stranger, (very tall and slim) and myself. A small soldier, my husband and three other men were at the oars.

"When the move began, the little soldier was very gallant and offered to carry the lady out. Finally, she agreed to try it and very bashfully got on his back, that being the only possible way he could carry her. Her arms were around his neck and her feet were dangling down. He went through water above his knees, and her feet were flopping in the water at every step.

"I was convulsed with laughter, but my mother, whose turn came next, was shocked and in a quandary as to what she was to do. My husband offered to take her in his arms—as he was very strong and tall—but she thought she was too heavy. Finally, she concluded to get on his back, and she went off with her feet hanging down, but not in the water. Then came my turn, and I was carried out in my husband's arms as if I were a child, for I was small and slight. We then took a stage for a cold, miserable ride of four miles to the town."

With the trip to Baltimore over, Epifanio resumed freighting over the Santa Fe Trail. He had contracts to honor, or face losing his business. So once again, he joined his brothers on the trail, and Mamie was left behind in Westport with her parents.

As a general rule, freighters made the bulk of their trips in the spring and fall because freighting was easier in those seasons. Winter snows often lay deep in the mountain passes and, in summer, the water holes dried up, leaving men and animals without water. The usual pattern for New Mexican freighters was to plant crops in early spring, then leave for Missouri with their freight trains and, when they returned, their crops would be ready to harvest.

The summer of 1863 was a difficult season for the Bernard family. Daily skirmishes had once more erupted along the Missouri-Kansas border. Being in the final stages of her pregnancy, Mamie was often confined to her room, because women with her "sickness," as the condition was called, could not be seen in public. Recalling this period of time, Mamie wrote:

> "On June 26, 1863, my son, Pedro, was born in Westport, Missouri. Both just before and just after his birth, small battles were fought near Westport, and we heard very distinctly the firing and screams and general uproar of the battle.

> "The wounded and dead were brought into Westport and the Harris House was turned into a hospital where the Blue and Gray were tended with equal care. Men were taken out of their homes by the 'Jayhawkers' (northerners) and shot down before the eyes of their wives and children. The famous (and infamous) Order #11 was given about that time, and the people had to leave their comfortable homes and take refuge in town. The stables around Westport were the winter homes of many who had lived in comfort and plenty all their lives."

On July 31, 1863, General Thomas Ewing, Jr. established military posts at Westport, Shawnee Mission and Little Santa Fe. Ewing stated that this was "to protect Kansas from Missouri guerrilla raiders." Yet, Mamie believed the opposite was true: it was the residents of Missouri who needed protection. Each day, the atmosphere around town grew more strained as hoards of Union soldiers streamed into Westport and, much as Mamie loved Westport, she now prayed to escape from the sorry little town.

Thankfully, her prayers were answered when Epifanio

returned to Westport on August 5, 1863, that being the day his homecoming was reported in the *Kansas City Journal of Commerce*. To quote the journal: "Epifanio Aguirre's wagon train, of ten wagons, arrived at Westport Landing, carrying wool from Altar, Sonora, a town within thirty-five miles of Port Liberated (sic) on the Gulf of California."

If Epifanio was overjoyed at the sight of Mamie and his month-old son, then he was equally shocked to see armed troops on every street corner. In his absence, Westport had become a concentration camp—the residents prisoners—and, although he was a Mexican and unlikely to be attacked, he was extremely concerned for his wife and new baby.

Shortly after this, even more upsetting government orders went into effect. Epifanio was an intelligent man, and his anxiety grew as he watched the effect the new legislation had on his wife's friends. The first ruling implemented was Order #11. An explanation of this order is given in the *"Annals of Shawnee Methodist Mission,"* published by the Kansas State Historical Society:

> "August 25, 1863—Thomas Ewing, Jr., issued Order No. 11, ordering persons living in parts of Jackson, Class, Bates and Vernon counties, Missouri, to remove from their place of residence. The Reverend Johnson was said to have brought seventeen families home with him after this order."

Among the families affected by this order was the Elkins family. In compliance with Order #11, Stephen and his mother were ordered off their farm. This left Mrs. Elkins homeless, until Mamie's parents invited her to live with them, which she did for the duration of the war. As for Stephen, don Epifanio came to the rescue by allowing Stephen to accompany the Aguirre mule train on the next trip to New Mexico.

Less fortunate was Cole Younger's mother. The following winter of 1863-64, she had not yet complied with Order #11, so Union men were sent out to evict her from her home. They came at night, when the snow lay deep and, before they allowed her to leave, they forced her to set fire to her own house. The terrified woman fled to Harrisonville accompanied by her four youngest children and Suse, a former slave girl who had chosen to remain with the family. Later, in an attempt to locate Cole, the Union men followed the family to Harrisonville. When questioned as to Cole's whereabouts, Suse refused to answer, so the soldiers put a noose around the girl's neck and left her dangling from a nearby tree. Had it not been for Cole's mother cutting the rope, the former slave would surely have died. [1]

If towns, such as Harrisonville and Westport, had not already been designated as prison camps, then Order #11, sealed their fate [2] More Southerners were rounded up and moved into town to be kept under surveillance. Just when the people of Westport thought they had suffered every possible oppression, along came another cursed piece of legislation—Benjamin Butler's order, calling for the jailing of Confederate women.

Butler was a Union army commander with a reputation for cruelty. He once had a man publicly hanged for tearing down an American flag, and prided himself on starving Southerners by torching their granaries. "Instill terror" was his motto and, in keeping with this, he masterminded the Woman Order—a law which brought untold grief to Westport in August 1863. The order, first issued on May 15, 1862, decreed that "if any woman should insult or show contempt for any officer or soldier of the United States, she should be regarded and shall be held liable to be treated as a woman of the town plying her avocation." [3] In other words Confederate women who refused the attention of a Union soldier could be arrested as a whore and treated in like manner.

As a result of Butler's order, more than one hundred Westport females were arrested and jailed. Many were wives or sweethearts of Confederate soldiers. They were confined in a makeshift prison in the Union Hotel, three miles north of Westport. [4] This old hotel towered to a height of three stories and was said to be owned by George Caleb Bingham. The first floor housed a Jewish grocer (the term grocer being synonymous with saloonkeeper), the third floor housed girls of easy virtue, and sandwiched between (on the second floor) were the prisoners—the Southern girls. The "bad" girls came and went as they pleased, while the "good" girls were locked up. [5] Nannie Harris, and three of Cole Younger's sisters, Josie, Caroline and Sally, were among the young women held in the tottery old building. Joining them were several of Cole Younger's cousins as well as Mary and Josephine Anderson whose brother, Bill, had been their protector after their father's death. [6]

On August 12, 1863, the liquor vendor on the first floor complained that hogs were burrowing under the hotel to get out of the oppressive summer heat. He swore the building swayed with the motion of the pigs. A day later, in response to the complaint, a sergeant was sent to the hotel to conduct an inspection. The sergeant reported the building was safe. However, on August 14th there was a terrible grinding as bricks and mortar shot out from the building. Then, with a deafening crash, the structure collapsed. Heavy timbers, holding up the third floor, came tumbling down, crushing everything in their wake, including the Southern girls. Several died, others were seriously injured. Among the dead were fourteen year-old Josephine, Bill Anderson's sister, and Charity Kerr, Cole Younger's cousin. [7]

Word spread among the Confederates that the building had been deliberately undermined by Union troops. Three days later, Bill Anderson gathered a group of friends and relatives together. Denouncing the Union, he swore Kansas would pay dearly for his sister's death. He would enlist the help of William Quantrill, and together they would attack the town of Lawrence—the enemy's stronghold—kill every man, burn every building. They would show no mercy!

The resulting raid August 21, 1863, on Lawrence was not a battle, but a blood bath. The townspeople were taken completely by surprise as two hundred armed rebels led by Quantrill and "Bloody Bill Anderson" charged through the streets. Citizens scrambled to get out of the way of stampeding horses and flying bullets. Young men, old men, choir boys or cripples—it made no difference—they died where the rebels found them. Before the sun set that day, Lawrence's dead numbered over one hundred and forty with approximately a hundred homes and seventy-five businesses destroyed by fire. [8] It was a terrible day of slaughter which no respectable Confederate could take pride in.

Union vengeance was swift to descend on Westport. Once again, any man suspected of being a rebel was dragged into the street by Union troops and shot. It mattered not that wives were clinging to their husband's shirtsleeves, begging for mercy. "An eye for an eye and a tooth for a tooth!" Guns barked and citizens fell on Westport's dusty streets.

Chapter Eight—On The Santa Fe Trail

When Epifanio returned to Westport, Joab was greatly relieved. Young Aguirre and his vaqueros were well armed and, even as guns blazed around town, Joab enjoyed a certain sense of security.

However, Epifanio would not be staying long in Westport, and he made that very clear. Mamie had just presented him with a precious infant—and Westport was a war zone. This was no place for a baby, especially a baby whose mother helped make a Confederate battle flag. Just as soon as she was strong enough to travel, he was taking his wife and baby home to Las Cruces, New Mexico.

With a heavy heart, sixty-three year-old Joab listened to Epifanio's ultimatum. By now, Joab had grown accustomed to rocking his first grandson and, on occasion, entertaining the child with comical antics and lively hymns. He also worried about his daughter's welfare. Mamie was only eighteen. Physically, she was so small-boned, so short in height that she could pass for being much younger. To a doting father, she seemed far too immature to hand over to a race of people so different from his own.

After some discussion, it was decided that Joab and Mamie's sister, Margaret, would go with the Aguirres to New Mexico. Joab would then be able to see for himself what life in the territory would be like for his daughter and grandson.

Another reason for Joab and Margaret's visit to New Mexico was to avoid retaliations from the Union. Margaret and Mamie had sewn Confederate flags and, with their father, had been involved in Confederate rallies. Joab believed that if he and his two rebel rousing daughters were in New Mexico during this latest political upheaval, then the rest of his family could live without being constantly hassled.

Arabella, the family anchor, would stay at home, in the house the neighbors called "Fort Bell." She would not be alone; Mrs. Elkins, the permanent house guest, and her five youngest children would keep her company.

Nothing fazed Arabella; she had reliable friends, a strong faith in God and former slaves who were still loyal to her. If anyone could brave Westport's hostilities it was Arabella. She was a stern, arrogant, plucky woman who simply straightened her shoulders and set about the task of packing bags, boxes and trunks for her departing loved ones.

In the last days before Mamie left, she and Margaret visited friends and relatives, saying "good-bye" to the Harris girls, Florence Price and Cousin William and his family—those who were still in Westport. However, their list of acquaintances had been drastically reduced in the past few months. Living on the border had become so hazardous that a full scale exodus had begun the previous year. Even one of Mamie's favorite cousins, Cornelia Hamilton, and her husband, James, had made a temporary move to San Jose, California, with their large family, in April 1863.[1]

In fact, the Civil War had such an impact on Westport that parents begged Epifanio to take their sons to New Mexico. Most of the young men had no money to pay their way, but they could drive teams, wrangle horses—anything—as long as Epifanio would rescue them from the almost certain death young men faced if they remained on the Missouri-Kansas border. Among Mamie's childhood friends to go to New Mexico with the Aguirres were Joe Bernard (Mamie's cousin), Stephen Elkins, Dory Jones and Johnny Behan.

"In September 1863 we made preparations for another trip," Mamie wrote. "This time it was to be to the unknown lands across the plains and by the 19th, all was ready, and we started from Westport in ambulances (which were used to transport passengers)—quite a party of us.[2] There was my father, my sister, Margaret, my husband and myself and Pedro, then not quite three months old, and his nurse girl, Angeline, only thirteen years old.

"In another ambulance was Stephen Elkins, then a young man of twenty-one, just beginning in the world with no money in his pockets, but plenty of brains in his head from which to coin money to fill his pockets. He had a sunny temper and no end of grit and a loving, kind heart and with him came a member of Governor Goodwin's party."

1863 was the year the Federal Government made Arizona an independent territory, so the newly appointed Governor Goodwin and his officers were traveling in another mule train led by Epifanio's youngest brother, Yjinio. [3] That mule train left Missouri a few days ahead of Epifanio's, but was overtaken in Santa Fe. After this, both trains traveled together as far as Albuquerque.

"In another small wagon were two young men, Messrs. Wells and Giles," Mamie recalled. "In another, a family by the name of Kitchen—a mother and three little children and their cook. [4] The provision wagon was driven by Dory Jones, a young friend of ours, about sixteen."

Mamie had been acquainted with Dory for several years. After his mother's death, Dory's father married the niece of James and Cornelia (Bernard) Hamilton; thus Dory was raised by Mamie's relatives. Dory's father, Henry, owned a farm seven miles south of Westport where the Aguirres pastured their mules, and where Dory learned to speak Spanish from Jose Ortiz, a Mexican farmhand. This gave the sixteen year-old quite an advantage on the trail, for he could easily converse with Mamie, Epifanio and the Spanish speaking vaqueros. [5]

There were ten freight wagons and four ambulances in the train. Each of the ten freight wagons were drawn by ten large mules and loaded with 10,000 pounds of freight. Customers shipping freight to Santa Fe, New Mexico paid 15 cents per pound of merchandise. Pertaining to this trip, *The Council Grove Press* reported that "the large mule train of Epifanio Aguirre passed through Council Grove, Kansas, with mining machinery on October 5, 1863."

Mamie was surprised to find how convenient her living arrangements would be on the long journey. Always before she had traveled in small carriages, but the ambulances were much more spacious, or as she said,

"The ambulances used then for crossing the plains, or any long journey, were marvels of comfort—we thought—being arranged for sleeping as are Pullman sleepers on (railroad) trains nowadays, the seats built so they could be made into beds at night. We rode in the ambulances and found them as comfortable as any carriage, costing $500 apiece. There were toilet arrangements of all kinds under the back seats and in pockets in the doors. It looked from the outside like a rather long carriage and the doors opened on the sides and had windows in them like hacks. They had boxes in the back seat for clothes and sewing boxes, pockets on the sides in the doors which opened as hack doors do; in these pockets were brushes, combs and a looking glass. Under the front seat was another box and there were two seats facing each other so that six people could be comfortably seated. We had tents and camp chairs, a mess chest furnished as completely as a lady's china closet, and the top of this was arranged so it would spread out and make a nice table. We had canned goods galore and all sorts of comforts that money could then buy or loving kindness suggest. So, we started on that journey with every prospect of it being a happy one so far as temporal comforts of this life were concerned. I was like a child, with no more knowledge of the responsibilities of life or the care of a baby and only glad to leave that cruel war and its horrors behind.

"Our road lay through Kansas which was then in a fearful state of exasperation against the Bushwhackers (South) on account of Quantrill having just burned the town of Lawrence and murdered a great many people in revenge for something the Jayhawkers (North) had done to his people. So we could literally feel the 'blood' in the air."

Cautiously, Epifanio guided the mule train through hostile, mid-Kansas countryside. This was a route he had traveled often and knew well, but never before had he been so concerned for the welfare of those in his care. Political killings had become commonplace on this stretch of road, and since Joab, Margaret and Mamie were labeled as "Southerners" by Jayhawkers, and "Turn-coats" by Bushwhackers, they might be considered fair game by either North or South.

Epifanio kept a constant vigil. Whenever he felt uneasy, he would swing his tall frame out of the carriage, mount his horse and ride on ahead to scout the trail. Nothing in the world meant more to him than his tiny wife, the high spirited girl who dared wave a Confederate flag. Loving her as he did, he could not blame her for her patriotism, but knew there was good cause to worry.

On the evening of the fifth night, Epifanio made camp at 110 Mile Creek. The wagons were brought up in their regular circular formation and the tents set up. As usual Mr. Enders, an elderly German cook—one of the best cooks in the country—prepared the evening meal of beef and hominy. The night was sultry and warm and Joab retired early. The moon, when it rose, tinted the camp with streaks of silver light. The leaves of trees, the rims of wagon wheels, pots, pans and metal accessories—all reflected the moonlight. The sounds were of hobbled horses and mules grazing nearby, the hoot of an owl and the yodel of a coyote. Several vaqueros sat around an open fire, exchanging yarns. Their Spanish words interspersed with bouts of laughter were music to Mamie's ears—a melodious sound which suddenly fell silent at the sound of approaching horses. And, judging by the pounding hooves, there were many horses.

"We were thrown into a terrible state of excitement," Mamie said, "by the arrival one night of a company of soldiers when we were one hundred miles on our way from Westport. It was late when they arrived and my husband, sister, Mr. Elkins and myself were in the tent. The soldiers had quite a talk with my husband and Mr. Elkins."

Epifanio and Stephen quickly stepped outside to face the mounted men, while the frightened young women huddled inside the tent, scarcely breathing. Mamie could see the jagged shadows of armed men stretched across the tent and hear the seriousness in their voices. *Why had the Union soldiers come, Mamie wondered. Did they believe one of the Aguirre travelers had been involved in the Lawrence raid? Perhaps they thought her father and his flag-waving daughters had come to Kansas to stir up trouble? Would she and her family be killed as traitors?*

"And finally we found out that the soldiers had been sent, ostensibly, as an escort to keep the 'Bushwhackers' from getting our mules," Mamie explained. "But the real cause was someone had gone to Kansas City, saying we had several ambulances in our train. The soldiers suspected that we were to be met near the line and the ambulances were to be sent to Union enemies in the South. We really did have three ambulances, besides our own, but they were for parties in New Mexico."

Doubtless, it was Epifanio's quiet diplomacy that saved the day. He assured the soldiers that he was not involved in any illegal activity. Without raising his voice or summoning his men to draw their guns, he had alleviated a crisis, and in the days to come, the soldiers were nothing more than a nuisance.

"Those soldiers and lieutenants went with us for weeks," Mamie grumbled, "and my husband had to give them rations for which he never received a cent. We journeyed on, went through Council Grove, Fort Larned and many points where there are towns now, on the Atchison, Topeka and Santa Fe Railroad, but then there was only a wilderness. There was nothing to be seen but grass for miles—one long unending road with not a shrub and never a tree except for an occasional small one, near a water hole.

"We traveled very slowly, never making more than twenty miles a day, which was the fastest time ever made by mule wagons, but we seldom made more than fifteen miles. The day's journey was made to reach certain well known watering places, which were mostly only deep holes made by the rains. The plains I speak of are the prairie lands, five hundred miles of rolling grassy land, that looked boundless as the sea and, when the wind blew over the tall grass, it looked like the waves of the ocean—those long, smooth, green waves we see in water.

"The tall grass was turning gray with the cold that came upon us very gradually. The very monotony of it became pleasant at last. There seemed nothing more to expect, nothing to look forward to and nothing to do. I got so I could sew and read and make myself as comfortable as if I were in a house. Pedro grew and thrived and was the pet and delight of the company. Angeline studied Spanish and made fun for us all through her mistakes.

"We journeyed on and on until we received word from Fort Larned of my sister's death."

The news of Kate's death came as a terrible blow to the travelers. Kate's wedding, the previous February to Rezin Worthington of Diamond Ridge, Baltimore County, had been such a happy occasion. Mamie was stunned. For Kate to die was unthinkable!

As the sad news traveled from one to another, shock reverted to tears. And then, much to Mamie's dismay, her father and Margaret decided to leave for Westport. Watching them go and knowing she could not accompany them was almost more than Mamie could bear. For her, there was no turning back; she was a freighter's wife and must go on alone, without the family she was born into.

Surely a pall fell over the travelers as, once again, the mule train set out on the trail. Onward they went, the miles stretching out behind them in a column of dust, whips cracking and mules braying, but this time without the usual songs or laughter of the vaqueros. For the first time in Mamie's young life, death had claimed someone near to her. Never had she felt such grief or loneliness. But fortunately she had a husband who could comfort her and sometimes distract her from her saddest thoughts.

"About this time we began to meet herds of buffalo," Mamie said, recalling one of those distractions. "They looked like the herds of cattle on Arizona ranches we see today. Our fresh meat was furnished from those herds by hunters of the party who hunted on horseback. We saw droves of antelope and they, too, were to supply us with quantities of fresh meat. The tongues (of the buffalo) were delicious after they were pickled. We had plenty of them as my husband was a great buffalo hunter and kept us well supplied. I can never forget the first buffalo I saw. It had just been killed and we rode to where it was, off the road. I had a curiosity to measure the hair on its neck which I did with my arm, and it covered my arm from my finger tips to my shoulder.

"When we neared the crossing of the Arkansas River there commenced talk of difficulties—as that river used to be very uncertain—until I was anxious for it to be over, having that aforementioned horror of swift muddy streams. By the time we reached the crossing—the old Cimarron crossing it was—the weather was quite cold and we had several dust and wind storms. There was quite a formal camp made on the bank of the river. The wagons were lightened of their loads, the beds raised up, and then twenty mules were hitched to each wagon. They were started with men driving, and two men on horseback were on each side of the teams. When they started (across the river) the teams were never allowed to stop, for if they did, the treacherous quicksand caught the wheels and the feet of the mules and held them. So a good teamster never let his team stop, even for a moment. When about half of the train was over, the ambulances were rushed over because the sand was steadied somewhat. But the horror of it—that awful muddy water! It took two days for the train to cross, and there was quite a jubilee when all were on the other side, and the men sang and had a glass of whiskey all round. The whole camp was gleeful and sat up around the fires, telling yarns late that night. The teamsters sang a sort of chant, a long drawn-out song.

"The first drive after the crossing had to be made a short distance and then they made camp and brought the mules back to the water because there was a forty-five mile journey ahead without water. The afternoon after that first short drive, there came up a terrible wind storm. The wagons were put in a circle by driving one wagon up after the other, each one stopping just a little behind and to one side of the one in front—half of the train on one side, and half on the other—and the ambulances were put in the center. Well, this had been done when the storm came up, and the wind blew with such force that it nearly upset the ambulance in which I was with Pedro and our nursemaid, the redoubtable Angeline. Just as the wind was doing its worst and the men were holding the ambulance, Pedro took the colic. The louder he cried the more frightened Angeline became, until finally she howled outright and commenced to say her prayers and declare the baby would die—almost in the same breath—which I suppose was more than human nature could stand, and I too, commenced to cry. So that when the storm passed and the door was opened, there we were in the depths of woe, the three of us.

"The weather had been so cold that my husband concluded to leave the train and go ahead to Las Vegas where we would wait for the train. So we started, taking the ambulance and the baggage wagon only. We rode right into a blinding snowstorm the first night. My husband knew the country so well that he took the reins of our ambulance himself and drove ahead for dear life, the others following us as fast as they could."

It took all Epifanio's skill (as well as a bull whip) to drive his horses blindly into the eye of the storm, but he knew he was on course. He could feel the jouncing effect of metal-rimmed wheels in ruts on the well-used trail. Mile after mile he raced through the blizzard. Afternoon turned to dusk, dusk to the black of night, or as Mamie recounted:

"We went on and on that whole night, through the blinding snow storm until near day when we were in sight of Wagon Mound, New Mexico, which being such a landmark made us feel safe. Then came the anxiety for the others who were struggling along behind the best they could."

Once in New Mexico, Epifanio found relief from the punishing wind in a grove of pine trees. Wagon Mound, the prominent hill, shaped like a huge loaded wagon, lay far to the south and miles beyond that was the small town of Las Vegas, New Mexico. Epifanio brought his exhausted team to a halt, set up camp and made Mamie and the baby comfortable. Anxiously, he and Mamie waited for the rest of the wagons to come into camp—and come they did. Guided by the blazing fire, the rigs straggled in, one by one. The drivers, white ghosts of men, hopped down from their perches and, knocking snow from their clothing, were drawn like moths to the fire. Then came an appreciative chorus of "Gracias! Gracias! don Epifanio," as tin mugs were handed out to the weary men.

In the flickering light, Epifanio took count of the men as each came to squat beside the fire. It soon became apparent one was missing—young Dory Jones.

"¿Dónde está Dory?" he asked.

But no one had seen Dory's wagon.

Epifanio stood, shaking his head. *How could that be, when ten freight wagons were traveling behind Dory? Each one would have had to pass the young driver on the trail. And then the obvious struck home; the teenager had wandered off the trail and was lost in the blizzard.*

Epifanio knew that he couldn't ask any of his men to go back into the storm to look for Dory. Every man, mule and horse had been pushed to their limit. Yet, his conscience would not allow him to sit by a warm fire while a sixteen-year-old froze to death. Stopping only to check on his wife and child, he set out on foot with nothing to guide him but the feel of the rutted trail beneath his feet.

He called as he walked, but was answered only by the wind's wild cry as the storm continued to cut an icy path across the plains. He trudged on, in total darkness, until the first pale glow of daybreak came to him through the falling snow. By this time, the snow was deep and he was fatigued to the point of resting every few steps, but he would not give up. Then, quite suddenly, he saw the baggage wagon covered so heavily with snow that it almost blended into the landscape. The horses, still hitched to the wagon, were standing quietly facing into the storm. *But where was Dory?*

Epifanio circled the wagon, calling Dory's name and increasing the size of the circle until the teenager was found. Removing his serape, Epifanio wrapped it around the young man, loaded him into the wagon and drove back to camp.

"Dory was put into the wagon more dead than alive," Mamie said, "and my husband drove into camp getting in just after daylight. The snow was still falling, but we could see a house nearby, so we started for that, but we went almost immediately into a marshy place so covered with snow that we could not see the road.

"Into this, our horses floundered and fell, and I had to be carried to another ambulance along with Pedro and Angeline. But we finally arrived at the house which seemed to me like a palace, so tired and cold was I. And it was the first house I had been into since I left Westport, two months before. The owner, Mr. Raber, was kindness itself and although the breakfast was cornbread, fat bacon and black coffee—three things I detested in my normal condition—they seemed like nectar to me, and the way I ate and drank astonished my husband and the rest of the party. We stopped there two days, and then we went on to Krenigs' ranch (La Junta, New Mexico) where there was an old fort, and we stayed all night.

"The next day we arrived in Las Vegas and, at last, I was 'across the plains' and into some semblance of civilization once more. There we stayed a week in very comfortable quarters. The weather was like summer, so warm was the air. We rode to the hot springs which were six miles away up in the mountains. There was only one building with one little room in which was a wooden tub. But the springs were a curiosity to me as was the sight of burros loaded with clothes coming and going, to and from Las Vegas.

"All of the washing for the town was done at the springs, and the women sat around the large spring, rubbing out the clothes on stones.

"From Las Vegas we went on to Santa Fe, taking two days to go seven miles and traveling through those lovely mountains all so new and strange to me—whose eyes had grown used to those unending plains.

"Can you imagine yourself being two months going on a journey that nowadays is made in two days? It took us two months to go from Kansas City to Santa Fe, New Mexico, and then our journey was not yet over. We still had many more miles to travel and eventually lost track of time.

"We stopped at a place called Kosloskeys for the night (before reaching Santa Fe), and for supper and breakfast had fine trout, caught in the mountain stream right there. Just beyond that ranch is the Pecos Church, and there we stopped to see the ruins, then in very good state of preservation. The rafters still held up part of the roof and were beautifully carved at each end. We could trace the outline of the town for a long distance."

The ruins of Pecos Mission remind visitors of the great Spanish explorer, Coronado, who visited an Indian village on this site in 1541.[6] Pecos, being the richest and most powerful pueblo in New Mexico, imported carpenters to erect this particular mission in 1710, but earlier missions existed. The modern traveler is also reminded that a crucial Civil War battle, the Battle of Glorieta Pass, was fought a short distance from the Pecos Ruins in March 1862 (the year prior to Mamie's visit to the ruins). In this skirmish Northern troops, comprised of Colorado and New Mexican volunteers, defeated Confederate forces and officially put an end to all Civil War activities in the Southwest. This military action was another reason why Epifanio was reluctant to take his new bride home to New Mexico in the autumn of 1862. However, by the latter part of 1863, Santa Fe, New Mexico, was alive with all sorts of peacetime activity.

"We arrived in Santa Fe the last of November where we met the rest of the Arizona party and I met Mr. McCormick," Mamie said. "Quite a number of dances were given for Governor Goodwin and his party, and they had quite a lovely time. We stayed there a week and then went down the Rio Grande River in company with the Governor's party. Arizona was then part of New Mexico and almost an unknown part. The Federal Government was established in Arizona that year (1863) making it an independent territory, that being the reason for Governor Goodwin and his officers to come across the plains at that time.

"While in Santa Fe, I saw the first installation of Navajo Indians brought in on their way to the reservation just given them at Bosque Redondo (Fort Stanton). They were the first of 7,000 who were afterwards put on that reservation.

"At Albuquerque we stopped two weeks where the whole party were right royally treated by the natives. One ball was especially elegant. It was given at Peralta not far from Albuquerque—20 miles about—and we had to travel right on the banks of the river. In some places the road was so narrow my hair fairly stood on end.

"From Albuquerque my husband sent Governor Goodwin's party across the country to Prescott with his train. They passed over what is now the line of the A&P Railroad, encountering awful snow storms. In one of the storms, nearly all of the mules were lost—seventy mules in one night—and each one was worth a hundred dollars. Mr. Elkins was intending to go on to Prescott, but was persuaded by myself and my husband to go on to Las Cruces with us. Dory Jones went with us, also.

"We went down the Rio Grande in the ambulance, crossing the river several times to my dismay, finally crossing at Paraje the last time. This was the starting place across the dreaded Jornada del Muerto (Journey of Death). We stopped at Fort Craig near where the town of San Marcial is now. The Jornada is a desert of ninety miles without water and is the 'abomination of desolation,' for even the earth looks like ashes. As the Indians were bad, it was not safe for us to go alone, so we waited for the stage and the paymaster, Major Davis. There were others too, so we joined company and crossed the Jornada together.

"We went into Fort McRae which is on the river and there rested the first night. The next day we went on and arrived late that night near Dona Ana (six miles from Las Cruces), a small town on the Rio Grande River."

Wanting to make a good impression when she met her new in-laws, Mamie scurried around that evening, unpacking her prettiest dress and little Pedro's most appealing baby gown. The great day was at hand and she looked forward—with a certain degree of apprehension—to seeing her new home for the first time.

Chapter Nine—A New Home

The next morning, as the travelers approached the Aguirre hacienda, Mamie wondered what lay ahead. There was no denying the beauty of the landscape. To the east, the Organ Mountains rose in tall, serried peaks, resembling the pipes of an organ and, from which the mountain range took its name. The rock faces were lustrous with various shades of blue, purple and pink and, in fact, appeared to change colors at will. At lower elevations giant yuccas dotted slopes that stretched toward the fertile Mesilla Valley, where the flat-roofed adobes of the Aguirre hacienda could be seen to skirt the banks of the Rio Grande River.

With an all encompassing motion, Epifanio waved a hand. "Do you like? Do you like?" and Mamie nodded, hoping to get the right accent on a newly learned phrase. "¡Hay qué bonito!"

She and her husband had been on the road over three months and were arriving at their destination just one week before Christmas. Mamie had never met Epifanio's parents before and silently prayed that her Spanish speaking in-laws would accept her as part of their family. She found herself wondering if she would be able to adapt to a Spanish-Colonial life-style. Living in New Mexico was going to be quite different from anything she had known: the Spanish language; the Catholic religion; the adobe buildings; the Mexican clothing—it was frightening to think of the contrasting lifestyle and what the future might hold. Yet, she made a conscious decision not to grumble. Instead she would busy herself learning the Spanish language and appreciate the new and interesting things New Mexico had to offer.

As the mule train made its way toward the Aguirre hacienda, friends and relatives came out to greet the travelers. Introductions were made along the way, with much talk and laughter, until finally the ambulances rolled to a stop in front of the main house and Mamie was presented to Epifanio's father and step-mother.

Mamie was greatly relieved when she and her baby were welcomed with the spontaneous exuberance spawned by a long-awaited homecoming and were soon settling happily into their new surroundings. As Epifanio's wife, she was exempt from manual work and given her own personal Moza, a servant who assisted her in all things, and organized daily events. Other servants cooked, cleaned and tended the baby. This left her free to read, do needlework and learn equestrian skills, the latter being very important. In the 1800s, the Spanish descendants who topped the Mexican hierarchy were expected to be skilled riders. The upper-class señorita always rode sidesaddle, either on her own mount or perched in front of her handsome "caballero."

For Mamie, an afternoon's ride was great fun, cantering along paths which wound through creosote and mesquite bushes, tall yuccas and low lying, cacti. At such times, she might catch a fleeting glimpse of a roadrunner, lizard or snake. The occasional Javalina or desert puma provided a thrilling sight for the "Chiquita" from Missouri. It was great fun to go riding with her beloved Epifanio on the mountain trails. Sometimes they dismounted and stretched out in the sun like desert cats; at other times they would actually hunt for game. Later, when Mamie found this poem in a newspaper, she cut it out and pasted it in her scrapbook. It was a reminder of those special moments. (The title and author are unknown.)

> Like tigers we stalked the desert
> Where the antelope came to drink;
> Like a bolt we sprang upon them,
> Ere they had time to shrink...
> Come to my arms my hero:
> The shadows of twilight grow,
> And the tiger's ancient fierceness
> In my veins begin to flow.
> Come not clinging to sue me!
> Take me with triumph and power,
> As a warrior that storms a fortress!
> I will not shrink or cower.
> Come, as you came in the desert,
> Ere we were women and men,
> When the tiger passions were in us,
> And love me as you loved me then!

The New Mexicans were high-spirited people, noted for

being generous with one another and proud of their horses and women. Their culture, inherited from old Mexico, had been handed down from the Spanish Conquistadors and amalgamated with aboriginal customs. Residents of the Las Cruces area loved to celebrate, to hold fiestas, to gamble and stage wild displays of horsemanship. Whether racing horses or feasting, their laughter was spontaneous, their music lively and their dancing frenzied. No one could appreciate this carefree lifestyle more than a young woman who had just fled from the Kansas-Missouri border wars.

"On Christmas day we had a family dinner," Mamie reported happily. "One of the eatables was an immense watermelon as fresh and crisp as if it had just been cut. It had been gathered late and hung in the rafters of a storeroom along with many others of its kind and bunches of grapes also, which, though not quite fresh, were not quite dry and were very nice. They raised quantities of grapes in the Mesilla Valley from which the celebrated El Paso wine was made. These grapes were so sweet and kept very nicely till late in the winter packed in chopped straw. That first winter was delightful to us all. The weather was so warm and the constant sunshine so lovely that we 'States' people enjoyed it to the fullest extent, staying out of doors most of the time.

"We rode on horseback and in the ambulance all over the country. I found some old friends in La Mesilla, the Colonel Jones family and Judge Hackney, who were kindness themselves to me. [1]

"On New Year's day (1864) my husband and myself were invited to be 'Padrinos' (godparents) for the New Year's high mass, which we attended sitting in chairs in front of the altar with highly decorated wax candles in our hands. These were lit, and my whole attention was devoted to keeping that candle straight. For I was so interested with the newness of everything that, should I forget the candle for the moment, it would bob over to the imminent danger of my hat. This was a special attention we were shown because my husband was much beloved in this town.

"Next came Pedro's christening which was a grand affair. For three days before there was a baker and two assistants in the house. They baked no end of cakes and confectionery, roasted fowls and pigs and were highly entertaining to me, on account of the way they made and baked things. Everything was baked in one of those bee-hive-shaped adobe ovens that opened into the kitchen. It was heated red-hot and then all the coals scraped out and things put in on flat pieces of tin and shallow pans. The number of eggs that were used was a marvel, and in fact it was all a wonder to me. There were two hundred guests. People from far and near were invited, some coming from El Paso, sixty miles away. All the officers from California Column, who were stationed there at the time, were on hand.

"First of all, Pedro was taken in state to Mesilla to be christened in the afternoon, his grandfather and grandmother standing for him. Then came the supper and afterwards the dance. Pedro was set at the head of the table and crowed and laughed in a wonderful way for a six months old baby. His health was drunk in champagne by all standing, he being held up by his proud father and then the supper commenced. The dance was kept till the 'wee hours' and everyone enjoyed and long remembered Pedro's christening.

"New Mexico was wonderfully interesting in those times. It always reminded me of the Bible lands and the customs were certainly of Bible times. The plowing was a great curiosity to me. The plows were two poles crossed so one made a point to the ground which was covered with steel (or an iron-shod pointed stick). The oxen were hitched by the horns (they always used oxen), and as many as twelve plows followed each other in one furrow. The furrows were deepened by one yoke of oxen following the other, until there were twelve plowing in the same furrow and until the required depth was reached. The strongest yoke of oxen and man led the furrow.

"Do you remember an expression in the Bible where it says, 'And Jacob led the furrow?' I never knew what that meant until I saw that long line of plows following each other in the same furrow.

"The carts were made of wood entirely, not a piece

of iron in them. The wheels were immense round pieces of wood with holes in them, and the way they creaked and complained as they moved along was comical.

"In those days there were no board floors or unnecessary wood work. The rafters of the houses were unhewn logs; the windows had wooden bars up and down and shutters outside, rough hewn. There were no glass windows. I had the first glass window of any size in Las Cruces. The panes were very small, and there were a great many of them in each sash. The window, which cost sixty dollars, was the comfort of my life and the admiration of the town. The natives would stand, two rows deep outside, looking in at me as I sat on the broad adobe windowsill.

"Then the babies were not dressed as they are now. They were wrapped in swaddling clothes, a succession of wide and narrow bands, beautifully embroidered. The little hands and arms were strapped down tightly with bands. When a child was six months old, tight-waisted shirts for the boys (made like men's with collars and cuffs), and long sleeved dresses for girls, were put on them. Their hands were put in bags, but the swaddling bands were still used underneath. When a new baby came, word was sent out to the immediate friends by a 'mozo' (man servant) that another servant was at their command.

"My babies' clothes were the first American ones anyone had seen in Las Cruces, and their little dresses were borrowed and copied and used over the swaddling bands. Afterwards the people began to dress their babies as I dressed mine, so I started the fashion of American baby clothes in Las Cruces.

"There was something new to see all the time. The annual feasts came on in due time. Each town has its patron saint whose day was celebrated by high Mass and then a week of games and bull fights and dancing in the open air by the populace. There were three towns close together—Donna Ana, Las Cruces and Mesilla whose feasts came in January, February and March and we attended all of them.

"At the Mesilla feast, held in March, there were many more elaborate preparations. I was again invited to be the 'Madrina.' (My husband had gone back to the States, leaving me at my own request, to spend the winter). Again I had to sit in front of the altar with a candle in my hand. I was attended by Steve Elkins, Miltie Jones, my sister-in-law (Lola) and Mrs. Jones, and was dressed in a way that would be astonishing nowadays, for part of my attire was an elaborate cloak which reached to my feet. It was made in the City of Mexico and embroidered a half a yard wide on three capes. I also had to go to the vespers, and the evening was cool. The coat was brown satin and the embroidery white. So you can fancy my astonishing appearance as we sailed up that church aisle, climbing over the kneeling crowds—for there was no seats, and all sat on the floor—till we reached the chairs set for us before the altar. Someone remarked that I must be the Virgin Mary.

"The next afternoon we attended a bull fight. The ring was in the church plaza built of logs tied together with raw hide. Above one side were the private boxes; 'palcos' they were called, which were made of boards loosely put together and covered with canvas. These were reached by ladders of the rudest description and the widest apart rungs one could imagine. It was terrible climbing for short folks like me. When we ladies started up that ladder (me in that wonderful cloak) two men held blankets over us as we went up. When we arrived at the top, the boards of the floor were so wide apart that we came near to stepping through. But we all enjoyed the bull fight immensely, though there were no bulls killed and no blood shed.

"After we got settled in Las Cruces, Steve Elkins commenced the study of law and was admitted to the bar soon after. His first case was intensely interesting to us all and was something about a division of goats. His next case was an assault and battery case, and the next a divorce case for which he got a twenty dollar gold piece and a government pistol. He then went on to success and was sent to the Legislature at Santa Fe."

The Aguirres had given Stephen Elkins a new start in life, and there were fond farewells when Stephen departed from the

Las Cruces hacienda. After becoming a district attorney for New Mexico, he became a territorial delegate to Congress. He married Sara Jacobs of Wellington, Missouri, on June 10, 1866, and they had two daughters. [2] After Sara's untimely death, Stephen moved to West Virginia where he married Hallie Davis, daughter of US Senator Henry Gassaway Davis, the richest man in that state. Eventually, Stephen became a wealthy US senator in his own right, serving as Secretary of War under President Benjamin Harrison.

Mamie went on to say, "I lived in Las Cruces seven months and then went to Las Vegas, New Mexico, with my husband who had, what was then called, an 'interior freight contract' with the government to supply all the military posts of the territory with provisions and freight. The shipping point was Fort Union, and Las Vegas was the closest place to reside. There I lived happily, going occasionally to Santa Fe during the winter of 1864."

In the mid-1860s, the US Government awarded most freighting contracts to local residents. Epifanio submitted a tender for transporting military supplies from Fort Union to the interior posts and, to qualify, he moved his family to Las Vegas, New Mexico, where they lived from July 1864 to February 1865. Mamie and one year-old Pedro traveled by stage to Las Vegas on a winding trail some three hundred and fifty miles or more. Accompanying them was Delores (Lola) Aguirre, Epifanio's half-sister, who was on her way to Kansas City to attend school. By this time, Mamie and Lola had become good friends, so the long trip was kept lively with a generous amount of vivacious chatter.

The contract, awarded Epifanio on June 1, 1864, called for him to freight 5,000,000 pounds @ $2 per 100 pounds (per 100 miles) during peak freighting months, and $2.25 the other months. When he completed the contract at the end of January 1865, he was paid $138,177. This was good money in the 1800s. True there were expenses to be paid: wages, repairs and replacement of livestock, yet it appears the Aguirres enjoyed a prosperous business year. [3]

While Mamie was living in Las Vegas, Pedro's nursemaid, Angeline, married and moved to Fort Union. Mamie was clearly upset by the fifteen year-old's decision to marry, but there was no reasoning with the girl. Angeline was determined to do as she pleased, reminding Mamie that she was "no longer a slave." Yet, Mamie knew full well what Angeline's future was likely to hold: poverty, hard work and birthing babies, one after another, until the poor girl was old before her time. *If that wasn't slavery, what was it?* Mamie wondered.

Dory Jones continued to work for Epifanio for some time. Later Dory found work in Tucson, before moving permanently to Pueblo, Colorado, where, as Mamie said, "he was well-to-do and highly respected by all." Other Westport friends came to New Mexico, and Epifanio, being a generous husband, thought nothing of inviting them—lock, stock and barrel—to his hacienda where many of the young men quickly succumbed to the charms of dark-eyed señoritas and became western ranchers and business-men.

While the Aguirres lived in New Mexico, Joe Bernard, Mamie's first cousin, joined Epifanio in the freighting business. Earlier, Joe had attended the Aguirres' wedding and his signature appears on Epifanio and Mamie's wedding certificate. He was the youngest son of Thomas Bernard and shared the same name as Mamie's father, "Joab Mitchell Bernard." During the Aguirres stay in Las Vegas, he married Louisa Des Marais.

Another important happening took place while Mamie lived in Las Vegas. Her father came to visit, prompting Arabella to send him a firsthand account of the "Battle of Westport."

This bloody conflict was Confederate Sterling Price's last stand and considered a major battle in the Civil War. General Price arrived in Westport with about twelve thousand men, four thousand of which were unarmed. Samuel Curtis, the Union general, met Price with approximately eighteen thousand men; three thousand, six hundred of these were Kansas State Militia, hurriedly mustered in for emergency service. The battle was fought in a series of encounters on October 22 and 23, 1864. Here then, is an eyewitness account of the battle, as recorded by Arabella in a letter to Joab on Oct. 25, 1864.[4]

"Dear Husband:

"Since I wrote great events have transpired. Price has come and gone. The battle was fought on Saturday and Sunday. All day Saturday, troops by the thousand were passing out to meet him, but on Saturday afternoon, Westport saw another sight. Those same troops were in full retreat through the town of Kansas City. They came past the Baptist Church. I watched them from Mrs. Jones' porch—men, horses, wagons, cannons—pell-mell. Later in the evening they made a stand just before our door waiting for the Rebels who they said were just behind them. Dr. Vance was at the gate as merry as ever. I told him I did not want the battle before my door, or I did not think it right, or some such remark, and he said, 'They must fight somewhere!'

"One soldier saw me shutting the shutters and said a cannon ball would go through them. But after awhile the troops moved on down the road, and the women came flocking for protection to the cellar. Old Fort Bell sustained its reputation. So doing all we could, we got supper and settled a little. About eight o'clock, here came the rest of the Federal army, whooping through. Roe was with them. They whooped so loud we thought it was the Confederates, so when they went through we thought we might rest, but about four o'clock, there came some soldiers for supper. We were afraid to let them in, and we were debating what to do when they commenced to batter the green door down; they had off the outside slats. Mrs. Elkins and I went trembling down. I asked them what they wanted.

"We want supper," they said. "We were sent here."

"Who sent you?"

"Colonel Jennison, and you'd better give us supper rather than one hundred." So we opened the door and sat them down to what we had, hominy pork, bread, coffee— and there were seven. We told them we had been feeding soldiers all the evening. They were very civil after they were well filled.

"The next morning, Sunday, the Federal army passed through again, and such a day. The Confederates made a stand about Wornalls' and the fight was at Brush Creek and all around there from Gannets' out. We could see the fed troops on the hill opposite Neely's place where they have cut off the timber all on the hills back of

McCutchens' and the cannon booming and the shells in the air. It was a most beautiful day, and the window in my room was a good place to see, and people were on the wood house and stable. Mr. Simpson's woodshed was filled and was the best place. William (Cousin William) and our girls were up there.

"About the middle of the afternoon, Price commenced retreating. Pleasonton reinforced the Feds and the Rebels got off as fast as they could, leaving their wounded and dead on the field. Fresh troops went through to follow him, and the victorious army straggled home. One soldier called to me, 'Pap Price is gone to hell, and I'm going home.'

"Soon the soldiers were calling for supper, and Margaret and I had to go to work, but I tell you we did not stop to question. We let them in quick and were as polite as could be. Each soldier was a hero, and each had done such good fighting. Most of our company were Jennison men, and I don't think they even saw the fight after Saturday. All think that Price had a large army, but the wounded Confederates say there were not over three thousand; some say twelve hundred and the Feds army were ten thousand here.

"And Pleasonton came up with a great many. It was Shelby's Cavalry, and there were very few Missouri troops mostly Arkansas men. Roe is one of the heroes, too, and declares there were thirteen thousand rebels, but the accounts are different. No two men tell the same tale. There are quantities of wounded and dead brought in all the time. They made the Harris House a hospital and Confeds and Feds are nursed there, but the women as usual (Sally Purdee and company) were quite hard on the rebels and on any who pitied them. I was hardhearted enough to stay away and kept the girls at home, too. Joe Boggs (Dr.) was there and pronounced secesh. She (Sally Purdee), had to leave, but eventually the women kept up such a clatter that in mercy to the men, they turned them all out, but a few. Susan and William (Cousin William Bernard) went down, but it did no good. Some folks are hard on them.

"We were not very well off for flour. Neither was

Susan. There was none at the mill and no stores open for about two weeks, but I never saw anything last like it did. I said, it was like the widow's cruise. I am in hopes I can get some tomorrow. Susan says she must have cooked for a hundred. And eleven stayed there one night.

"There has been a great rush to the battle field. Roe took Innie and Bell this afternoon. She told me to tell you about it, the dead horses are on both sides of the road from Ganets' way out on the Prairie, and such splendid animals—all blooded horses—all their heads toward Westport. One out Wornalls' gate. Charlie Polk was at Mrs. Wornall's and was a Colonel; he sent all the women and children into the cellar, and there they remained during the fight. She went up once to see him, and he was gone and the Federals were there.

"There were Confederate wounded and dead in her house, and it is said they are in the houses around there. I do not know the amount of dead on either side. They find them all about, nearly to the mission. The Confeds took off. Goodwin and his son ran away from them. Jake Booker, too, and he got home today. He left them about six miles from Harrisonville. John Campbell was taken out of Bents' house and shot, some say by rebels, some say by the other party. George Todd is killed [5]. I've some relics of the field for you. John Harris is to be married this week; the cards are out. Susan and Will are invited.

"Wed, This afternoon, Roe put the horses to the carriage and took the girls out to the battlefield and went to Wornalls'. They saw bursted cannon and shells and heard incidents of the fight. There was a much larger force of Confederates than was thought at first. Price was himself on the hill near Wornalls' and was at Boston Adam's place. They left twenty-five wounded there in care of a Rebel surgeon. They were badly wounded. Roe was in the fight and stood his ground well. So, "good-night to Price!" I hope he will make no further attempts to come on the Blue. I hear they are fighting still, and still worsted."

"Dear Mame:
"Today, your letter to Nan of the 10th and Pa's

came. I am glad you are all well and that Pa has some idea of coming home. I commenced this to him, but as he tells me not to write anymore letters to Vegas, I thought I would send it to you, so you and Joe can see how fared the fight in Westport.

"The wounded and dead are still being brought in; many brave boys have fallen. One boy about seventeen, (Rebel) has his leg taken off yesterday at the Harris House. I am so sorry they ever came up, and so many have been killed and buried, and no one will ever know who they are.

"Innie and Roe are in tonight. Innie has been here since last Friday. It was thought the (Shawnee) Mission would be attacked, and Roe had to go with his company, so she came in, and after the fight he came. Things are very unsettled here; yet, the stores are still closed."

"P.S. Ask Joe, don't he wish he had been here to fight? You appear to live well at your house. We seldom make good things now. Everything is so dear and scarce. There are no vegetables, hardly any butter or eggs. I never missed your Pa so much before. We have nothing laid in for winter. We have only three cords of wood and that is green. I have gone about a great deal trying to get things, but if you ever saw desolation, you can see it here.

"I would have had plenty if your Pa had been here. I have felt often how hard it is for him to be away and we getting along so badly. I want to go somewhere where I can get things myself. Every man here, finds it as much as he can do to attend his own family. If I lived where I could get things myself, your Pa could travel till he was satisfied.

"I hope this finds you all well. Pedro will get better as the weather gets cooler. You have been highly favored. He is such a large child and his second summer, too. You would have had a great deal of trouble with him I expect if you had been here. I think I would like to live in Las Cruces better than Las Vegas. You seemed to enjoy yourself so much more there. I send you three ledgers this week. Good-bye. Love to Epifanio and Joe and, if Pa has not left, lots of love to him, too.

"Post script: Nan is very pleased to hear Lola is crocheting on her behalf. She will write next week. We will send the pictures as soon as we get time to pick them out. Goodnight, Good-bye, your mother, A.M. Bernard."

Being a sensitive young woman, Mamie's heart ached as she read her mother's letter. Mamie had long since stopped championing "political causes." Now, all she wanted was to see an end to the Civil War. *What good had all the killing done, she mused. Left women without husbands, children without fathers! Why, oh why, had such a terrible war been allowed to happen?*

Sadly she pasted another poem, *"The Blue and The Gray"* in her scrapbook. It was written by F.M. Finch.

"From silence of sorrowful hours,
The desolate mourners go,
Lovingly laden with flowers,
Alike for the friend and the foe.
Under the sod and the dew,
Waiting for Judgment day,
Under the roses the Blue,
Under the lilies the Gray."

The Civil War was not yet over and, during the next few weeks, news of recent battles continued to filter through to Mamie in New Mexico. Prisoners of war were dying by the hundreds of starvation and disease in makeshift prisons. It was a pitiable situation, and Mamie joined others in prayer for the prisoners and their families.

In the days to come, Mamie's father returned to Westport, and life in Las Vegas continued with Mamie recording the following highlights in her journals:

"We made a trip (from Las Vegas to Santa Fe) about the middle of December. We expected to stay a week and be home for Christmas, but a big snow storm came on and blockaded the mountain roads. This meant we could not leave, so we spent Christmas in Santa Fe. It was exciting! I was going constantly, visiting and receiving visits. The military were very gay and the Governor's (Arny) family, though quiet people, were very cordial. So, the time passed pleasantly.

"On Sunday Steve Elkins and I went to high mass at the old Santa Fe Cathedral, and I was dressed in my best (but not in the aforementioned cloak). I was dismayed when we found there were no seats in the church, and we had to sit on the floor with many inward qualms (on my part), about my nice silk dress. Down we sat on that dirt floor, Steve doubling his feet under him, but this soon grew irksome, and we grew more and more uncomfortable. We were too well bred to leave the church, so we varied our position by kneeling once in a while till church was over. By this time we could scarcely stand and felt as if we had a spell of rheumatism of long standing.

"When we left Santa Fe the roads were splendid, the snow being packed down solid and we enjoyed the lovely scenery.

"I went to a marriage in Las Vegas that was typical of those times in the middle classes. I also attended one of the upper ten.

"For the first wedding, we went to the church to see the ceremony, then went in a sort of procession with the bride, groom, attendants and a dozen men with fiddles and guns. The men played, and the guns were fired off at intervals all the way to the groom's house, where a fine breakfast was prepared. At night there was a dance, the musicians singing verses complimentary to the dancers as they played. Each singer made up the words as they went along, bringing them in to suit the occasion in a wonderful way. The bride changed her dress three times in both cases, the only difference being in the value of the dresses and jewelry, and that of the upper ten did not go in a procession to the church.

"The old Bible custom of a man serving a certain time for his wife, as Jacob did, was carried on in New Mexico, then. Only instead of serving seven years, he served seven months. The bride had to make three changes in her dress from the time she was married until twelve o'clock midnight. If she was poor the bride's maid (always a married woman), had to borrow dresses for her, and they took great pride in getting handsome ones.

"Wheat was threshed out with loose horses turned in upon the stacked wheat which was in an enclosure where the mud floor had been pounded hard. Just as a man now takes his threshing machine from farm to farm, men took their herds of horses to thrash wheat then. Afterwards the men threw the wheat up in baskets, and the wind blew away the chaff. And there were gleaners in the wheat fields—just like in Ruth's time.

"Do you remember how the Bible says, 'He shall tread the wine press alone'? Wine was made by the grapes being put into large rawhide bags with holes in the bottom. These bags were hung from a beam and bare footed men, one to each bag, trod out the juice which ran into large copper kettles of home manufacture. The sweet wine was made by boiling down the juice till it was the consistency of apple butter, (arrope) and with this the wine was sweetened. Think of the concentrated essence of dirt!

"Furniture was homemade and very scarce and priced high. We wore our dresses in one fashion for years, till they wore out. Books were impossible to get, unless we brought them with us. Newspapers and letters came once a month in winter and every two weeks in summer.

"Now I am only telling about the part of New Mexico that was settled, but (at that time) in our beloved Arizona there were not even the few comforts I speak of."

In late April of 1865, more news of the Civil War reached New Mexico. At long last the war was declared over—the Confederates had been defeated. Almost in the same breath the Aguirres heard another shocking report: President Abraham Lincoln had been murdered in Washington on April 15, while attending the Ford Theater. By the time the news filtered down to Mamie, the assassin, John Wilkes Booth, had already been shot, and his accomplices rounded up and hanged.

Most disturbing for the sensitive Mamie was news of a stately old Southern lady being sent to the gallows along with those who had actually planned Lincoln's assassination. Mrs. Mary Surratt, had given Booth shelter, and that appeared to be the old lady's only crime. Since she had been a prestigious socialite, a European traveler and highly respected by her Southern friends, hanging this elderly woman ignited more rebellion.

Once again, Mamie heard of a new rash of retaliatory kill-ings and concluded that if the Civil War was over, it was only on paper. Peace had not really come to her old home in Missouri, or anywhere else in America. Ill feelings were still rampant, as Cole Younger and Jesse James would demonstrate by "looting and shooting" at Union targets for years after the declaration of peace.

Chapter Ten—Life in New Mexico

The huge wheels of Epifanio's freight wagons rolled on, through rain and sleet, through sunshine and storm. Dust flew, black flies and mosquitoes hovered over water holes, and as often as not the vaqueros cursed the day they were born. Theirs was a dangerous job—if accidents didn't end their days, the Indians might. It was said the vaqueros blew their wages as quickly as possible, fearing they might not live long enough to spend them.

Like the vaqueros, Epifanio knew the dangers of hauling freight, but he had to make a living, and freighting was a paying proposition. Consequently, he was more than pleased to have his mule trains freighting from Fort Union's dispatch; there was good money to be made on government contracts, and when he completed his 1863-64 contract he submitted a bid for the coming season. However, William Moore, the Fort Union's sutler, underbid him and got the contract. [1]

It was by this disappointing turn of events, that Epifanio's government contract ran out, and there was nothing for him and his family to do but go back to Las Cruces.

"I remained in Las Vegas till February 1865," Mamie said, "when I returned to Las Cruces in a buggy, stopping at different points on the Rio Grande as my husband's business demanded. We crossed that dreadful Jornada del Muerto (Journey of death) again.

"We traveled in our own conveyance with a stage and did not touch at Fort McRae but stopped for water at Point Rock. Here the United States government had tanks for water which were filled from the river. The water was brought thirty miles in wagons made as tanks. We arrived in Las Cruces in the early part of March. And on May 12, 1865, our second son, Epifanio, was born."

Life in New Mexico was certainly not without hazards for

either Epifanio or Mamie. Sandy Wardwell, a pioneer stagecoach driver, told of an Apache attack south of Socorro, New Mexico, which involved the Aguirres. According to Mr. Wardwell, Epifanio Aguirre, his wife, their two small children and two servants were riding in a carriage, directly behind the stage Wardwell was driving, when Apaches began shooting at the party. Wardwell described what happened. [2]

"On the second night, and just as day was breaking, right at the big laguna, two or three hundred Apaches jumped us, and the "balacera" opened. I was in the lead with the coach, and this man (Aguirre) and his family came next, while the escort (of eight soldiers) brought up the rear. I thought two or three times we were gone.

"One Indian had an old musket, and he knew—and so did I—that if they could stop us, we (travelers) were dead to rights. But I was on my job, as the fellows say, and when the old devil downed a mule, I would jump down and cut it loose and keep going.

"This man Aguirre would take a six shooter in each hand, and his bridle reins in his teeth, and make a dash on ahead and open the way for us, empty his pistols and dart back to his carriage, and his wife (Mamie) would hand him two more loaded. I never saw a man with more nerve in my life. He fought like a demon, and the escort fought well. The passengers were firing all the time, and the top of the stage looked like a porcupine's back, it was so full of arrows. Well, we fought our way to within six miles of Paraje, and then they gave up and left us. I got to the station with three mules in the lead and none on the tongue. The Indians had killed both wheelers.

"It was a pretty close call for us, and I think this Aguirre was the means of saving the whole outfit, for he kept the Indians from closing in on the lead, and the soldiers kept them from the rear."

That same year, November 19, 1865, Mamie's father-in-law was killed when a wagon pole crushed his chest and the Masonic Order, in which don Pedro held a long standing membership, arranged his funeral. [3] Family and friends were liberal with their praise for this great pioneer who had established farms and ranches, developed mines and built a flour mill. He was a man who believed in hard work, had set his sons up in business and sent his younger children to American schools. Following their father's death, Epifanio, Pedro and Conrado dissolved the family partnership, and for the next four years Epifanio and his brothers went separate ways. [4]

Traditional protocol dictated that Epifanio, as eldest son, was now head of the family hacienda. As such, he was also heir to his father's responsibilities. From this time on, until his death, Epifanio would financially support his step-mother and her family. It was also his duty to be a "father-figure" to all of his father's children, which meant making sure his younger stepbrothers and sisters received a good education. It was a sizable task to inherit, but one that was not entirely foreign to him. He had been trained for the job of "el gerente" from birth and was accustomed to supervising his younger brothers, Pedro, Conrado and Yjinio, as well as providing food for the hacienda.

With all the graciousness of her Southern upbringing, Mamie accepted her husband's commitments and gladly set to work mentoring Epifanio's younger stepbrothers and sisters. She was especially fond of Lola and Santitos who were intelligent, cheerful girls, and they soon came to regard Mamie as a second mother, as well as a trusted friend.

Apart from minor worries, the years Mamie spent in Las Cruces were among her happiest; she had many social events to keep her busy and, after the children were bedded for the night, she enjoyed reading the newspapers, even if the news they carried was outdated. Many newspapers ran poems for their readers' entertainment and, if a certain poem was relevant to her own experiences, Mamie clipped it out and pasted it in her scrap book. This poem entitled "*Our Baby*" was written by N. Bairnes and reminded Mamie of baby Epifanio, a roly-poly little fellow, lovingly nicknamed "Butchie," by his father.

Two little shoes, out at the toes,
Trotting about where'er mother goes:
Soiled gingham dress, put on just now,
They do get so dirty, no one knows how;

Black each wee hand;
been making mud pies and playing in sand.
Dear precious head, tousled and rough;
Bright laughing eyes, can't see enough;
This is our baby.....All day.

It often seemed that when life looked the rosiest for the family, hard times lay just around the corner. In December of 1865, Epifanio suffered a sizable loss when Navajos stole eighteen of his mules valued at $3,500. Mamie touched on other problems when she continued her story:

"...I remained (in Las Cruces) till March of the next year (1866) when we again made preparations for a return trip across the plains to Westport, going as we had come with wagons, but not by the same route...

"...This time we went by way of Tularosa, passing through Fort Stanton, Texas, and going south by a nearer way that was to bring us to the Arkansas River at Fort Dodge. There was quite a party of us. We had our ambulance and a baggage wagon and two riding horses—my husband's and mine. There were four other large wagons filled with harnesses for two new trains that were to be bought when we reached our destination. Loose mules were driven by herders. That was the way the trains generally went to the States in the spring, and they traveled fast. We were just forty days from Las Cruces to Westport.

"We went through Comanche country and were a week without a road—just going by compass and sending men ahead to look for water. As the Comanches were then at war with the whites we were in some danger, but were not molested at all. We crossed the Arkansas River at Fort Dodge, and I was surprised to see the changes made in three years time. All the country through Kansas was settled up—trees growing and houses where nothing but grass had been three years before. We encountered some severe weather—had two snow storms and some mules were lost, but on the whole the trip was pleasant."

Considering she had not been "home" for three years, this was a very happy reunion for Mamie. What an exciting time it was when the family finally reached Westport, with Grandma Bell raining down hugs and kisses on two-year-old Pedro and baby Butchie. For Mamie this was also a time of catching up on news, hearing about all the changes which had occurred in the past three years. The town had not yet recovered from the Battle of Westport, so most changes were not for the better.

Mamie's sister, Margaret, had abandoned her "Southern idealism" in favor of marrying Andrew Johnson, the Unionist. Their wedding had taken place on March 10, 1864. Mamie sympathized with her sister because she knew what an emotional struggle Margaret must have had, especially when climbing to the roof of Duke Simpson's woodshed to watch the Battle of Westport and knowing full well that Andrew was doing his bit for the war effort—fighting fellow Southerners.

Harder still for Margaret, was the murder of her father-in-law, Tom Johnson, the former Shawnee missionary, and Mamie was horrified as she listened to the details of his death. On January 2, 1865, the old missionary had been lured out of his house by strangers who were asking their way to Kansas. Once outside, the strangers rushed him, but Johnson managed to get back in and bolt the door. However, his assailants were still able to kill him by firing a volley of shots through the door. [5] Johnson's killers were no doubt seeking revenge for his part in the Civil War. A good many Southerners held him personally responsible for the deaths of their loved ones. They accused him of swapping sides in the middle of a war, ridiculing the South in public speeches and billeting Northern troops at the Shawnee Mission—any one of these perceived sins may have sealed his death warrant.

On a happier note, cousin Neely (Cornelia Hamilton) had returned from California with her husband, James, and family, and what stories they had to tell! Since returning to Westport, the Hamiltons had built a home surrounded by flowers and apple trees, similar to the homes they admired in California. Prior to the Aguirre's arrival, cousin Neely had given birth to her tenth child and, much to Mamie's delight, cousin Neely had named the baby Mamie.

The Hamiltons no longer had slaves. Several years before the Civil War began, James had told his slaves they were free to go, yet they chose to stay. Strangely enough, overzealous Northerners spirited them away one night, but as a last gesture of appreciation the former slaves laid the fires, and set out breakfast dishes just as they had done for so many years. Mandy, the children's nurse, had definitely not wanted to leave the Hamilton home as she considered the Hamilton children "her own." Later Mandy would recall how she took with her an infant's silk nightcap as a souvenir, "to remember her babies by." [6]

Mamie, Epifanio and their boys were always welcome at the Hamilton home and many good times were had during this visit.

"We stayed in Westport a year," said Mamie. "And there on February 4, 1867, Stephen was born. When he was three months old, we started to cross the plains again, this time with a mule train.

"By this time there was a railroad to Junction City in Kansas, so we went by rail that far. My younger brother (eight-year-old Allan) was with us. Our ambulance this time was different—larger—as it behooved the larger family I had. It was what the army used for moving the wounded, had a nice easy spring and was very high from the ground. It had a stove in one end and an open space for a wash stand, etc. We had carpet on the floor and our bed and trunk at one end, with pockets on the side. In fact it was like a little room, out and out, and covered with canvas and oilcloth. And that was my home for the next three months. We had so much rain that for nine days they would only move the train a short distance out and make camp again. After that came continued dry weather and the wheels dried up so they were easily broken. Twelve wheels had to be made on that trip.

"When we got to the Rio Puerco the rains commenced again, and then we had no end of it. But the children were well and hearty and happy, and we got along nicely. From Las Vegas we went by way of Fort Stanton, crossing a corner of the Staked Plain. We traveled through the narrow valley called the Missouri Valley in which we were three weeks and crossed one river seventeen times."

"One day two teamsters had a quarrel, and one of them was killed. The last I saw of the other man he was running up the mountain side like a deer. The dead man was buried where he fell. It rained so much, and the roads were so bad they had to be made as we went along, and it was wearisome to the flesh before we arrived at Las Cruces on the fourth of August, after three months of constant traveling."

As the little ones squirmed and jostled each other, Mamie tried to keep them entertained, tried to ignore the dust seeping into the carriage and the grime tracked in after rest stops. Keeping active children happily occupied in cramped quarters was no small task. There were bumps and bruises, quibbling and tears, and mud—lots of mud, but Mamie chose not to dwell on these things, saying only that the trip became "wearisome to the flesh."

Among other events occurring in 1867 was the wedding of someone Mamie considered very special—Lola Aguirre. After completing her schooling in Kansas, Lola had fallen in love with a freighter by the name of Mariano Samaniego and the couple were married that summer. Mariano was a round-faced, well-educated man with a pleasant disposition, and he and Lola were extremely helpful, when anyone needed assistance.

One evening, after Mamie had settled down from the day's activities, she opened *The Prescott Miner* and found that her relative, Johnny Behan, was in the news. [7]

"Johnny Behan bade adieu to his numerous friends in Prescott last evening and started for Missouri on a visit to his people. Mr. Behan is a young man of good moral character and excellent business qualifications. He has been Acting Deputy Sheriff of this County for a long time past. We wish you a pleasant trip, Johnny, and hope you will soon return in company with a better half."

Mamie smiled when she read the tribute and imagined Johnny's arrival in Westport. *Why he'll be the talk of the town! And all the single girls will swoon when he walks down the street. Imagine Johnny, a Deputy Sheriff, and only twenty-two years old!*

On arriving in Arizona in 1863, Johnny Behan had found employment with the Quartermaster Department of the California Column before going on to Fort Whipple to cut hay for forage. Later, he joined a Prescott freighting company hauling freight to mines with bull teams. It seems Mamie's former playmate had lost no time in establishing himself, and three years later he was serving as Prescott's Deputy under Sheriff John Bourke. But if life seemed to be coming up roses in 1867, the following decade would thrust Johnny Behan into some very unnerving events.

Another item in the newspaper amused Mamie, and this one she pasted in her scrapbook. Written by an unknown author, the story depicts a typical parlor game enjoyed by young people in the 1800s, and is entitled "The Mum Sociable."

" 'Lend me your revolver,' said the young man, who had just come into a West Side Saloon. His nose was skinned, his eye blackened, his white tie was twisted around his ear, and one tail of his dress coat was torn off.

" 'What's the matter with you?' asked the bartender giving the younger man a scowl. 'Do you suppose I'm going to give you a revolver to kill somebody, and then be arrested for being an accessory? Not much!'

"The young man took a wet towel and sopped the blood off his nose and then said, 'You look like a man whose advice can be trusted in an emergency so, I'll tell you about the murder I'm contemplating. The problem is, our lodge is giving a mum social this evening. You know what a mum social, is, don't you? Young people sit around all evening and keep their mouths shut and never say a word till a signal is given; then they make up for lost time and talk for all get out. Is my nose still bleeding? Thanks!'

" 'They invited me, and I just came from there. That is I came from the house next door. You see, I went to the wrong house and rang the bell. A man came to the door. 'Good evening,' he said, but I wasn't going to be caught speaking, because you have to pay a forfeit if you speak, so I just walked in and pulled off my overcoat and hung it up, and hung my hat on the hat rack. The man looked a little bit annoyed, but he asked me if the weather was not softening up a little. I smiled, but didn't say anything, just walked right in and sat down in his sitting room. I thought I was the first one there and felt very awkward. The man watched me closely and finally said that I had the advantage of him; and I smiled again, but didn't say anything. Now that I think of it, I did notice that he unbuttoned his shirt sleeves and began to roll them up.

"He asked me what circumstances he was indebted to the honor of my visit, and I thought he was trying to get me off guard, so I smiled one of my best two-for-a-quarter smiles, and looked at him as much to say 'you can't play any of your games on me.' The man came up behind me and hissed in my ear: 'What's your little game, anyway?' Well I wasn't going to speak and give myself away, so I gave him a look of contempt, and then I thought lightening struck me. He took me by the throat and choked me so my tongue hung out and his wife screamed, 'Don't kill him,' as the man hustled me out the hall, opened the front door, picked me up bodily, and threw me into a snow-bank—which was five feet deep. I struggled a little going out the door, and ran my nose against the door casing, and I guess he forgot to let go of my coattail when I went out. I stuck head first in the snow bank and before I could dig my head out, the door closed. So I couldn't have explained my conduct even had I been so inclined. Just as I stood up, and shook myself off, the door opened and the man threw out my overcoat, hat and overshoes and he told his wife to hurry up with the shotgun, and he would take me on the fly as I went over the fence.

"Well, I didn't wait for no shotgun and grabbed my things, and came down the street at a gallop. I met a lot of young people going up, and as I turned the corner, I saw them going into a house, which was next door to the one I visited, and that was the first I knew of my mistake. So, now what I want is for you to tell me whether I had better shoot that man or kill him with a club. I was raised in the South, and my warm Southern blood will not stand for any such treatment."

Mamie had a keen sense of humor, and practiced the old adage, "laugh a little, and you won't cry as much." Sadness, in those turbulent times, came at the least expected moment, and shortly into the New Year, Mamie received devastating news. Her youngest sister, Bell, had been accidentally shot. Unable to go to the funeral, Mamie was forced to wait several more weeks before she learned the cause of her sister's death. A Missouri writer covering the event wrote:

"In 1868 in Missouri, bandits and post-war criminals were not uncommon, and most young men were trained and equipped to defend themselves. On January 27, Arabella Wilson, the Bernard's sixth daughter, a beautiful seventeen-year-old, was accidentally shot and killed. She was making her brother's bed when the loaded pistol he kept under his pillow discharged."

Bell, with her sweet disposition, had been very special to Mamie, as was Kate who died in 1863. *Two sisters dead* in *less than five years!* They had both been so young and beautiful, and Mamie wondered why God allowed such things to happen.

Chapter Eleven—The Road To Altar

After the shock of losing another sister subsided, the remainder of 1868 passed with routine events—nothing out of the ordinary—and could be described as the calm before another terrible storm.

The first unfortunate event occurred in 1869, while Epifanio was making a trip on the Santa Fe Trail. One of his mule trains was ambushed close to San Marcial, New Mexico, by Indians who killed some of the teamsters and mules. The wagons were ransacked and the livestock driven away. No sooner had that loss been tallied when another train was lost in a fire caused by a careless army officer who dropped a lit cigarette in the dry prairie grass. The wagons had been full of merchandise when they burned. The Aguirres had suffered losses before, but never quite as crippling as these last two.

The harsh reality had to be faced: Epifanio's business was ruined and his money had run out. The family had grown accustomed to an affluent lifestyle, but under the present circumstances he would not be able to provide even a basic livelihood if he stayed in New Mexico. Realizing how discouraged her husband was, Mamie tried to compensate by being cheerful, resolving that no matter how difficult life became she would never complain, but would buckle down and help her husband find solutions to their financial problems.

Since Epifanio had an investment in a store in Mexico, he decided to make a temporary move to Altar, Sonora, where his brothers were living. It was Epifanio's intention to refurbish his freight lines from the sale of his Mexican assets. Young Pedro had just turned six the previous June; Butchie was four and Stephen was a toddler of eighteen months. The ranch life of Las Cruces, and all the trappings of wealth the family had once enjoyed, were left behind as they set out on another long journey through territory Mamie had not yet seen. Epifanio, ever aware of dangers on the trail, made arrangements for the family to accompany others going in the same direction. There was safety in numbers and men with rifles were sure to be needed in the days ahead.

"We went from New Mexico to Tucson," Mamie wrote. "And from there to Altar, Sonora, traveling in our own conveyance, along with a wagon train to Fort Bowie for protection, because the Apache Indians were so bad.

"We left Las Cruces, New Mexico in an ambulance with a train of wagons that were bringing wheat and other things to Fort Grant, Arizona. There were also fifty men coming to hay near Fort Bowie to fill a contract made with the US Government by Stephen Ochoa. These men were well armed and had wagons for their provisions. They rode in the wagons part of the time, but most of the way they walked.

"We had a baggage wagon with two big American horses and an ambulance drawn by a good pair of horses. Besides these, we had two saddle horses which were ridden by mozos (personal servants). "We" were my husband, myself and three children and two young ladies, my husband's sisters (Dolores and Santitos). We had a tent, lots of bedding and provisions and were a well satisfied crowd. Our first day's journey was rather hurried and we had to catch up with the train that had gone ahead. My recollections of the journey is coming across the Rio Grande River near Mesilla and then going miles and miles on a sandy desert sort-of road, till near sundown. Then we caught up with the train and camped with them that night out in the middle of the plains.

"The next day we went along slowly, feeling the heat intensely—it was the last day of July. But at last we reached Fort Cummings and there were shade trees and water and a restful time for a day. The young ladies and I hunted moss agates of which we found a goodly number, and we washed handkerchiefs and righted up things generally before starting out again.

"We started out again near nightfall. As a storm was brewing and, because we were to travel all night, the owner of the train offered us the use of a wagon that was loaded with wheat. If you have never had the good fortune to see one of those old "Prairie Schooners" you can have no idea of their size. They were as long as an ordinary room and about eight feet wide. The wagon bed was six feet high and the bows, covered with wagon sheets, were about six feet high. This particular wagon was loaded with wheat to within two feet from the top, and before we started from the Fort our bedding was arranged on top of the wheat, and we were lifted into the wagon and comfortably settled for the night.

"Just as we were settled and ready for bed, someone suggested that wheat always had weevils in it. This struck horror to my soul, and I fancied my poor little ones getting weevils in their ears. So we hunted up handkerchiefs, doubled them, three cornered, tied a knot in the end and there we had night caps. So we presented a comical sight when my husband looked in upon us to see how we were feeling.

"Soon all was ready and the train pulled out. When our wagon began to move it was like a ship getting underway. It rocked and swayed back and forth in a lumbering way, but never a hard jolt did we feel. Just a heavy swaying which gave me the most peculiar feeling—as if being on the water and the loose wheat slipping away under us in a soft sliding way that was indescribable.

"The storm I mentioned before was coming on, and it came upon us with great force when we got well into the canyon. (Magdelena Cañon, I believe they called it). That canyon is so narrow in places and the rocks so immense on all sides that the thunder was appalling. It crashed and reverberated among those rocks till we were deafened and the lightning was something fearful—and never to be forgotten. Our 'schooner' rocked and reeled along for awhile in the rain and the crash of the storm. But soon the train had to stop and there we stayed for an hour. Even the children could not sleep. My husband came into the wagon with us. He had stayed out to help guard the train and our 'schooner' especially, for the road was dreadful and the Indians so bad, too, then."

It was little wonder Epifanio burst out laughing when he

lifted the canvas and saw his "querida esposa" and her three little ones in such strange head gear—they looked funny to say the least. But then, Mamie's solutions to annoying problems often had a humorous twist, and Epifanio found his cheerful little wife was a pleasure to have on any trail, no matter how long or rough. Later that evening, with his clothes soaking wet from riding shotgun, he climbed into the wagon, settled down beside Mamie and quietly teased her about "las gorras cómicas," the comical caps.

Years later, the memory of this dark, stormy night, with Epifanio and her young sons cuddled together in the wagon, became very precious to Mamie. It was a moment in time when the tension of traveling in dangerous country was broken by a sense of togetherness. And most certainly, on that night of July 31, 1869, they were surrounded by danger, for they were traveling through Apache Pass—a narrow gorge lying between Dos Cabezas and the Chiricahua Mountains.

The original trail connected the eastern San Simon Valley to the western Sulfur Springs Valley and ran through narrow cliffs and rock strewn slopes. This terrain lent itself to Indian ambush, which happened to be a regular occurrence that autumn, being that Cochise, chief of the Chiricahua Apaches, was camped in and around the pass with an estimated 500 warriors. [1]

Single travelers attempting to maneuver Apache Pass invited an almost certain death, while large groups seldom escaped some form of harassment. One of the first recorded Indian attacks in Apache Pass occurred sometime between 1854 and 1858 when a wagon train from Texas started into the pass. The train was destroyed, thirty persons were killed and some women taken captive. The bodies of the dead were discovered some time later, stripped of clothing and mutilated beyond recognition. After that, Indian ambushes were recorded in Apache Pass on a regular basis for the next twenty-four years. There can be no accurate count of travelers who were killed by Apaches in this pass, but they numbered in the hundreds.

On one occasion, thirteen men were found dead, one of them having been stretched naked on a Spanish bayonet with hands and feet staked out. The sharp points of the bayonet leaves were passed through his body and, writhing from pain, he was left to die. Another was stripped naked, tied upside down on a tall soap weed and roasted to death. [2]

Terror was a constant companion of those venturing through the Apache Pass. And some travelers were so frightened they would actually go out of their heads. Stage drivers called these panic attacks "the starts," and would leave the sufferers at the next stopping station until they recovered sufficiently to resume their journey.

Mamie had heard all of these horror stories, but realized that Epifanio had to take the family through Apache Pass; there was no other route from Las Cruces to Tucson.

"As soon as the storm ceased, we rolled and rocked on again," Mamie recounted. "We were soon all fast asleep and spent a restful night. After that day nothing of interest happened till we came to Burro Canyon and Springs. Most of the time we traveled at night on account of the Indians. So it was night when we passed those springs. There had been a house there at the time of the old Overland Stage Line and the walls were still standing and made a fine place of ambush for the Indians. Not long before two mail carriers had been killed there and mail matter, such as Congressional records and newspapers, were scattered all along through the canyon, but we had seen no letters.

"But this night it was bright moonlight, and we were driving slowly along when I saw a low hill ahead of us covered with white things. We all exclaimed and wondered what they were. And soon found out—for there was a buckboard thrown over on its side and mail sacks cut open and letters strewn over the ground—all opened. My husband hastily gathered up all he could, and we came on fearing every moment an attack from the Indians. But we came on unmolested.

"When we got to Steins Pass great preparations were made to guard against a surprise from the Indians. Men were sent out to reconnoiter and were scattered on the hills above the narrow rock walled canyon through which we had to pass. Two big wagons went ahead of the ambulance we were riding in, and the rest of the party came behind. My husband drove the ambulance with his hand on his pistol, and there was never a word spoken as we passed through that awful walled canyon. As we passed along the men on the rocks above scrambled along ahead, and finally we came out into a wider place, and then the men on foot came to walk beside the ambulance. Finally we came out of the canyon and never stopped until we were in San Simon. There we stopped and stayed all night.

"We were soon in Fort Bowie where we stayed for three days, the guests of the commanding officer, Colonel Bernard, who is 'kinfolk.' We were royally entertained with the best the Fort could supply, and when we left were supplied with an extra escort of soldiers who came with us to Tucson. We were entitled to an escort. All parties of travelers were given escorts, but there were some old running gears of wagons to be turned over to the commissary at Tucson, so Colonel Bernard took this occasion to send them, and they had to have an escort—so our escort was doubled. A party of young men had been waiting at Fort Bowie for an escort, so they came on, too—on horseback—so we made quite a large party. One of the young men was W.C. Davis.

"So, from Bowie we went to Tucson: the escort of soldiers, the men on horseback and ourselves. On the way we saw dead men, wagons deserted, the mail cut open and letters scattered around, and in fact traces of Indians all along the road. Around all the water holes were fresh tracks of Indian, so we expected hourly to be attacked.

"We came through safely, traveling mostly at night and camping in the day time, but never felt quite safe until we reached Tucson. [3] We had rooms in the building on the corner of Main Street and the alley that runs back of Zeckendorfs. That alley was then a good street with some large houses. Our meals were brought to us from the Cosmopolitan Hotel. The hotel was then kept by Captain Thayer whom we had known in Las Cruces, New Mexico, in 1863. Tucson had one long street only—Main Street. And where the Hall house now stands (in 1897) was way out of town."

The Aguirres arrived in Altar, Sonora, Mexico in August, 1869, and were welcomed by Epifanio's brother, don Pedro, and his wife, doña Ana Maria Redondo de Aguirre. Ana was the daughter of a prominent Mexican family, and as such was used to hosting upper-class functions. So, now she graciously opened her doors to the new arrivals and Mamie soon felt at home.

The autumn passed quickly and once again Christmas came, bringing with it the traditions Epifanio had known from birth. For nine days before Christmas visitors came to the Aguirres' door and, just as the Virgin Mary had requested a place to lie down, so the visitors asked for *posada*. Eight times the visitors were refused, but on the ninth day they were invited into the "big house" to celebrate Christ's birth. For Epifanio, it was like old times—the way it used to be when he was a child—except the laughter of little ones came from a new generation. What a large, happy family! And what good memories!

Then came New Year 1870. Beginning as a time of renewed hope, January would bring Mamie and the Aguirre family more than their share of sorrow.

Chapter Twelve—Death On The Trail

January 16, 1870: Daylight was at least two hours away with the darkest part of night pressing hard against the dusty streets of Altar, Sonora, Mexico. A raw wind was busily picking up debris and tossing it in the air, so that the man hurrying from the stage-stop to one of the hacienda's flat-roofed adobe homes, shielded his lantern in the fold of his cloak. On reaching the door, he rapped loudly. "Don Epifanio!" he called, his voice carrying an unmistakable note of urgency. "Acudes, por favor!"

Inside, Epifanio, Mamie and their three small sons slept peacefully, completely unaware of the drama unfolding around them. The man continued to thump on the door until it opened and his employer stood in the lantern's flickering light.

"Buenas noches, amigo. Qué pasa?" Even in his night shirt, thirty-six year-old don Epifanio bore an air of competency—calm, yet self-confident—in every sense a master of men. His copper-brown hair lay in soft waves, while his blue eyes and sensitive features contrasted pleasantly with a firm chin and rugged, muscular build. "Es algo grave?" he asked, then listened attentively as the young man explained the problem.

A team of horses, six horses in all, had been hitched to Aguirre's stagecoach; the freight was loaded; passengers were waiting to board. However, there was a problem, one very large problem. The driver, hired several days before, had not put in an appearance.

The young man waved the lantern worriedly in the direction of the stables, his words coming in a flutter of Spanish, "Tell me how can a stage travel one hundred and twenty miles from Altar to Tucson without a driver, Señor?"

Above the moan of the wind, came the sound of horses blowing nervously in the dark. It was going to be a dirty day—not a good day to travel. Yet the stagecoach must leave at six o'clock sharp. Don Epifanio was faced with a problem. Who in the hacienda could be recruited on such short notice to fill in as a relief driver? Reason told him he would not be able to send just anyone; he needed an experienced driver. It took muscle to work the stiff brakes of a stage, not to mention a great deal of skill to handle a six-in-hand on a road that was no road at all, just a narrow trail winding through a series of rocky gullies.

There was only one person he could rely on—himself. With the abruptness of a man used to making snap decisions, Epifanio sent the messenger to wake up his brother don Conrado, then turned back to get dressed, just as Mamie tiptoed out of bed and stood beside him. She was twenty-six years old, but looked much younger, an elflike woman with long auburn ringlets and the inquiring eyes of a child. Not wanting to disturb the sleeping children she took her husband's arm and pulled him closer, "Do you have to go?" she whispered.

"Sí, mi amor."

"Why?" It was a question she had often asked when they lived in New Mexico, when Epifanio's trading ventures forced him into dangerous encounters with Apaches. But this morning, Mamie's "why" was not driven by fear for her husband's life. No, she had every reason to believe the stage would travel safely for its route lay in friendly Papago territory. Still her dark eyes coaxed him to stay home. "Send someone else."

"I can't. It wouldn't be right to ask an inexperienced man to drive on such a windy day. Besides, Conrado will come with me."

Seven and a half years of marriage, and it seemed to Mamie that her husband was always putting other men's comfort before his own—his work before her and the children. The thought annoyed her. "How about us?" she asked impatiently. "You promised to take us riding."

"And so I will, when I return, but today it is much too windy to go pleasure riding. Now back to bed, my little one. You will need to be well rested for our outing when I return." He gave her a peck on the forehead, turned her towards the mound of bedding and reached for his serape.

Disappointed, Mamie bounded away, not bothering to respond to his cheery, "Hasta mañana."

When Epifanio arrived at the stable, three male passengers

were waiting. One was Clito Elias, the brother of Conrado's wife. After checking the stage to make sure all was as it should be, Epifanio swung himself up to the seat on top of the stage and took the reins. Clito, known as "Blind Elias," had very poor eyesight, so Conrado assisted him into the belly of the stage, then scrambled up to sit beside his brother.

It would be good, Epifanio thought, to have his younger brother along, a jovial companion, a spare driver. "Si, muy bien."

A crack of the whip and the stage was off, the team prancing, pulling hard on the reins, as anxious horses will on a windy day. They would be kept at a fast trot until the next stopping station where a fresh team waited to relay the stage on another leg of the journey to Tucson. [1] As the day wore on, the wind continued to fan a large column of dust from the wheels. This was not a good thing, and Epifanio knew it, for such high rising clouds of dust alerted others of their presence. Hopefully there were neither Apaches nor bandidos in this part of the country. Conrado must have been thinking the same thing for at sunup he loaded a rifle and placed it within easy reach. [2]

They had just crossed the border between Mexico and Arizona when it happened—about two o'clock in the afternoon—under the watchful eye of Mount Baboquivari, sacred mountain of the Papago. The stage was approaching Sasabe Flats, less than a mile from La Posta de Aguirre, the next stage-stop. Epifanio felt the pain of the bullet ripping into his flesh, before he actually heard the shots. And then he felt himself falling, falling, falling into a strange kind of darkness he had never known before. Instantly, the team he had been skillfully urging on, turned and started galloping, full tilt in the direction they'd come.

When Conrado heard the shot and saw his brother fall from the stage, he attempted to grab the reins, missed and was hurled to the ground. For a split second he lay gasping for breath. Miraculously he was uninjured, but he could see Epifanio's body—a lifeless heap, pooling in blood, sprawled on the dusty trail. [3] The shocking sight cleared the younger man's head and brought him to his feet.

The Indians, busy pursuing the runaway team, failed to notice Conrado pick himself up and run for cover. From his hiding place the younger Aguirre watched an Indian drop the lead horse with a bullet; saw a huge cloud of dust as stage and horses piled up; heard the splintering of wood, the squeals of terrified horses, the crazed yipping of Indians, but worst of all he heard a sound which would haunt him for the rest of his life—the screams of men being dragged from the stage and gutted.

The following day was January 17, 1870. Back in Altar, the wind died down and dawn broke with its usual winter crispness. Mamie awoke from a troubled sleep to hear hoof beats thundering past her door. Then came the sound of voices, raw with hysteria, followed by a woman wailing. *Something was wrong! Some tragedy had occurred! What could it be?*

Dressing quickly, she stepped out of the door, only to be met by her brother-in-law, Yjinio. His hands were shaking as he broke the news that Conrado had returned to Altar, alone.

Mamie had but a single thought: "¿Dónde está mi esposo?" (Where is my husband?)

"He is dead!"

There are no words powerful enough to describe Mamie's grief.

Yjinio Aguirre was the same age as Mamie, and it had fallen to him to deliver the news of his brother's death, prior to setting off to La Posta de Aguirre to bring Epifanio's body back to Altar for burial. Before leaving, Yjinio attempted to recruit sharp shooters from Altar's townspeople to accompany him on the trip, but no one stepped forward. They were terrified of the Apache, so he was forced to travel alone. To Yjinio's dying day, he never forgave the men of Altar for what he called "cobardía" (cowardice). [4]

Nothing had prepared Mamie for the horror she felt when Epifanio's body came back to her, wrapped in a blanket, cold and stiff in the back of Yjinio's wagon. Somehow she managed to console her three small sons. Then, with the help of grieving in-laws, she endured the doleful mass and watched as her beloved husband was buried in Altar's cold, gray earth. Numbed by shock, she scarcely heard the mournful dirges, sung with all the sorrow the Mexicans could wring from their heavy hearts.

It would take a very long time to accept the fact that Epifanio was not coming home. Never again would she see his smile in the morning, nor hear his approaching footsteps at the end of a day. Her deepest regret was that she could never tell him how sorry she was for the times she was out of sorts and had taken him for granted.

To onlookers, Mamie appeared stoic—square-shouldered and stiff—kneeling in church in her black attire. From an early age, she had learned to suppress her emotions. When she was growing up, her mother had never allowed her to make a public spectacle of herself. Such indiscretions as weeping openly or laughing too loudly were a sign of poor breeding—and simply not done. Yet, in the sanctuary of her home, Mamie shed many tears as she immersed herself in a private world of poetry. The previous year, her mother had sent three discarded ledgers (salvaged from Colonel Boone's Westport store) and, in one of these, she pasted pictures of garden scenes and romantic verses. This poem, entitled *"Our Own,"* was written by Margaret E. Sangster. The words held special meaning for Mamie because they reminded her of the last time she saw Epifanio alive. Many a lonely night she read the verse over and over again, each time the hurt clinging to her heart as if she had penned the words herself.

"If I had known in the morning
How weary all the day
The words unkind would trouble my mind
I said when you went away,
I had been more careful darling
Not to give you needless pain;
But we vex our own with look and tone
We might never take back again.
How many go forth in the morning
Who never come home at night;
And hearts have been broken
With harsh words spoken,
That sorrow can never set right.

The Weekly Arizonan carried the following report of the ambush on January 29, 1870, under the caption, "Murdered by Indians."

"Again we are called upon to picture a fresh scene of blood and robbery, in which an additional four have been placed upon the list of Apache victims for 1870. We have the particulars of the sad affair as follows: On the 20th inst. (correction: Jan. 16, 1870)[5] two of the Aguirre brothers, Conrado and Epifanio, with three other men, enroute from Altar to Tucson, were attacked at Sasabe Flats by a large body of Indians and four of the number were killed, Conrado alone escaping. The Indians were concealed by the roadside, within the distance of half a mile from the station and, as the stage drove up, fired into it, killing the driver and another man, both of whom fell from the stage as soon as shot. Conrado attempted to seize the reins, but stumbling in the effort likewise fell from the stage, while the horses turned and ran furiously in the direction of Altar. The Indians, seeing three men fall from the stage, doubtless believed them all dead and accordingly turned their attention to the horses, which, by firing a volley into them, they soon maimed them and the stage overturned. This incident gave Conrado a chance to run for his life—which he did—and reached the station safely, but the unfortunate two, still occupying the stage, were taken and butchered on the spot."

Many locals wondered if the ambush was the work of the Apaches or a handful of renegade Papagos. The mystery remains today. The Apaches were initially blamed, however a Masonic ring and the serape, worn by Epifanio at the time of his murder, were found in possession of a Papago Indian a year later. One explanation is that the Papagos acquired Epifanio's belongings from a dead Apache at Camp Grant in 1871. This is highly probable because other stolen property was recovered at the site of the Camp Grant massacre, such as a brooch belonging to Trinidad Aguirre and a pair of easily identified moccasins belonging to Trinidad's husband, Leslie Wooster. (Both Trinidad and her husband had been brutally killed by Apaches shortly after don Epifanio's murder.) [6]

The desert sands have long since blown over the spot where Epifanio fell. Only the Indians involved could have identified his killers, and quite possibly they died at Camp Grant.

For Mamie the event was too sad to speak of, so she simply wrote: "In January my husband was killed at Sasabe, Arizona, by the Apache Indians. He and three others, only one escaped." Later, she pasted another verse in her scrap book.

Entitled *"At Last,"* the writer of the poem is unknown.

"Poor beating heart now rest;
Sorrow and pain no more
Shall make thee sore distressed;
Thy restless care is o'er.
Go still sweet session keep
Of blissful sleep,
And no more throb and ache—
T'is living hearts that break."

Mary Bier Bernard and don Epifanio Aguirre

United in Marriage — August 21, 1862

Above: Mamie's Tea and Coffee Service—a gift from don Epifanio to his new bride in 1862. The service and cutlery are engraved with the couple's intertwining initials. Also shown here are two native baskets from Mamie's collection.

Below: A tiny Confederate flag made by Mamie's beloved sister, Kate, who died in 1863.

The Pecos Mission Ruins, N.M. dating back to 1710

The church of San Miguel, oldest church in Santa Fe, New Mexico.

Ruins of Fort Union (1851– 1891) The women of the fort welcomed Mamie into their parlors as the wheels of don Epifanio's huge freight wagons creaked up to the fort's ware house.

Mamie's personal scrapbook and photos.

Epifanio and Mamie's home in New Mexico.

Mamie Bier (Bernard) Aguirre as a young woman.

Hand embroidered, Madrina cape, worn by Mamie in New Mexico.

Mamie as head of the Spanish Department at The University of Arizona.

Sasabe Flats, with Mount Baboquivari in the background, where stage driver don Epifanio Aguirre was ambushed on January 16, 1870.

Aguirre Peak, named after don Epifanio Aguirre.

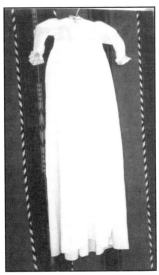

Pedro's christening gown.
Worn by his grandchildren,
great-grandchildren and
great great-grandchildren.

Mamie's sons: Left Epifanio Jr.
and Pedro Joab Aguirre.
Epifanio died at age 13, struck
by lightning while riding his pony.

Mamie's sons:
(l-r) Stephen and
Pedro J. Aguirre

Mamie, her mother, Arabella, and unknown child.
(Taken in the 1880s)

Pedro poses with a boy rescued from
Apache Indians in 1886.
(see page 169, *Journey of the Heart.*)
Courtesy of Arizona Historical Society, #17869

Noah and Allan Bernard with Mamie's sons,
Stephen, Epifanio (Butchie) and Pedro Aguirre.

Johnny Behan and his wife Victoria
Courtesy: Arizona Historical Collection 30223

Cole Younger
1844-1916

Senator Stephen B. Elkins
1841—1911

Left to right: Four generations - Mamie's son Stephen with his sons, Stephen Epifanio & Benjamin Aguirre, Great grandmother, Arabella Bernard and Mamie Aguirre, taken in the sitting room of brother Noah's home.
Courtesy of AHS# 30223

Brother Noah's house in Tucson, where Mamie lived between 1890 and 1906.

The sitting room . The same cozy room as it appears today, as viewed by the author.

Noah Bernard 1854—1907
Mamie's brother.

Joab Bernard 1800-1879
Mamie's father.

Mamie's son, Pedro J. Aguirre 1862-1907.

Mamie's grandson,
Pedro (Pete) Aguirre,
son of Pedro J Aguirre
1908-1982.

Mamie Aguirre

Mamie (center), her sister, Jesse (left),
on route to Ensenada, Mexico.

Courtesy of Arizona Historical Society #17827

– Bear Valley Picnic

Edwin (Ned) Bernard.

Bear Valley Picnic
Mamie, standing on right,
Noah, holding the horse.

Standing: Epifanio
(Butchie),
Noah and Allan Bernard.
Front: Pedro and Stephen

Mamie's great granddaughter, Rowene Aguirre Medina, examines one of the original interior adobe walls of Noah's Arivaca store & post office The building now houses a feed store.

Noah Bernard's Store, Arivaca, Arizona,
as it appeared in the 1800s.

Arivaca School in which
Mamie taught.
Built in 1879 by
don Pedro Aguirre, this
is now the oldest standing
school in Arizona.

Mamie's greatgranddaughter
Rowene in Arivaca School.

Train wreck at Edenvale, California, May 9, 1906
Ultimately responsible for Mamie's death.
Courtesy of Arizona Historical Society 24,357 & 23,644

An Aguirre mule train — huge freight wagons which carried trading goods from Westport, Missouri, to Guaymas, Mexico, in the 1800s.

Note: Yjinio Aguirre posing with his pet mule, "Macho Grullo." Macho Grullo was a familiar sight on the Santa Fe Trail; he seldom worked, but accompanied Yjinio wherever he went for forty-one years.

Epifanio's grandnephew, Yginio F. Aguirre, taken in 2003.

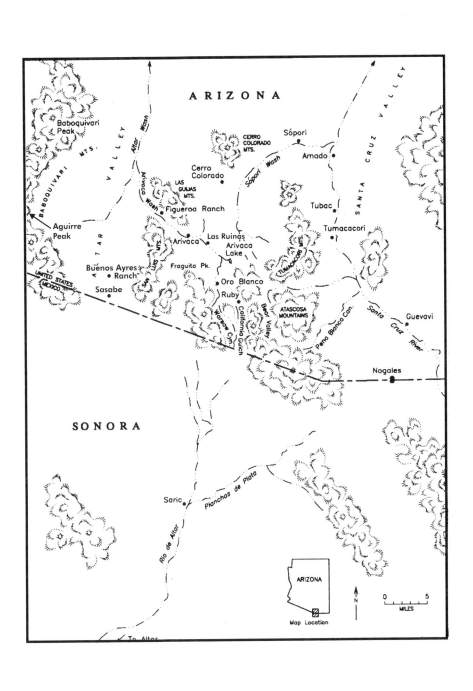

A R I Z O N A

Baboquivari
Peak

BABOQUIVARI MTS.

Altar Wash

VALLEY

Arivaca Wash

Aguirre
Peak

ALTAR VALLEY

UNITED STATES
MEXICO

Buenos Ayres
Ranch

Sasabe

CERRO
COLORADO
MTS.

Sópori

Cerro
Colorado

LAS
GUIJAS
MTS.

Figueroa Ranch

Arivaca

Las Ruinas
Arivaca
Lake

Fraguita Pk.

Oro Blanco

Ruby

SAN LUIS MTS.

Morena Cyn.

California Gulch

Bear Valley

Sópori Wash

Amado

Tubac

Tumacacori

TUMACACORI MTS.

ATASCOSA
MOUNTAINS

SANTA CRUZ VALLEY

Peña Blanca Can.

Santa Cruz River

Guevavi

Nogales

S O N O R A

Saric

Planchas de Plata

Rio de Altar

To Altar

ARIZONA

Map Location

N

0   5
MILES

Fall round-ups haven't changed a great deal on the Arivaca Ranch. Spring calves are still brought in from the hills on horseback prior to shipping to market. A bladeless windcharger, used in Mamie's day stands with a modern power pole as a reminder of the past.

(81 year-old, Emeterio Hermandez and his appaloosa put in a full day's work).

Author Annette Gray, on the Arivaca (Las Ruinas) Ranch where Mamie spent her summers. Some of the original ranch buildings can be seen in the background.

Chapter Thirteen—The Aftermath

Mamie stayed with her in-laws for five months before deciding to take her three little sons back to Westport. Always before, Epifanio had been with her when she traveled, and she had trusted him implicitly with her life. Now, she felt it would be impossible to travel on the overland route, via the Santa Fe Trail—it was far too dangerous. So, she chose to go to Missouri by a longer, safer route.

With the help of her brother-in-law, Yjinio, she loaded her belongings in Epifanio's carriage and joined a wagon train leaving for Hermosillo, Mexico. On reaching, Hermosillo, Mamie and her three sons boarded a stage and traveled to the seaport at Guaymas, Sonora, where they embarked for San Francisco on a steamship. Yjinio traveled as far as San Francisco with them. Then, after delivering Mamie and the children to the railway station, he returned via the same route to Altar.

Recalling the journey to Westport, Mamie wrote:

"In June 1870, I started again for the States by way of Guaymas. The Indians were so bad all through Arizona that it was unsafe to travel anywhere in Arizona—especially for women and children. I had been prepared to go overland to Yuma in my own conveyance and from there take the stage across the desert to San Diego, and from there the steamer to San Francisco, and carry on east by train.

"But, just as I was ready to start, a friend came from Tucson and told us such tales of the horrible sufferings we might have to endure on the road to Yuma that I concluded to wait awhile and go to Guaymas to catch the monthly steamer from there to San Francisco, which I did, going from Altar to Hermosillo (300 miles) in my own conveyance and from Hermosillo to Guaymas (90 miles) in the stage that made tri-weekly trips to that place.

"I had three little boys, the oldest seven, the youngest three, so I had my hands full. We spent a week in Hermosillo with some friends, waiting for the steamer and when it was due we went to Guaymas.

"In the meantime news had come of a startling nature. A small piratical vessel (a steamer) had come into the port of Guaymas and fairly taken the town. The pirates went into the Government buildings and offices and helped themselves to all the money they could lay their hands upon. They took official papers of some kind also, and carried off, as a prisoner, a young man named Mejia. Mejia was the son of General Mejia who was shot with Miramon and Maximilian. [1] The young man had been married two weeks earlier to a sixteen year-old girl, the daughter of a German consul living in Guaymas.

"So, when I arrived at the hotel in Guaymas everyone was excited, and I was advised not to go on that steamer. Supposing it escaped the pirates coming up (it had not yet arrived and was overdue), it would surely fall into their hands going down. But it escaped 'coming up' and arrived the day after we did. There were US troops aboard from the Fort at Yuma, so they were taken on up to the mouth of the Colorado River. This meant we had to wait another week in Guaymas for the steamer to return. And in that week, I met the wife of Mejia, a girl with hair like gold, blue eyes in a fresh German face and an unformed childish air about her that was pitiful to see, considering she was only at the beginning of life's sorrows. She wore her hair in two braids down her back which hung far below her waist. She hardly seemed to comprehend what had happened—for she was very cheerful."

"Well, the steamer came at last (it was the old Continental) and we left Guaymas about the 21st of June. The trip was fine. We rolled and tumbled around in crossing the Gulf (as we did several times). We stopped first at Carmena Salt Island to take in salt water as ballast. There were salt works to see and we gathered such lovely shells. The steamer laid there three days and many of the passengers went on shore and we sailed around in a yacht.

"And at night we could hear the most dismal moans—sounding as if some giant was bewailing the dead. The Mexican steward told me it was supposed to be the wail of lost drowned souls praying to be let out of purgatory, and only at night and at certain places could they come near the shore. And then they would come on the waves, and as the waves went back they would try to catch hold of the rocks and sand with their long hands, but could not hold on, so they would go slipping back with a cackling sound and then that awful heartbroken, bloodcurdling moan would come. I stood on the deck looking out on that black waste of water, hearing the moans and listening to the steward's story, until my heart fairly ached. I have never heard those moaning sounds anywhere else on the ocean or near it."

So soon after her husband's death, the story of the moaning spirits was extremely upsetting for Mamie, especially when she thought of Epifanio's Catholic upbringing. Reflecting on the church's view of purgatory and listening to the mysterious wails, she could not help but wonder if his spirit was at rest. After a sleepless night, she watched the sea transform itself into a maze of color and later wrote about its beauty.

"Those waters are full of colors, especially at sunrise. As it grew lighter the steamer seemed to be plowing through fire. The long lines of sporting dolphin would leave waves of fire behind and around them and the whole ocean seemed to be on fire at times. It was lovely and beyond my power of description. We went from Carmen Island across the Gulf to La Paz. That is a lovely bay, but seems impenetrable to the uninitiated. A pilot came out to meet us, and we followed him into the wildest, rockiest, narrowest passage through which a steamer ever went. We seemed almost to graze the towering rocks at times. But all at once, just about sunset we were in a calm, lovely, landlocked bay, with hills all around and the water an exquisite rose color from the pink clouds of sunset. After we got to our place of anchor and things settled, we could see the flying fish taking long leaps out of the water and sort-of skimming around like birds.

"We stayed there three days, going ashore to see the quaint little town built under a hill close to the water with lovely coconut and palm trees all around it. There we took on the most wonderful lot of things—sacks of silver bars, boxes of silver dollars (a boat load of them), gold in nuggets, pearls, fruit of all kinds. There the steamer unloaded flour upon which they told me no duty had to be paid. From there we went across the Gulf of Mazatlán, and there we stayed three more days.

"There, too, we learned the end of the pirate's story. As we neared Mazatlán we saw a large steamer lying there, and upon coming nearer we saw the US flag at half mast. As soon as we got near enough I saw it was a US man-of-war, the 'Manongehela.' After we stopped and anchored, two long boats put off from the man-of-war. They came along side and a coffin (a large pine box) was lifted up and then eight wounded men were sort of swung up in canvas hammocks.

"We soon found out what had happened. The piratical steamer which carried the money and man from Guaymas had gone up into an arm of the sea near San Blas. The man-of-war had gone up after the steamer, hoping to rescue the man Mejia. The Manongehela, being a large boat could not get near to the pirates, so a young Lieutenant and some soldiers took boats to go nearer. As soon as they got in range the pirates fired upon them and killed the Lieutenant at first fire. The next volley wounded the men. Then the pirates were seen putting off for the shore in two boats and in a few minutes the little pirate steamer was afire. (It is assumed the young man, Mejia, was burned to death in the pirate ship.)

"So the soldiers went back to their own boat and came crestfallen and sorrowful back to the gulf to wait for the monthly steamer to take their dead and wounded to San Francisco. This had happened only a week before we came along. And the man-of-war left the next morning after we arrived.

"At Mazatlán steamers have to stand three miles off from shore and keep up steam all the time they are there. A regular saw-tooth line of rocks run out from the shore in a curve, and immense rocks stand straight out of the water, like tops of sunken mountains. So it's a dangerous sort of place. But it was all very interesting to see the yawls with gaily colored awnings coming and going all day long.

"And such a variety of things were brought on board. The most important were bars of silver by the boatload and a big boatload of silver dollars put in small boxes and marked $250 each. Then there were boatloads of beautifully spotted leopard skins; a boat load of turtles weighing three to five pounds each; parrots and other lovely birds; pottery; bright blankets; liquors; sugar in the rough as panocha (unrefined brown sugar) and piloncillos (powdered brown sugar). In fact, it was like a show to see it. From there we went to San Blas, but before we got there an alarm was given. Pirates had been sighted, and all women and children were put in the cabin. The doors were tied outside with ropes, and there we huddled, scared to death, for almost an hour, but nothing happened, so we went on to San Blas. At San Blas the sea was so high that a whole family had to be tied in a big arm chair, one by one, and let down over the bow of the steamer and dropped into a boat, which tossed and tumbled around in a frightful manner.

"The steamer could not land because it was so rough, and there was a storm coming up, too. So we hurried out to sea. But, while we were waiting for those passengers and their luggage to be taken off, the steamer gave a lurch that sent us all sprawling in the middle of the cabin. Near San Blas are some awful points of rock standing straight out of the water and they are called 'Le Tres Marias.'

"We hurried out so we could pass them before the storm came, which we did. What a storm it was! We tossed and tumbled, rolled out of our berths three or four times and had a rough time generally.

"The next stop was at Cape Lucas where we stayed two days. There we took on some beef cattle. They were tied by the horns, one to each side of a boat, and brought to the steamer. Then they were put in a sort of harness with a broad band around their middle and hoisted clear up into the air, before being dropped down into the hold.

"All told, we were eighteen days making the trip for we had to stop at all the ports on the gulf. But finally we arrived at San Francisco where we boarded the train to go by rail to Westport."

Chapter Fourteen—Life in Missouri

The autumn leaves were spectacular in the fall of 1870, the late flowers and foliage so bright, the river so wide and blue; it was as if Westport opened her arms in a valiant attempt to welcome Mamie home. But, in those first awkward minutes when she faced her parents, Mamie was overcome by sadness; Epifanio was not at her side and the town had somehow lost its magic.

Stifling her emotions, she exchanged hugs and kisses with her parents and siblings, who seemed genuinely pleased to see her. Nan, Jesse, Noah and Allan were still living at home, and had gladly set to work, heaving furniture aside to make room for their sister's arrival. Arabella was particularly happy to have her daughter home, doting on her three grandsons, handing out knitted toys and rag balls, each item fashioned by her own hands. How the little ones adored Granny Bell and clambered up on her knee to whisper in her ear, to tell her of their adventures on the boat and train. It was surprising to see how Granny had mellowed, how she nodded and pretended to understand the tumble of Spanish words, all foreign to her ears. She was not the stern mother Mamie remembered—at least not for the time being.

The Civil War was a thing of the past, as were Westport's heydays. Although buildings had been repaired and gardens planted, the town would never regain her former glory. If not dead, Westport was dying, her vitals being sucked out by the growing city of Kansas.

Westport—beautiful little Westport—how could this possibly have happened to such a wonderful little town! A poem, captioned as *"Westport,"* by an unknown writer remains in Mamie's collection; it reads:

> Oh! Westport, thy fame spread far
> Across the plains;
> Thy name is known in peace and war,
> And on thy street many made their gains.

Joab Bernard was no longer rich or politically influential, but his household was running smoothly—or as smoothly as could be expected with so many under one roof.

Mamie's sister, Annie (Nan), was twenty-two and getting married on October 17, 1870, which meant Mamie was just in time to help with wedding preparations. Her sister, Jesse—a favorite of Mamie's—was a boisterous, fun loving twenty year-old, and currently dating Louis, a young man her parents disliked.

Sixteen year-old Noah was taking his final years of schooling, and his serious brown eyes told Mamie of the guilt still haunting him. It was, after all, his pistol that killed his youngest sister. The experience had drastically changed him from an irresponsible youngster to a man who would do everything possible to protect his remaining sisters. Then there was eleven year-old, Allan. Only four and a half years older than Mamie's own Pedro, Allan had a smile for everyone and was at that pernicious age when he was either getting into, or coming out, of mischief.

Mamie's eldest sister, Margaret, the Confederate flag maker who had actually married a Unionist, was living close to Westport on the old Shawnee property. She and Mamie had shared many experiences in their formative years, and now Mamie was back home to indulge in lengthy heart-to-hearts.

As for Cousin Cornelia, she was overjoyed to see Mamie and her boys. Similar to Mamie, Cornelia was a recent widow. James Hamilton had died two years previously after contracting typhoid fever. But the apple and peach trees he had planted were producing a bumper crop and were a living tribute to a man who had driven a large herd of cattle to San Francisco, then came home to plant his California dream orchard in Missouri.

Of course Mamie was especially fond of her little namesake, Mamie Hamilton, Cornelia's daughter. Sadly, two years after Mamie's return to Westport, the little brown-eyed girl died on September 19, 1872. She was just seven years old, the same age as Mamie's own Butchie.

At the time of the child's death, Cornelia was still grieving the loss of her husband. Yet, comforting her youngest son, she was heard to say, "Won't Papa be glad to have Mamie with him!" Such brave words inspired the following poem, entitled *Mamie*, written by Rev. Schenck:

" 'Won't Papa be glad to have Mamie with him?'
Was breath'd from her sorrowing heart,
As she saw the eyes of her child growing dim
From the stroke of a mystic dart.
"Mother felt, as she held her half-orphaned boy
O'er the couch of his sister's pain
That Papa was waiting, with radiant joy,
To welcome his Mamie again." [1]

Thankfully, there were happier events in store for the family. For instance there was the wedding of Cornelia's eldest son, James, a quick-witted young fellow known to entertain the family with his off-beat sense of humor. As a youngster, he kept the family diary when the Hamiltons went to California. Now he was a handsome cowboy, headed for Colorado.

As for sister Nan, her wedding went off without a hitch, and by 1871 she was expecting her first child and still living at home. Her new husband had taken himself off to Colorado and was planning to go ranching if he could get enough money to buy cattle. These condensed versions of love letters written by Nan and Phidelah described the comings and goings at the Bernard household during Mamie's stay in Westport. [2]

Westport, July 27, 1871—Annie (Bernard) Rice to husband Phidelah Rice

"My own precious Husband:

"Received your letter Tuesday morning. Mr. Bryant told Pa he did not have the money to invest in cattle and was going to write you that he did not have the means to buy cattle on shares.

"Westport is in quite a state of excitement tonight. Miss Anna Neilson is to be married at 11 o'clock tonight to Mr. Willie Millo. And the ladies of the C.P. Church are going to give Mr. Barchanan a donation party.

"I am invited to both but could not attend either on account of my size. I did think for a while that I would go to the donation party and commenced to dress, but I did look so large to myself, so concluded to stay home and write to you, my dearest dear.

"Mamie, Jess, Flora (Florence Price) and Allan have gone to the wedding. I will not seal this until I hear how the wedding comes off. Ma had the honor of flowering the cakes for the wedding. She ornamented them like she did for our wedding, but they are not quite so pretty.

"Tomorrow the young ladies and gentlemen of the town are all going to a fishing party on Indian Creek about ten miles from here. Jess is going and expects to have a fine time of it. She expects to meet Louis there.

"Mrs. Bryant, Dr. Bryant's wife, has come over to stay all night with us. The rest of the family are not home. And I must go down and talk to her awhile.

"Well, my dear, Mrs. Bryant has retired and Ma has gone upstairs, too. And as I have to wait for the girls, I will pass the time off writing. Allan came just now and "boy-like" he could not tell much about the wedding. I expect they are having a nice time by the way they are laughing and talking. You can hear them over here very plainly. I expect I ought to tell you how smart your wife has been lately. I've just done lots of sewing for the "expected" and then I got some nice blackberries to put up and did most of the work myself, too.

"Yesterday Ma had a rag party. Cousin Nealy (Cornelia), Susie, Lou and Emma came to help Ma cut and sew rags for her carpet. We had a nice dinner and a pleasant time generally."

The next day Nan finished her letter by saying:

"We have been having frightful weather until the day before yesterday. It has been a little warmer since then, but we still have a cool breeze. I do wish you were here now. We are having so many fresh vegetables and I just know you would enjoy them. The peaches are getting ripe, too.

"Jess has just left in a spring wagon. Mamie is getting ready to go. And who do you think she is going with? Why, that good-for-nothing Ed Price. I don't know what in the world she does mean. If I was her I wouldn't be caught in a buggy with him. I don't think Pa likes it one bit. I expect he thinks his troubles with his daughters will never cease, don't you think? Ma has found out that Jesse has been writing to Louis and she was very much displeased indeed. So Miss Jesse is not to write to the young man anymore. I don't know how she is going to manage about hearing from him. I expect they will fix some plan today to hear from one another.

"I almost forgot to tell you about the wedding. The bride looked very sweet and pretty. She wore a blue poplin. Wreath and veil were white, the veil was Innie's. It is quite a handsome one. And they had a nice supper, too. The girls say that everything was very nice.

"Jim (young James Hamilton) was here the other evening, just talking on about Miss Eliza. (the former slave who accompanied James and his wife to Colorado) He said he asked her if she smoked, chewed or dribbled snuff, but said he forgot to ask her if she ate beans or snored and, if she did, he wasn't going to have her. I never heard such talk as he has. It makes me laugh every time I think of the way he talks. I believe he has concluded to start for Colorado about the 20th of next month. Let me know in your next letter what you want me to do. Ma thinks I had better stay here until you have a house of your own to take me to. Do as you think best, dearest. How I long for you to come home soon to your devoted wife, Nannie."

From the Ranch in Colorado, Phidelah writes:

"Well, Pet, this week is passing slowly. The days are so very, very long, and we rise so early. But then I always find something to do to pass the time, between reading and writing and working and riding and fishing. And now I have a new source of amusement. Lou has a fine filly, a present from her Pa. I have undertaken to break her to ride and am to have her for my saddle horse for the summer. She is going to be no trouble at all to break and will make the best saddle horse in the territory—perhaps.

"I let her loose awhile ago with a long rope to her. She started off and I after her. I ran her a mile and gave up the chase. Will followed her on horseback and caught her. Yesterday we moved back to Francisco's ranch and today are quite busy preparing to start to Canon City. We are to camp out. Now won't that be grand this splendid weather. We will take a tent and Will, Lou and Mrs. Yager will sleep in it and I in the wagon. They are cooking up a perfect wedding of nice things, cakes, custards, venison and c & c. Lou came in just now with a nice pound cake and said, "When your wife can bake a nicer cake than this…" I forgot the rest. I told her, "When she comes out Will and I will have frequent cake-baking contests."

"We have still something else to relieve the monotony. There are a hundred Apache Indians camped just below us a mile. Some of them are at the ranch almost every hour. The dogs bark to apprise us of their coming and then we close all the doors, will not allow them in the house. They are a great nuisance, most unblushing beggars and thieves. About twenty came up this morning, headed by the chief and asked first Francisco and then Will to give them a beef, and when they refused to do it talked quite saucy.

"They will no doubt steal half a dozen before they are done. They dare not do anything openly, or we would subtract a dozen or so from their number. They are most loathsome creatures and all the nice fancies I once indulged and which were encouraged by sundry writers on 'The noble and heroic traits of the Indian' are fast giving place to a feeling of disgust, amounting almost to hatred. But then I must repress such a feeling. Such is man without the elevating influence of the Gospel.

"We had a fine mess of trout for breakfast. Andrew, Francisco and I caught them. Wish you could have shared it with us.

"Now darling, you see I am doing well, and while I am cheerful I cannot avoid missing you constantly. And heaven guard, cheer and comfort my heart's treasure is the constant prayer of your own Phidelah.

"PS: We will go by Badito tomorrow and I will mail this."

From Nan to Phidelah: July 30, 1871

"My own dear husband:

"How very, very precious your letters are to me, but I do long to hear your dear voice again. It seems as if it is such a long weary time to wait for you to come home.

"Thanks to cousin Susie, (Susan Harris Bernard, Cousin William's wife) we have plenty of nice apples to eat now. She sent us peaches, too. They are not very good yet. It is rather early for them. If you come home in September you will be just in time for the nicest fruit.

"Another thing I mentioned in my last letter was the fishing party. Jess went and met Louis there and had a great time of it. Talking of Ma not letting Jess write to Louis anymore, he was awful angry and wanted to do all kinds of desperate things! I believe he wanted her to run away with him, but she had the good sense to refuse. She told him she would marry him just as soon as he could support her. I don't know what will become of Pa and Ma if she was to marry him. They are so very unwilling for the match.

"You will see by the date of this that it is Sunday. Mr. M. is here as usual. Jess is enjoying herself, talking to him. I don't know how she can stand him; he is always so tiresome to me.

"I did not go to church this morning. I do not like to go out in the daytime anymore. I look so large to myself. I expect to attend church tonight. I want to go hear Mr. Wheatly if he preaches. He is a favorite of mine. Heaven bless you dearest and bring you home to your wife, Nannie.

"*Postscript:* *31st*. I'm real sorry I said anything about the way None (Noah) done. He has changed since then and is very kind to me. As for my coming out there before I'm sick, Ma says I mustn't think of it. She cannot bear to have me leave her until I am entirely well. It seems to distress her to hear me talk of going until I'm well. But dearest, I will do as you think best."

Initially, Mamie enjoyed being in Westport, but as time passed she began to feel ill at ease. Living in her parents' home was like reverting to childhood. At times her younger sisters squabbled and, when her sons got into mischief, they were reprimanded by everyone in the house. Besides that, Pedro and Butchie still spoke with a strong Spanish accent and were sometimes teased at school. In the Southwest they were treated as upper-class Spaniards—but here they were considered "different."

More exasperating was the role she was expected to play as a widow. Eyebrows were raised if she should so much as talk to a man. Even sister Nan had taken her to task for accepting a ride in Edwin Price's carriage. Mamie was not exactly sure why Nan objected. After all, the Price family had always been considered special friends. Together Mamie and Florence Price had sewn the controversial flag and, on Mamie's wedding day, Florence had been the perfect attendant.

It was also obvious, at least to Mamie, that brother Noah had his eye on Amy Price. *So, what harm could come from riding in Edwin's carriage with Noah and Amy—and playing cupid?*

If truth be told, Mamie found it refreshing to witness Noah's budding romance. Noah had been severely depressed, but since Amy Price appeared on the scene he was noticeably brighter, and for that Mamie was thankful.

As for Nan's derogatory remarks about Edwin Price, it infuriated Mamie to think her sister could be so cruel. Edwin was a family friend—nothing more—and, as far as Mamie was concerned, he deserved respect. Not only was Edwin the son of the great General Sterling Price, but he was a loyal Southerner who had joined the Confederate army, been taken prisoner and suffered a great deal before being pardoned by President Lincoln.

Mamie felt sorry for Edwin, just as she did for all the other young soldiers—Southerners and Northerners alike—who had fought in the Civil War. The conflict had produced no winners, only men with missing limbs and emotional scars that would never heal. *Yes, each one deserved respect and sympathy!*

Yet, in spite of her compassion, Mamie had no desire for a serious relationship with any of these men, no matter how heroic. She had once been in love and that would suffice. What she valued now, more than anything else, was her independence.

Perhaps she had lived too long with Epifanio's people, enjoying their spontaneity, the way the Mexicans laughed and danced and welcomed each day by stepping up on a horse and galloping off, returning whenever they pleased to feast on beans and corn tortillas and tell of their latest adventure. The Mexican lifestyle was full of action, while Westport's vitality had gone. The more Mamie pondered her dilemma, the more she realized that Westport had nothing to offer—no promising future for herself or her sons. There was only one solution; she and her sons were going back to the Southwest.

Chapter Fifteen—Teaching On The Frontier

Arizona's Governor Anson Safford was small in stature, five foot six, and self educated. Originally from Vermont, he knew little about Arizona when he took the oath of office on July 9, 1869 and, as an "outsider," got a cool reception from the residents in Arizona. Before long he won their hearts by showing genuine concern for their welfare, and they responded by affectionately calling him, "Our Little Governor." [1]

"The Governor is little...but, composed of the right sort of material," *The Prescott Miner observed.* "We need scarcely to say that our people are pleased with our new Governor."

Traveling about Arizona, sometimes at great personal risk, Governor Safford was quick to recognize the need for a comprehensive public school system. In 1871, during the sitting of the sixth territorial legislature, he pointed out the inadequacy of the existing school system and asked that money be set aside to provide free public school education. With strong support from Estevan Ochoa, Epifanio Aguirre's second cousin, Governor Safford's proposal was adopted, and the governor was made Superintendent of Schools.

The seventh territorial legislature held in 1873 found Safford promoting his dream of "free education for the children of Arizona." But school teachers were hard to come by. Safford was corresponding with potential teachers around the country and often advancing personal funds to bring them to Arizona. Two of Mamie's relatives, Johnny Behan[2] and Estevan Ochoa[3] were delegates at this 1873 territorial sitting, and it was during these sessions, when schooling was being discussed, that Johnny and Estevan suggested one of their own as a prospective teacher—Mamie who had let it be known she wanted to return to the "wild west."

The idea of teaching school in a remote area where Apaches were still threatening the white community must have seemed absurd to Mamie's friends, but the former Southern Belle needed money to raise her sons. She hated being dependent on handouts from relatives, and it was becoming more and more apparent that either she resign herself to a marriage of convenience, or go to work.

Mamie chose the latter and, in 1875, she set out for Arizona accompanied by her three growing sons and brother, Noah, who had just turned twenty-one.

When they arrived in Tucson young Pedro and Butchie fairly danced with joy for don Pedro had come to meet them. After their father's death, don Pedro had become the head of the Aguirre hacienda, as tradition dictated. He felt it was his duty to look after Epifanio's family, in the same way as Epifanio had cared for his dead father's next-to-kin. After some discussion it was decided that Noah and Mamie's two eldest sons would go to live with don Pedro. Noah would go to work while twelve year-old Pedro and ten year-old Butchie would go to school.

Living with don Pedro was very much to young Pedro and Butchie's liking. They still remembered the happy days with their father's people, but eight year-old Stephen could barely remember his father, let alone don Pedro. He begged to stay with his mother, and she gladly took him along when she went to teach school. Her first school was north of present day Benson, and of this experience she wrote:

"The first time I ever taught school was in the fall of 1875 at a little country settlement in Arizona called Tres Álamos on the San Pedro River where the people lived far apart. The ranches were scattered up and down the river at intervals of from three to five miles and the bulk of the 'town,' consisting of about a dozen adobe houses, was on the west side of the river and foot hills. About the center of this collection of houses was a one room adobe house, with a one sash window, a small door and an immense fire place. It belonged to some unfortunate who had been killed by Indians and had left no heirs. So the 'deestrict' appropriated it for a school house.

"One of the trustees came to Tucson to hunt up a teacher. I was asked to take the school and I did. I went from Tucson with an old friend of mine, Mr. Hooker, who owned a cattle ranch and store and a comfortable house on the river a mile from Tres Álamos. We went through in a day—40 miles—and I took my youngest son with me. We stayed that night at Mr. Hooker's and went the next morning across the river to Mr. Thomas Dunbar's where I was to board.

"I did not know Mr. and Mrs. Dunbar then, but afterwards they were my very dear friends. Their house was an adobe with a big corral attached and consisted of one large room which was Post Office, stage station and sleeping room for "travellera" going through the country, back and forth from the different Forts, Bowie, Grant, Apache and the San Carlos Indian Reservation. Back of this room was two smaller ones, with no doors between them. Lumber was scarce and high then and we had no board floors or unnecessary doors or windows in houses. So, the door between my room and Mr. and Mrs. Dunbar's was a blanket which, when there was an extra number of guests was taken down and put to proper use. Often Mr. Dunbar would come and ask me to lend him my door, which I cheerfully did. But everything was spotlessly clean and neat, and we were very happy together those six months of my first school.

"The kitchen and dining room were together in a sort-of annex to the main building, an after thought as it were. The meals prepared by Mrs. Dunbar were known far and near, and all travelers going and coming would strain a point to sleep and eat at Dunbars', such delicious meals they were, such coffee and biscuits and bread, such sweet milk and fresh laid eggs and cakes and pies as made one's mouth water. So, no wonder everyone made it a point to reach Dunbars'.

"Once while I was there, General Kouts came through the country and was wined and dined and danced in Tucson, and then went on a tour of inspection of the Forts. Relays of mules were sent from Tucson to the cienega and from Fort Grant to Dunbars' station. And the drive of about 130 miles was to be (and was) made in a day with the understanding that they were to dine at noon at Dunbars'. Quite a number of prominent civilians as well as officers accompanied General Kouts and nearly all were friends of mine. For two days before Mrs. Dunbar was preparing for the dinner which was to be extra nice, and all the 'pies and things' were ready when Thanksgiving day arrived, which was the day the general was to pass and all was bustle and life at the station. The house was cleaned nicely. I swept it myself while Mrs. Dunbar started dinner.

"Just in the midst of the bustle, Mrs. Dunbar was taken with a violent chill and had to go to bed. So there was great trouble in the house until I offered to finish getting dinner which, with the help of Mr. Dunbar, I did. And what fun we had! There was a window from the dining room to the kitchen and through this the eatables were passed. Mr. Dunbar stood inside the dining room and I passed the plates. Everything went off fine, and no one knew I was there for only my head showed as I handed things in. But one man who knew me well caught a glimpse of me as I passed to and fro, and he kept looking, much to Mr. Dunbar's amusement. Another man I knew came around to the kitchen to speak to Mrs. Dunbar and found me out. But dinner passed off all right, and we had a good laugh over it."

"But I'm not telling about the school. Mr. Dunbar and I went around the neighborhood and notified the scholars that school would commence on the next Monday, and then we inspected the room. And such a place it was! No seats, no desks or blackboards—not even a table. There were about half a dozen books, first readers and some slates and pencils. But we got some candle boxes and put boards across them for seats, then the trustee who had engaged me brought me a chair and a stool.

"The chair had been seated with raw hide that was not dry, so it had drawn up in the middle, throwing the back forward, and using it was out of the question. Instead, I took the stool which was also covered with raw hide. It was so high my feet did not touch the ground (I am a very short person), so there I sat with my feet on a rung of the stool, holding the books on my lap, while the scholars sat down on the ground and wrote on the boards. Afterward the school in Tucson got new seats, and they sent me the old ones. But I had a full school of girls and boys—some grown and others were little things with many sizes in between. There were twenty-three in all. I had to walk a mile across the valley to the school house, which I did accompanied by many of my scholars.

"One day along in April of 1876, we were detained on our way to school, so when I opened the door I left the key outside in my hurry. A little boy, Eddie D., went outside and had only been gone a few moments when he came running and screaming. As I looked out the window he passed and directly behind him came a big Apache Indian. The child, in his fright (or maybe it was the Indian) turned the key and locked himself out. So there we were locked in and the Indian and screaming child outside. The children looked like death, they were so frightened and I, no less scared, called frantically for Eddie to unlock the door. I suppose the Indian understood for he unlocked and opened the door, and poor Eddie tumbled in, a limp heap, almost unconscious.

"The Indian said, 'Good morning' and calmly walked in, seating himself on a bench beside a girl with a sore arm who gasped and rolled off onto the floor.

"At this I could not help laughing, for I saw he meant us no harm. He gave a grunt and a sort-of laugh, picked up the girl's book and began looking at the pictures in an unconcerned way. I had quieted the school by then and was proceeding along with the class to which Mr. Indian paid the closest attention. Finally, he grunted something and pointed all around. I then pointed all around and said, 'these are all mine—my children.'

"He looked all around slowly and then shook his head and said, "No, they are too black." The color seemed to be the only thing that made him doubt. That there were twenty-three did not seem to count.

"Less than a week from that time the Indians killed a family near where Benson is today, and I had to close my school because it was not safe for me to go back and forth or the scholars to leave their homes. So my first school was broken up by Indians. That Indian who visited my school was one of the three who went through the settlement, up and down the river, and were no doubt sent to spy out the country and see how the settlers were fixed with arms, etc.

"The news of the killing came before daylight the next Sunday morning. A runner on horseback was sent to warn the settlers, and he reached Mr. Dunbar's before day break. People who lived in those times were always on the lookout for Indians. So, when I was awakened that morning by a hoarse voice saying, 'Los Indios! Los Indios!' right at the little window of my bedroom, it did not take me long to spring out of bed and to my blanket door where I found Mr. Dunbar getting up and Mrs. Dunbar shivering with fright as I was myself.

"The man told a horrible tale of the murder of a man and his two sons who lived about six miles above us. Then he galloped on to warn the settlers along the river. So that was a terrible Sunday, and we all kept indoors closely. That night the mail coach (or buckboard) passed and brought us news of another man being killed near Fort Bowie, and the next day a company of soldiers came from Fort Bowie and camped right near the house. So we were safe.

"Monday night's mail brought me a letter from my brother (Noah) in Tucson telling me not to go back to the school house again, and that he was coming after me, which he and my brother-in-law and five other men did. They arrived at Tres Álamos with a buggy and an ambulance on Tuesday afternoon and we started back at dark Tuesday night and arrived back in Tucson the next afternoon. I went in the buggy with my brother-in-law and the others came close behind as escort.

"In the midst of our fright and trouble a comical thing happened. A lady had come from the ciénaga to visit Mrs. Dunbar and was there when the news of the Indians came. She had left her husband at home and, of course, was very anxious. The night the news came of the killing at Bowie, she and I were awake and listening at the door leading into the large room I have spoken of. We could hear every word because the stage driver sat on the door sill and Mrs. W. was leaning against our side of the door. Someone asked which way the Indians went after killing

Mr. Rogers at Bowie, and the driver said, 'They went towards the ciénaga.'

"That poor woman gave an awful screech and commenced pounding on the door and screaming like mad about her husband. And I heard the driver say, 'Good Lord, what's that?' There was such a commotion in that room and in ours that it was like bedlam let loose, for Mrs. W. fell down in a sort-of fit and kicked the door and carried on dreadfully. She was naturally a very violent woman and very large, so we had a time with her and we were all shivering in our nightgowns.

"I'm sorry to remember that I put my head on the pillow and laughed most shamefully when I heard that man jump off the door sill. We took Mrs. W. home as we went, and when we got to her home she discovered her husband had gone to Tucson, so she went on into Tucson with us."

Mamie left Tres Álamos in April of 1876. That same year her brother, Allan, and sister, Jesse, arrived in Tucson. They came much as Mamie had, in the company of a mule train. Their trip, via La Junta, Colorado had taken four months, traveling with Epifanio's brother-in-law Mariano Samaniego. Mariano was still freighting, despite some fairly large losses resulting from Apache raids.

Following Epifanio's death there had been many more murders and, in March 1871, the *Arizona Miner* printed three full columns of names of those killed by Indians between 1866 and 1871.[4] Most of these murders clearly implicated a band of Apaches living at Camp Grant, but government agencies refused to do anything to stop the raids. The brutal murder of Leslie Wooster and Trinidad Aguirre, who were farming south of Tucson, was the final injustice to set off an unprecedented uprising of Tucson citizens. The townspeople who, by this time, were both terrified and angry, elected Wm. Oury and Juan Elias to lead a party of 148 men (94 Papago Indians, 48 Mexicans and 6 Americans), to Camp Grant. Arriving at the camp on April 30, 1871, the Tucson party surprised and killed close to one hundred Apaches—many of them women and children. This much publicized incident became known as the Camp Grant Massacre and, although Indian raids decreased after the incident at Camp Grant, the Apache were still considered a very real threat in 1876.

In '76 a new era in public schooling was just beginning to evolve in Tucson. John Spring, friend of the murdered Leslie Wooster and Trinidad Aguirre, had moved to Tucson in 1870 and attempted to start a boys' school. Swiss by birth, he taught his first class of 138 boys in a long adobe building on the corner of Meyers and McCormick streets. Later he was to remember this class as totally undisciplined. They were "a perfect chaos of boys," he said, "mostly barefoot and speaking no English." He also recalled "a dirt floor, those two rows of uncouth, unpainted and unvarnished desks and the many bare feet of the youngsters dangling from the benches." [5]

Equally roughshod were the school authorities, and when Spring asked for help, he was refused. He resigned and the school closed, but a few months later a girls' school was established by Mrs. L.C. Hughes who, besides organizing a temperance league and women's rights movement, made no bones about the fact that she sanctioned Tucson's role in the crude and bloody Camp Grant Massacre. [6]

When on March 4th, 1872, the first public school opened in Tucson, it was heralded with serious opposition from the Catholic sector. [7] Two young ladies, Miss Wakefield and Miss Bolton, braved the primitive conditions and came from California to teach school in Tucson. However, Tucson's many bachelors were starved for companionship and Miss Wakefield married a merchant, Edward Fish, only four months after her arrival, while Miss Bolton accepted a marriage proposal from John Wasson. [8] Mamie explains those first public school undertakings as follows:

"The public schools in Arizona were established by Governor A. P. K. Safford about 1871 and they had a stormy existence for a while in Tucson. In 1874 there were two schools, one for boys and one for girls. The first teacher of all (for the girls' public school), was Mrs. Hughes about 1872, then came two young ladies for the second school year. In 1874 the schools were taught by John Spring and a Miss Parker. Miss Parker afterwards married. Then came W.B. Horton and Miss Nesmith in '74 and '75. I had taught in the San Pedro area in 1875 and 1876, at a small town called Tres Álamos, but my school was broken up by an Indian raid in April of 1876, so I came back to Tucson sooner than I expected.

"In May the lady teacher of the Tucson public school for girls was taken sick which left the girls without a teacher, and I was asked by the trustees to finish the term which still lacked a month. There were about twenty girls in the school when I took charge. With few exceptions, they were the most unruly set of girls the Lord ever let live. They had an idea they conferred a favor upon the school and teacher by attending. They had some reason for this as there had been such violent opposition to the public schools by the Catholic priests, and they were all Catholic.

"The recess bell was a signal for those girls to climb out of the windows into the street, to whoop and scream like mad and to generally misbehave. I let the first recess pass, but when the afternoon recess came, I would not allow a girl to leave her seat. Of course there was a rebellion and mutterings dire, but I told them that the first one who left their seat should go home and stay there. So, order was restored, and no one left the room. The next day my girls were like lambs, so far as disorder at recess was concerned, but several girls stayed at home. During the day, one girl, who is now a mother of a large family, made an ugly face at me during class. I immediately slapped her in the mouth and sent her home, which procedure kept order for that day. Next day another girl, almost a young lady (and now a mother of a grown son), was impudent to me, and I sent her home. The upshot was that at the end of the first week I had only five pupils, but I had order.

"Governor Safford, who had been a personal friend of mine since 1869, came to visit the school at the end of the first week. He asked me how I was getting along. I said, 'Governor, I have broken up your girls' school trying to keep order.' I also said, 'unless I can have order, I will not teach this school for five hundred dollars a month.' I was getting one hundred.

"He laughed until the tears came to his eyes, but I was in dead earnest. Then he said, 'Mrs. Aguirre, you just go on breaking up the school that way. You shall keep this school if you never have more than five scholars.' But the next Monday all the scholars returned, and before the end of the month many new ones came, so the school closed with forty girls. I was asked to take the school again and for the following years I was reelected without once asking for the school.

"The girls' school I taught in was ungraded, and I taught from the primer to the 5th reader classes. I taught in the old Congress Street adobe schoolhouse which was built in 1875 from proceeds from a one-night supper and dance, organized by the ladies. At the dance there was a cake auctioned off which brought in nearly a thousand dollars. Every bid on the cake was paid down. If a man bid five dollars he paid five dollars down. The next man's bid was raised to six, eight or ten dollars and was also paid down, and finally the cake went for two hundred and fifty dollars ($250.00) to Mr. R. N. Leatherwood who brought the cake to school the next day and divided it among the children."

Bob Leatherwood, Tuscon's "man-about-town," became one of Mamie's closest friends. [9] Described as having "grit and valor," Bob was only five feet, five inches tall, but his acts of courage clearly offset his lack of height. His record of public service was second to none: a Tucson councilman, a County treasurer, a member of the State Legislature and Captain of the Arizona Rangers. [10] At one time he was Pima County Sheriff, and as such was known to have tracked two murders to Death Valley and single-handedly brought them back in irons to the Tucson Jail. Another time, on September 9, 1875, Leatherwood, accompanied by the well-known Juan Elias and three others, set out to capture a horse thief in the vicinity of Fort Lowell. On this occasion only the horses were returned, as it was considered more expedient to hang the thief from a mesquite tree. When time was at a premium, the hanging made good sense to Bob Leatherwood whose busy schedule included building a school in Tucson. However, as Mamie explains, a new public school was not everyone's priority.

"... there was a great fight against the public schools in those days. The Catholics fought them with tooth and claws. Lectures were given against the evils of public schools by Judge Dunn and one of the priests Father Antonio. The better class of Mexican Catholic families would not send their girls. And the boys and girls, whose parents were broadminded enough to send them, were ostracized. I was pretty well known through Arizona and Sonora then—being one of the few pioneer women. So, when I took charge of the girls' school, there was a change came over the status of public schools for girls, and by degrees some of the better Mexican families sent their girls to me. And finally the priest's nieces came to me, and that settled the matter.

"But my troubles in the first year were many and sore. For instance, the first Christmas I had 'Tableaux Vivantes' as an exhibition, instead of 'speaking pieces.' Well ahead of time I engaged the services of our band at a certain price for Christmas Eve."

(Music had always been very much a part of the lives of those living in Tucson, with Mexican típica groups, string and brass, existing from the earliest times, along with small orchestras which played waltzes and polkas at local dances and parties.)

"There was a Catholic convent school (in Tucson) then as there is now, but then a large degree of rivalry existed between the schools. So, when a recent convert to Catholicism, Mr. P. N. Filly, heard that I had engaged the band for my exercises, he offered them more than I did—and got them. A Catholic friend of mine told me of this, the day Mr. Filly had taken the band from us, and the exhibition was to come off that night. It had been planned to break up my exhibition.

"So I got my friends together, young men then full of zeal and resources—they are old men now—and they hunted up King William, a fine musician, and he got someone who could sing.[11] They moved the school organ into the boys' school room (which was a very long room with a stage at one end), and we had the most beautiful playing and singing between acts. And the beauty of it was I had nothing to pay for it. The same young men had colored lime lights (purchased in San Francisco) which they set up and burned while the pictures were on stage, making them look lovely, and King William played soft or gay airs to suit the picture. The main hall being darkened made the pictures look lovely with those lights thrown directly on them.

"There was a romance begun that night of those tableaux which ripened into a marriage that ended in murder for one, and the slow awful death of the other. The picture of 'Night and Morning' was on stage. 'Night,' a lovely dark haired girl with a filmy black, star spangled drapery around her, was leaving the stage. She was half hiding her face, looking back towards 'Morning' as she came in filmy white, the morning star on her forehead and treading upon pink clouds. Her arms were outstretched towards 'Night' and she, a lovely pink Hebe of a girl, full of life and youth, really looked the part of a beautiful 'Morning' as she stood there.

"That was the picture that flashed into sight as a man reached the end door of that long dark hall. He was spell bound, he told me, although he had known the girl who represented morning almost all of her life, but he had never realized her beauty until then. He fell violently in love with her then and there, and in a year they were married. He was after some years murdered in cold blood and, a year after, she died a lingering death. 'Night' was always gentle and sweet and good, the very flower of maidenhood, and she became the idolized wife of our best beloved Governor and, although the Governor is dead, she is living a happy and useful life."

The beloved Governor, Mamie spoke of, was Governor Safford, a very caring person. While visiting John Spring's class one day, Safford noticed that one young lad, Ignacio Bonillas the son of the blacksmith, was too poor to attend school regularly. Safford offered to buy books and other school supplies for the boy, but his parents were too proud to accept charity. "Ignacio can keep the books only if he works for them," they said. So, Safford put the young fellow to work, polishing boots, feeding mules and sweeping floors. [12]

Later, Ignacio's sister, Soledad, the girl who played "Night" in Mamie's concert, became Governor Safford's third wife. Safford's second wife, whom he wed in Larcena Scott's parlor, died in 1880.[13]

The young lady who played the part of "Morning" was Mary Page, the daughter of Larcena Pennington-Page Scott,[14] Larcena's story is one of intrigue; it began in 1855 when her mother died, and her father Elias brought his family of twelve children from Texas, into what is now Southern Arizona. Three months after her marriage to John Page, Larcena and ten-year-old Mercedes Sais Quiroz (the daughter of a friend), were captured by Indians who took Larcena into the Santa Rita Mountains, stripped off her clothing, lanced her with spears and threw her down an embankment. Miraculously, the victim lived and when she regained consciousness, she found herself in a rock-strewn area with snow on the ground. Too weak to stand upright, she crept sixteen miles in nine days through rugged terrain, keeping herself alive by eating roots and wild berries. Finally she reached home, where a few months later she delivered a healthy baby girl. This infant was Mary, the pretty little girl who became Mamie's "morning star" fifteen years later.

Shortly after Mary's birth, Larcena's husband, father and three of her four brothers were killed in three separate Indian raids. Mercedes, the child captured by Indians at the same time as Larcena, was eventually rescued and married Sheriff Charles Shibell—the same Charles Shibell who appointed Johnny Behan as sheriff prior to Wyatt Earp's shootout in Tombstone .

Although Mamie taught Larcena's daughter, relations between Mamie and Larcena got off to a rocky start, due to the fact that Larcena's first husband, John Page, had been known to shoot Mexicans on sight. However, the old grievances were eventually forgotten, and Larcena was extremely pleased to see her daughter portrayed as a morning star and equally proud when Mary caught the eye of the eminent Dr. Handy, that evening.

Doctor Handy appeared to be a "good catch" for a young lady and Mary Page made a beautiful bride. In the next four years, little Mary bore the doctor four babies. Then came her addiction to morphine, and she had her children taken away. She was subsequently beaten and locked in her room by Handy who claimed to love her.

Later, when she filed for a divorce, her husband threatened to kill any lawyer who defended her, saying his wife didn't deserve a lawyer. "She is a morphine fiend and a slut," he said.

However, a lawyer by the name of Frank Heney began divorce proceedings which Mamie attended as a character witness. The court battle had grown to vicious proportions, when Dr. Handy encountered the lawyer on the street—a gun was fired—and, when the smoke cleared, the doctor lay dead, "killed when his own pistol accidentally discharged," said the lawyer. That put an end to the court case, but Mary (Page) Handy never saw her children again. A few months after her husband's death, she died of cancer.

Be that as it may, Mamie Aguirre had very little time to brood over the death of her former pupil, for she had troubles of her own. In her memoirs Mamie says only that, "My health failed, so I had to resign from my school in Tucson in 1878."

Yet, in 1878, her problems far exceeded a mere illness. Something terrible had happened—something far more tragic than anything her Christian faith had prepared her to deal with.

Chapter Sixteen—The Fatal Storm

Summer was Tucson's cruelest visitor, for it always brought searing hot days that turned Southern Arizona into an enormous oven. To work in the heat of the day was impossible. New residents quickly adopted the Mexican custom of working in the early mornings and late afternoons when the day was cooler. The majority of Tucson residents also took midday siestas and slept outdoors in the summer. And, as Mamie points out in the following story, many of the townspeople had some unique ways of dealing with summer problems. [1]

"One moonlight evening don Juan and his family were sleeping outdoors as was the custom in Tucson during the stifling heat of summer. Don Juan owned a large comfortable home with several smaller houses in back, one of which he loaned to an old woman and her daughter. The old woman was seriously ill, and daughter seeing no sign of life and thinking her dead, began to shriek. Hearing the commotion, don Juan imagined the young woman was being attacked, so he snatched up his pistol and ran to the rescue. When he discovered the old woman's prone body, he immediately knelt down in his night clothes and, in a loud voice, commenced to recite the prayer for the dead. Whereupon, the old woman opened her eyes and, seeing don Juan bending over her with his pistol, gave a screech and died sure enough. Don Juan, being a devote man, but totally uneducated, was blissfully unaware of having effectively helped the woman to a "buen morir."

"The next day, don Juan took charge of the woman's funeral arrangement, buying a coffin and seeing she was properly put into it. Throughout the day he paid several visits to it, and was quite satisfied with his work. Now at that time, there lived across the street a maiden lady, a woman in her twenties, "full of kind deeds and good works, but one of the simplest plants that ever grew. She had a large house and rented one of the outside rooms to a poverty stricken young couple whose newborn baby died the same evening as the old woman under don Juan's roof. The maiden lady was in a quandary as to how to bury the baby as the parents were so poor, but when she heard of the old woman's death, there popped into her head the idea of burying the baby with the old woman. Crossing the street, she tucked the dead baby comfortably under the old woman's arm, before setting off to tend to her household duties. But she had not counted on don Juan having a last look at the corpse before the funeral. Discovering the bundle under the old woman's arm, don Juan hauled it out and unwrapped it, and there was the poor little baby!

"This set him to raving and tearing around until the whole neighborhood was roused. He gave no one a chance to explain, but said dreadful things, demanding of the watchers, what they supposed St. Peter would think when the old woman got to the pearly gate with a young baby under her arm. This seemed to convince the crowd of their wickedness in allowing a poor old woman to run such a risk. He then tore across the street swearing to call the police. In the meantime, the maiden lady had been told and was just coming serenely across the street to get the baby when she met don Juan. And then, if she had not had a well-known physician to endorse what she said, she would have been in very grave trouble."

Mamie finished the story by saying, "The girl herself told me this and she very naively remarked that she thought she had arranged things so nicely."

Many of those living in Tucson would spend the entire summer sweltering in the heat, but Mamie was fortunate to have family living in the Arivaca Valley where temperatures were always several degrees cooler than those of Tucson.

When school let out in 1878, Mamie and young Stephen climbed aboard one of don Pedro's twenty-six passenger Concord stagecoaches bound for Arivaca, sixty-five miles southwest of Tucson. The stage from Tucson to Arivaca was pulled by six horses and made seven stops along the way to change horses.

Considered fast, the stage could make the sixty-five mile trip in eight hours, leaving Tucson at six in the morning and arriving in Arivaca at two in the afternoon.

Stephen was ecstatic; he and his mother were going to spend their summer vacation in Arivaca with his brothers and Uncle Noah and Uncle Pedro, and Mamie was equally happy. She would have her three sons together, for a change—and she loved to visit Arivaca.

In many ways, this visit was like a homecoming for Mamie, because several family members who had traveled over the Apache Pass with her now resided in Arivaca. Two of these young people, Indalecio and Santitos Aguirre, had matured while Mamie had been in Missouri. Both had moved to Arivaca with don Pedro and, in 1878, Indalecio (also spelled Yndalucia) was the postmaster at Providence Wells, a small post office located south of Arivaca, on Sasabe Flats. [2]

The hustle and bustle of Arivaca silver mining activity was something else Mamie liked. It reminded her of Westport's vitality, prior to the Civil War and, similar to Westport, the little town sat beside a winding stream in a picturesque setting.

The Arivaca Valley was, and still is, extremely pretty. Blessed with life-giving rain both winter and summer, the area supports a multitude of grasses, desert yucca, and agave. An abundance of wild life, such as pronghorn antelope and deer, can be seen foraging on hillsides. Overhead, hawks, eagles and falcons soar in the mountain air, while jackrabbits and coyotes bound across the road when startled by a passing vehicle.

Surrounded by mountains on all sides, the valley is cut off from Arizona's main thoroughfare; the rugged San Luis Mountains lie to the southwest; the Las Guijas lie to the northeast and, to the northwest, the Baboquivari Range rises to a majestic 7,730 foot granite peak—Mount Baboquivari—which can be seen for miles in all directions. One the most prominent landmarks in the Southwest, Epifanio always used this mountain range to establish his bearings when hauling freight from Mexico.

After Epifanio's death, don Pedro moved to Arivaca. There he built homes for his family and residents of the Aguirre hacienda, as well as a public school. Silver was being mined in the Las Guijas Mountains, and miners required services. So, don Pedro began catering to the miners' needs and the industry he created revived the town. [3] Soon Arivaca boasted six saloons, a hotel, two bakeries, two restaurants, a butcher shop, a blacksmith shop, a brewery and a small Mexican blanket factory.

From the time Noah arrived in Arizona, don Pedro assumed responsibility for the young man's welfare. In the Spanish-Colonial tradition, Noah was considered an extension of the Aguirre family and, according to Pima Census Records, when a head count was taken, don Pedro went so far as to register Noah as his son. Don Pedro was an industrious man with plenty of work lined up to keep the newcomer busy. Noah's first job was to manage don Pedro's store while the older man was busy tending a large herd of sheep for Lord and Williams on a nearby ranch. [4]

When Mamie and Stephen reached Arivaca in the summer of 1878, Noah was still running the store in conjunction with a post office which opened after Noah's appointment as postmaster on April 10 of that year. [5] Mamie was surprised and pleased to see how well her kid brother was doing. Noah had only been in Arizona four years, but already he was proving to be a capable businessman. Besides working in the Arivaca store and post office, he had also done some prospecting for silver. With the proceeds from these various ventures he had gone into partnership with a friend, John Bogan, bought some cattle and was in the process of setting up a cattle company.

It was plain to see that Noah earned every penny he got. As postmaster, he was working on commission and his original ledgers show that sales at the store were seldom for large amounts. Typical of a morning's sale was a seventy-five cent entry on July 18, 1878, and a three dollar transaction made by Indalecio Aguirre on August 21 of that year. [6] But having small amounts of money coming in from more than one source, proved to be enough for Noah to buy cattle. Now he was planning to set up a ranch on a parcel of land east of Arivaca. He would call the ranch "Las Ruinas," a name chosen because there were ruins of an ancient Spanish mission on the land.

Of course, when Mamie heard of the ruins, she was beside herself with curiosity and begged Noah to take her to see them. No doubt she believed, as others did, that the famous Father Kino conducted services here in 1698, during the time he visited the village of Quitobaquito. [7]

All that remained of the mission were a few crumbling

walls, a large corral and three miles of eroding irrigation ditch. Yet, Mamie loved to poke through the debris, discovering bits of pottery and wondering about the builders of the mission. She pictured them toiling in the heat of the day, placing brick upon brick, their faces lined with worry or flushed with future dreams. Now, their once strong bodies were only a scattering of bone in the desert, their cares and dreams—and even their names—forgotten.

Imagining them, living and dying in this strangely beautiful country, as Epifanio had done, saddened Mamie, but she quickly brushed the feeling away. She had resolved to be cheerful this summer, not so much for her own satisfaction, but for Pedro, Butchie and Stephen's. She particularly wanted them to enjoy their time away from school.

The boys had inherited their mother's inquisitiveness and, like Mamie, they were intrigued by everything in the Arivaca Valley, from the breathtaking scenery to the activities in the busy little town. Here, too, they had other youngsters to play with, as well as ponies to ride and fascinating places to ride them.

Summer was fast drawing to a close when don Pedro arranged a family picnic for Sunday, August 25, 1878. The picnic would be the final event of the season and, as always, the boys were looking forward to an afternoon of feasting and games. On the morning of the big event, a few gray clouds hung in the west. It was still the monsoon season—a time when violent storms could erupt without notice, bringing wild flashes of lightning as well as much needed rain to the rangeland.

Mamie felt uneasy. Perhaps the family should postpone the picnic, but the youngsters were certain the storm, if it actually materialized, would not amount to much, and so they started off to the designated picnic spot, with thirteen-year-old Butchie racing ahead on his pony. Afterward, Mamie could scarcely recall the brilliant flash that lit the afternoon sky or the crash of thunder that frightened the horses. She knew only that her darling Butchie had been struck by lightning.

Noah's store was closed that day to observe the Sabbath. Yet, sometime after the storm subsided, he took down his ledger and, with hands shaking so badly he could scarcely write, penciled this notation at the top of the page:

"Butchie was killed, today." [8]

Once again, Mamie could not bring herself to express her grief in writing, but this poem, by an unknown author, entitled *Are All My Children In*, can be found in Mamie's scrapbook, attesting to the heart-wrenching anguish she felt.

"The darkness falls, the wind is high,
Dense black clouds fill the western sky,
The storm will soon begin;
The thunder's roar, the lightning's flash
I hear the great round raindrops dash—
Are all the children in?
They're coming softly to my side;
Their forms within my arms I hide—
No other arms are sure;
The storm may rage with fury wild,
With trusting faith each little child
With mother feels secure.
But future days are drawing near—
They'll go from this warm shelter here
Out in the world's wide din;
The rain will fall, the cold winds blow;
I'll sit alone and long to know
Are all the children in?"

By some strange turn of fate, Butchie died a short distance from where his father—and namesake—had been ambushed eight years earlier. What a dreadful time this was for Mamie as she collected her two surviving sons in her arms. Another sudden tragedy—another heartbreak. Surely she thought she would lose her mind as her Mexican relatives whipped the edge of her sleepless nights with their mournful dirges. In memory of her son, she added another poem to her collection. Written by an unknown author, the last verse of this poem, entitled *Tired Mothers*, reads:

If I could mend a broken cart today,
Tomorrow make a kite to search the sky,
There is no woman in God's world would say
She was more blissfully content than I.
But ah! the dainty pillow next my own
Is never rumpled by a shining head;
My singing birdling from its nest is flown,
The little child I used to kiss—*is dead.*

Eight months later more sad news came. Mamie's father, Joab, the debonair gentleman who had wandered the continent as a politician, pastor and entrepreneur, died on April 30, 1879 in Westport. He was 79 years old. Shock and sorrow had begun to take its toll. The Civil War, the constant fear of Indian attacks, her husband's ambush, the death of sisters, the loss of her darling son—and now her father. It was far more than a human spirit could bear and, for the first time in her life, Mamie felt she simply could not go on.

Chapter Seventeen—Cousin Johnny Meets Wyatt Earp

Meanwhile up in Prescott, Johnny Behan heard the news of Butchie's death and relayed the grim message to his friends at the *Prescott Miner*. They, in turn, published a brief obituary, which despite a few errors, carried a genuine message of sympathy.

"Epifanio Aguierre (sic), second son of Mrs. M. Aguierre (sic) aged about thirteen, was killed by lightning at the Arivaca ranch in Pima County on the 26th (25th) ult. The father of this unfortunate young boy was killed by Apache Indians about eight years ago while traveling in a carriage (stage) from Altar, in Sonora to Tucson. Mrs. Aguierre (sic) is a daughter of a well-known and wealthy merchant, a Mr. Bernard, of Westport, Missouri, and a cousin to J. H. Behan and Price Behan, of this town." [1]

Even as children, Johnny Behan and Mamie traveled in the same social circles, and they remained on friendly terms throughout their adult years.

Johnny's story, as it relates to Wyatt Earp, is included here because, not only did Mamie receive firsthand accounts of the notorious "gunfight," but she sympathized with Johnny as he told his side of the story.

When Butchie was struck down by lightning in the summer of 1878, Johnny Behan is believed to have attended Butchie's funeral in Tucson. Sad as the occasion was, but similar to other religious functions, it was a time when friends and family renewed acquaintances and were introduced to new faces. During or after Butchie's service, an important introduction took place—one that set the stage for a series of murders.

While teaching at Tres Álamos, Mamie had become friends with the Tom and John Dunbar families, and she was the common link between Johnny Behan and John Dunbar, two of the key men in the homicides which were about to take place. When John Dunbar met Johnny Behan, Dunbar happened to mention that he was planning to open a livery stable in Tombstone—and Johnny quickly snapped up Dunbar's proposal to become a business partner. Johnny's life in Prescott had turned sour; he had just come through a nasty divorce, and wanted a change of scenery.

Having come to Arizona in 1863, the same year as Mamie, Johnny had first clerked in the Pima villages, before moving to Prescott where he had become a highly esteemed sheriff. A series of news items in Prescott's *Arizona Miner* refers to Johnny as a "true and good man," a "man who spurns the offers of bribery" and a "most generous soul." In fact he was held in such high regard that he had been sent as a delegate to the Territorial Legislature in 1873, 1877, 1878 and 1879. Later, Johnny was recognized for his humanitarian efforts when he proposed a bill for the care of Arizona's mentally ill. The residents of Yavapai and Mohave Counties liked him and referred to him as a competent sheriff and generous parent. [2]

Johnny had married Victoria Zaff, the step-daughter of his boss, Sheriff John Bourke, in 1869. The young couple were blessed with a daughter, Henrietta, and a son, Albert, and, for the first few years, the Behans appeared to be happy. Victoria was a socialite and a fancy dresser who enjoyed such functions as General Sherman's ball in 1878, when the *The Miner* reported that "Victoria Behan was dressed in a black silk en traine, trimmed with cardinal." [3] However, when five-year-old Henrietta died in 1874, the resulting grief played havoc with the couple's relationship. The marriage crumbled, and shortly after a messy divorce, Victoria married Charles Randall. [4]

For Johnny, death and divorce were sufficient reasons to move from Prescott and accept John Dunbar's partnership offer in the Tombstone stables." Unfortunately, the move plunged Johnny into a disaster of mammoth proportions. Erroneously called the Gunfight at the O.K. Corral, the incident pitted Cousin Johnny against Wyatt Earp—and eventually put Johnny in a bad light.

Around the time of Butchie's funeral, Johnny met a young woman by the name of Josephine Sarah Marcus—another key player in the upcoming murders. Josie was only eighteen, with long dark hair and the face of an angel. The fact that she ran away from home to join a theater group should have been a warning sign, but Johnny gave her a diamond engagement ring, and in 1880 they set up housekeeping in Tombstone.

Once again, Johnny seemed happy. He bought a town lot in Tombstone, on the corner of Seventh and Safford Streets, [5] built a small house and, imagining himself on solid footing, he brought nine-year-old Albert to live with him and his "intended bride."

Cousin Johnny had plenty of work and worries waiting for him in Tombstone. Besides establishing a home and operating the stables with John Dunbar, there were all sorts of unexpected expenses. Josie Marcus was not an easy keeper—she liked to gamble. So, in order to meet his financial commitments, he applied for the job of sheriff of the newly-formed Cochise County and, with impressive referrals from the counties of Yavapai and Mojave, he had no difficulty landing the job.

Johnny's appointment as sheriff was made by Charles Shibell, the man whose wife had been captured by Apaches with Larcena (Pennington-Page) Scott. All of Johnny's comings and goings were of interest to Mamie, and since Larcena was the mother of one of her pupils, it was an easy matter for Mamie to receive news of Cousin Johnny's activities in nearby Tombstone.

Then too, Mamie often saw Johnny when he was passing through Tucson. At such times she would share news from "home" and reminisce about Westport's good old days. Johnny also visited Jesse and Allan Bernard as they, too, were in the immediate vicinity. Allan was a government surveyor in the Tombstone area, and Jesse was living in Charleston, four miles from Tombstone—and there were few things Johnny liked better than visiting with the relatives from his hometown.

During the summer of 1880, Josie Marcus referred to herself as Mrs. Behan. [6] Yet there had been no wedding bells, and it was rumored she was entertaining other men when her betrothed was out of town. The moment of truth came when Johnny was playing faro in a local tavern. Doc Holliday, a man noted for his vulgarity and short temper, accused Johnny of gambling "with money I gave your woman." [7] Doc's words stung, as their meaning was all too clear. Not wanting his son to be influenced by Josie's promiscuity, Johnny returned Albert to his ex-wife, and moved out of the house he and Josie had been sharing. [8]

Sometime after Johnny moved out, the infamous Wyatt

Earp moved in with Josie. This was an unfortunate arrangement, considering Johnny was County Sheriff and Wyatt Earp was the town's deputy marshal, under his brother, Marshal Virgil Earp. This meant the two men had to work together. Even if "women problems" had not arisen, it was highly unlikely that Johnny and Wyatt would ever have been friends. They were as different as day and night—different physically and different morally. To put it bluntly, the only thing the two men had in common was a seedy affair the relatives did not condone.

Wyatt Earp had arrived in Tombstone in 1879, with Celia, his common-law wife, and his brothers, Morgan and Virgil. The young Wyatt Earp was tall, dark and handsome, characteristics which later qualified him for romantic fiction—but an honorable man, he was not. Even by "wild west" standards, his methods of extracting confessions from those he arrested ranked second only to the murders he committed. Reportedly, Earp was wanted for horse stealing in Arkansas. But, when he arrived in Arizona, he hired on with Wells Fargo to ride shotgun on express wagons; then a few months later, on July 31, 1880, *The Epitaph* reported he landed the job of deputy marshal.

Although Johnny Behan was not aware of Earp's past, he soon realized the newcomer was not cut out to be a federal agent. Wyatt Earp was too anxious to shoot first and ask questions later, and this went against Johnny's sense of justice. Johnny believed an accused was entitled to a fair trial, regardless of the crime.

To say the highly publicized "Gun Fight At The OK Corral," was a "gunfight," is a mistake—the word murder is more appropriate. It was an entirely one-sided affair which lasted less than a minute. There was a huge volley of shots from the Earp gang and a couple of stray bullets from a dying victim, and it did not occur at the O.K. Corral. Rather it took place in an alley which ran off Fremont Street. When the smoke cleared three men were dead: Tom and Frank McLowry and their friend, Billy Clanton—and only one of them carried a gun.

The story, according to confirmed records, is as follows: [9]

Between 2:30 and 3 PM, October 26, 1881, Johnny Behan was in the barbershop, having a shave and listening to customers expound on the latest events, births, deaths, horse trading and the like. As he listened, he discovered that an all night poker game between Tom McLowry, Ike Clanton and Virgil Earp had ended in a quarrel between Ike Clanton and Doc Holliday. The quick tempered Holliday was an observer, rooting for Virgil Earp and Earp had lost money—a lot of money.

Johnny mentally filed the information away, knowing this could lead to trouble. He had no sooner left the barbershop, when a man by the name of Coleman raced up, telling him that two sets of brothers (Ike and Bill Clanton and Frank and Tom McLowry), were in Dunbar's Corral, the horse corral owned by Johnny Behan and his partner, John Dunbar.

"Looks like trouble to me," Coleman said, "…and it's up to you to disarm them." [10]

With that, Johnny went down Fourth Street to Fremont Street, walked west to Fly's Boarding House where he saw Frank McLowry holding a horse in an alley (between two buildings).[11] Further down the alley four men were talking. They were Tom McLowry, Ike Clanton, Billy Clanton and Billy Claiborne. (All were in the alley; none were in the OK or Dunbar Corrals.)

Johnny later testified, under oath, that he said, "Boys, you must give up your arms." Then he physically checked the men for firearms and found that only Frank McLowry had a gun. "Go up to the sheriff's office, lay aside your arms and wait there until I get back," he told Frank. "I am going to disarm the other party." By the other party, Johnny meant Virgil Earp and Doc Holliday, for he knew they might try to recover the money they had gambled away the evening before.

Meanwhile, Coleman, "the informant," had gone as fast as his legs would carry him to tell the Earp brothers where the Clantons and McLowrys were. Then, having stirred the pot, Coleman ducked into Fly's photograph gallery to watch the proceedings and was joined by Billy Claiborne who also wanted a ringside seat.

Johnny was almost certain the Clantons and McLowrys would cause no trouble if left to themselves; after all they had the money. As for the Earp brothers and Doc Holliday, that was another matter. Returning to Fremont Street, Johnny saw the Earp gang coming. One glance at Doc Holliday told him the man had been drinking. (As Sheriff Bat Masterson recalled, "Holliday had a mean disposition and an ungovernable temper. And under the influence of liquor, he was a most dangerous man.") [12]

Squaring his shoulders, Johnny stepped in front of the

gang and asked them to stop, but they muscled him out of the way and kept walking. Johnny walked with the four armed men, imploring Wyatt Earp to reconsider. "Leave them alone! They don't want any trouble!" A few paces more and Holliday and the Earps turned the corner of Fly's Boarding House, and there were the men they were looking for, less than four paces away.

"Let 'em have it!" Doc Holliday was heard to say.

"All right!" answered Morgan Earp as they pumped bullets into the men they had surprised in the alley. Ike Clanton escaped by running into Fly's Boarding House, while Billy Clanton, Frank and Tom McLowry fell instantly. With a hand to his stomach, Frank, who had not had time to leave his gun at the office as Johnny instructed, drew his gun and fired. The bullet grazed Virgil Earp's leg.

Attempting to even the score, Billy Allen who was hiding behind Fly's photo gallery fired a shot and wounded Morgan Earp. At least the Earp brothers said it was Billy Allen, when they killed him later. [13]

The so called "gunfight" was over in seconds, and Johnny Behan had not been able to stop it. As Wyatt Earp loaded his slightly wounded brother into a wagon, Johnny went to tend to the dead and dying, but there wasn't anything he could do to help them; they were too badly wounded. Tom McLowry had been carrying the poker winnings when gunned down—almost four hundred dollars in cash as well as checks and certificates amounting to nearly $3,000—enough to die for. [14]

Strange as it may seem, Wyatt Earp convinced the judge that his victims died resisting arrest. Judge Wells Spicer exonerated the Earps and Holliday, but the bloodshed continued. On December 1881, Morgan Earp was shot by an unknown assailant, setting Wyatt off on another retaliatory shooting spree. On his hit list were Frank Stilwell, William Brocius, Charlie Cruz, Billy Allen and John Ringo, all of whom were shot down in cold blood within a short period of time.

The killing of Frank Stilwell (an under sheriff), clearly put Wyatt outside the law. When a warrant was issued for Wyatt's arrest, Johnny Behan headed a posse and rode out to track him down. Thus newspapers carried one of the most unusual stories of the decade, concerning a sheriff who was chasing a deputy marshal. However, Wyatt Earp escaped and lived to the ripe old age of eighty-one, going to his final judgment on January 13, 1929.[15]

Josephine Marcus, the bane of Johnny's life, apparently never married, but followed Wyatt Earp from pillar to post and became a peevish old woman. No doubt her unhappiness stemmed from the fact she wished she had married Johnny Behan. She was bound to tease herself with such thoughts, since the newspapers were full of Johnny's successes, while Wyatt had given her nothing to hang her pride on. The aging Wyatt Earp was anything but handsome and Josie, who grew more cantankerous by the day, became extremely difficult to live with. So, it seemed Earp may have reaped his just reward after all.

Johnny left Tombstone in 1882 and never looked back. Among his long list of accomplishments—and the list is extensive—he served as a Brigadier General in Cuba, the Superintendent of Transport, had a government posting in China and headed the Commissary Department at Empalme, Sinaloa. [16] It may also be noted that Johnny Behan, Will Barnes and Bucky O'Neill were among the first to be sent overseas with Teddy Roosevelt's Rough Riders to aid the Cubans in their fight for independence, a valiant cause which heaped a great deal of hardship on the boys from Arizona and saw Johnny's good friend, Bucky O'Neill, killed in the Battle of San Juan Hill.

Wyatt Earp never served his country in any worthwhile capacity nor did he come close to matching Johnny Behan's valor and sense of fair play; yet there are many blind sighted, fiction lovers who reverse the honors—even today.

After Johnny's death on June 7th, 1912, Albert Banta, Arizona pioneer, editor and historian wrote:

"The life history of John H. Behan is a part of the state of Arizona. Johnny Behan was a most generous soul; always ready to share his all with a friend, or anyone in need, however, he never accumulated much of this world's goods. This writer and Johnny Behan were lifelong "pards" and chums. Both came to the territory in 1863, Johnny coming via the southern route and the writer via the northern route. In his death the state has lost one of its best and truest citizens and one of its most honored pioneers." [17]

The late Will C. Barnes told about an exciting incident, involving himself and Bucky O'Neill, along with Johnny's brother, Price Behan. [18] Similar stories could well have been written about Johnny, for both brothers were made of the same grit. (It was shortly after this incident, that the three friends: Barnes, O'Neill and Johnny Behan joined the Rough Riders.) Here, then, is a condensed version of Barnes's story which also serves as an exposé on stagecoach travel during Mamie's era:

"Six o'clock in the morning, dark and cold, a foot of snow on the ground. The huge Concord stage stood in front of the hotel at Prescott. The passengers were already climbing into the dark depths: two middle-aged Catholic nuns in their distinctive garb; tall dark handsome Bucky O'Neill; Will Barnes; Price Behan and a stranger, a young fellow making his first trip to Arizona—all told six passengers and a driver.

"Every nook and corner of the lumbering vehicle was filled with US mail and Wells Fargo Express matter, leaving limited space for the passengers, who crowded in best they could. Under the weather conditions, the driver had the seat on the top all to himself. The first few miles were upgrade making for slow progress. Once at the top of the grade, about six miles from Prescott, the driver pulled the team to a halt and clambered down from his high seat. Looking out, O'Neill saw him pull a bottle from an overcoat pocket and take a long drink. A minute later he took his seat on top, gathered the reins, threw off the brake and gave a wild yell. The team started off down the steep grade at a keen trot, the coach swaying and rocking along the rough road, skidding recklessly around curves, while the driver wielded his whip. It took but a few minutes to convince the passengers the driver was drunk and would not, or could not, control his team.

"Inside the coach the men formed a hasty plan of action. Behan, a deputy US Marshall at the time, sat inside on the left side. The drunken driver sat on the opposite side, half hidden by the coach. Behan opened the door carefully, grasped the iron railing outside and with help from O'Neill boosted himself to the top. Behan's left hand shot around the worthy's neck in a choking grip, while his right grabbed the reins. O'Neill, closely behind, gave the Jehu a clout on the head and pulled him from his seat.

Then as the team stopped, handcuffs were snapped in place, the boot of the coach was opened and the gentleman bundled inside where he created no further trouble.

"At noon, under Behan's expert driving, the stage reached its regular station. The drunken driver, not yet sober, was turned over to the station keeper to be sent back to Prescott as a prisoner on the upstage.

"As a general rule a fresh team and new driver were furnished at this stop, but no other driver being available, Behan agreed to drive the team down to Gillett thirty-five miles away.

"The new team was a notable one in that region— four perfectly matched snow white mules, one of the most picturesque and unusual stage teams in all the far west. Young, lively and full of pep, they were rarin' to go when hitched up. The road ran down the mountain side on a narrow shelf cut from the rocky walls. There was a maze of sharp curves and dangerous corners. As the stage dropped to lower altitudes the weather warmed; the snow melted and the roads turned to mud. Rain fell in torrents; progress was slow and it was midnight when the stage rolled out of the dark canyon onto the gravely bank of the Agua Fria, the lively mountain stream which had to be forded to reach the stage station on the southern side. Behan, soaked through and half frozen, stopped the stage a few yards from the water's edge. The river was surely booming and across the boiling, turbulent water could be seen the wispy lights of the stage station. Over there warmth and food awaited the chilled and weary travelers.

"The four men stood on the water's edge in the pelting rain, studying the situation. What a scene! The pouring rain; the occasional flash of lightning, the sound of thunder; the stage with its dim lit candles emphasizing the darkness; the four white mules like great ghosts and the dripping men. Adventurers all, they personally were willing to take the risk, but what about the Sisters?

"Back the men went to ask the ladies who were huddled together, shivering with cold. Clear-eyed and unafraid the elder of the women replied, "Gentlemen, we are but two frail women. You men must decide. We leave it to your good judgment and our Heavenly Father."

"Thus encouraged the four men discussed a plan of action. Just below the crossing the river entered a canyon. No one knew how deep the water was, but if it was deep enough to float the heavy stage the whole affair might be swept over the falls and lost. Cold and numb, the travelers could not possibly hope to swim in such a swift current. A water bucket hung at the rear of the stage which O'Neill filled with small rocks to hasten the speed of the mules should there be a need. Behan and O'Neill would ride atop while the other two men, each with a Sister of charity at his side were to stand outside on the upstream side of the vehicle. Holding tightly to the rail on top they were to lean back as far as they could to counterbalance the stage against the tremendous pressure of the swift flowing water. They hoped the combined weight of the four would keep the stage from overturning. In the event it did happen, it was agreed each man would grab the Sister at his side and devote his best efforts to get her safely ashore.

"Behan and O'Neill climbed to the driver's seat, with Behan at the reins."

"All ready?" queried O'Neill, looking back at the four figures clinging precariously to the side. With that, Behan loosed the brake and, with a wild yell, the mules lunged into the whirling water of the stream. O'Neill did his best by pelting the animals with rocks, both men yelling at the top of their lungs and Behan lashing the team with his whip.

"As the gallant little leaders struck deep water and began to swim they were swept downstream with the current. The longer legged "wheelers" kept their feet a little while, then they too were forced to swim. Finally the huge stage itself floated free. The water was up to the knees of the four clinging to the side of the coach. Each was leaning back as far as their arms would allow to keep the coach from overturning. Behan, cool and collected, did his best to keep the team headed towards the far bank and also keep them from becoming entangled in the harness and draft rigging. As the stage swung around in the water, the wheels on the lower side struck a submerged rock. The stage began to rise slowly and for one or two agonizing minutes it seemed it would turn over and all be lost. Just at that crucial moment when it looked as if nothing could save them, the two little lead mules touched the bottom with the tips of their hooves. How those little fellows did claw and tear at the steep bank. Gradually they got the stage to move ahead. The longer legged wheelers also touched bottom and they clawed and dug at it as if they realized the need of using every ounce of power available.

"Inch by inch, second by second, the heavy stage began to move through the water towards the bank. Gradually it settled back onto even keel. The going out was very steep and it took the last rock in O'Neill's water bucket, plus much yelling and slashing of the whip, to get the whole outfit safely out onto solid ground. Three minutes later Behan drove the team through the cottonwoods to the station. The door flew open in a flood of light. Once inside, the two Sisters, wet and cold as they were, dropped to their knees, while the men—those tough, staunch frontiersmen—whipped off their hats and went to stand beside them in silent, thankful prayer."

Chapter Eighteen—Life Goes On

"To everything there is a season," and so it was with Ma-mie; grief came, time passed and once again life took on new meaning. As she regained her emotional and physical health, she adopted many of her mother's dominant traits, becoming a strong goal-setting woman who valued her independence. Her suffering had merely reinforced her philosophy of life—a philosophy captured in the following shortened version of one of her favorite poems, *A Psalm of Life,* written by Henry Wadsworth Longfellow.

Tell me not in mournful numbers,
Life is but an empty dream!
For the soul is dead that slumbers,
And things are not what they seem.
Life is real! Life is earnest!
And the grave is not its goal;
Dust thou art, to dust returnest.
Was not spoken of the soul.

Lives of great men all remind us,
We can make our lives sublime:
And departing leave behind us
Footprints in the sands of time.
Footprints that perhaps another,
Sailing o'er life's solemn main,
A forlorn and shipwrecked brother,
Seeing shall take heart again.

Let us, then, be up and doing,
With a heart for any fate
Still achieving, still perusing,
Learn and labor and to wait.

Before long Mamie began teaching again, and a new chapter of her life began. The next ten years saw her career bear fruit as a strict, but well-loved teacher in southern Arizona. At San Xavier she was fondly remembered by one of her pupils, Higinio Aguirre (don Yjino's son). [1] In 1879, don Pedro Aguirre built a school in Arivaca with his own money (now the oldest standing school in Arizona), and Mamie taught there. [2]

Arivaca held a special place in her heart. Each morning at daybreak, when she visited brother Noah at Las Ruinas Ranch, she would throw open the curtains to watch the sun's first rays gild Mount Baboquivari's rocky peak. It was an awesome spectacle that she never tired of seeing, and it gave her a feeling of closeness to Epifanio and Butchie who died so near the mountain the Papagos considered sacred.

Mamie discovered that something positive always emerged from every negative experience. An example of this occurred when the family returned home for her father's funeral. During their stay in Westport, Noah renewed his friendship with Amy Price and, shortly after, he and Amy were married. The young couple took up residence on Las Ruinas Ranch, and their first two children were born while they lived on the ranch: Noah Jr. (Nonie) Bernard and Edwin Price (Ned) Bernard.

The ranch was beautiful in summer, especially when the rains came, when water tumbled through a hundred wooded canyons. Then, as if by magic, the desert sprang to life. Cacti, which in dry periods were a brownish-gray mass of thorns, were suddenly covered in blossoms, some a brilliant yellow, some orange or mauve, with petals as delicate and fine as wind-blown cobwebs. Huge ivory bells dangled from spiked yucca, and blood-red teardrops dripped from the tall, thin branches of ocotillo.

The ranch included portions of a lush ciénaga, which held a year-round supply of water—Arizona's most precious commodity—and this bubbled up from eight separate underground springs. With this life-giving flow, wild grass grew belly-high to a saddle horse and an abundance of oak, ash, walnut and cottonwood trees lined the streams that wound their way through the Arivaca valley.

A man by the name of George Pusch was Noah's partner on the ranch. So for business purposes, the ranch was originally called Bernard and Pusch Cattle Company. It soon grew to be one of the largest ranches in Arizona, controlling 92,000 acres in four townships and ran about 5000 head of cattle and 300 horses. Noah's brother, Allan, and friend, John Bogan, also ran cattle on this ranch, as did the following generation of Bernards.

Besides being a business partner, George Pusch was a good friend. He had come from Germany to America as a young man in 1865 and, having heard about the wild west, bought a pair of red, high-topped boots and headed for Arizona. He and a young German friend, John Zellweger, first bought the "Steam Pump Ranch." Unable to sell his beef, Pusch opened a butcher shop, patrons flocked to his door and his financial worries were over. He was both a good businessman and shrewd judge of cattle, but never pretended to be a cowboy. Once, while inspecting cattle, a wild steer took after him. Being on foot, he started running. However, his belt came loose, his trousers slipped down and he fell flat on his face. Luckily, a cowboy was watching and shot the charging animal just as it reached Pusch's bare extremities. Regaining his feet, Pusch gave the onlookers a broad grin and exclaimed, "Py Gott dot vas close!" The incident was never forgotten by Noah's ranch hands and Pusch, who was an amiable jokester himself, became the recipient of some good natured teasing. Later, when local cowboys swapped yarns, they often ended with, "Py Gott dot was close," knowing the punch line was sure to bring a laugh.

One of Mamie's greatest pleasures was watching the annual cattle roundups at Arivaca. A roundup was as exciting as a town fair and young Pedro and Stephen were always anxious to participate. Since there were no fences, all of the ranches, big and small, ran their cattle together—thousands of head of cattle on thousands of acres—from the Mexican border on the south to the Papago Reservation on the north. When the cattle were rounded up and the calves branded with the mother-cow's brand, the large calves were herded to market by their various owners and the rest turned back to pasture. [3] These roundups were huge events with at least seventy men—mostly Mexicans—taking part. Every ranch in the country sent their extra men. For the carefree Mexicans it was the event of the season, a social and sporting event they would never think of missing. Many riders were not on payroll at any ranch, but they came anyway and worked for nothing. It was a chance to show their roping and riding skills and have fun in the process.

This is where Noah's foreman, Ramon Ahumada, excelled. Ahumada was one of the greatest cowboys ever to swing a reata and, under his capable hands, Noah's ranch flourished. It was said, "No animal moved in the Arivaca or Bear Valley, no blade of grass waved, no water hole filled or went dry without Ahumada knowing it." [4] Many marveled at Ahumada's knack of handling men in the spring and fall roundups. He was a natural born organizer and was always elected as roundup boss at these communal events. Ahumada could take seventy or eighty men and cover a forty-mile sweep of flats and arroyos, gathering up as many as five thousand head of cattle in a single day. He assigned jobs to the various owners and cowboys with such tact they seldom realized they were being bossed.

To a greenhorn a roundup seemed like total confusion, for the Mexicans were wild, tough cowboys who loved to gallop about, roping anything they could find to rope. They roped their horses, cows, calves, the tail of another rider's horse, the rider himself. Everything imaginable had rope burns. To the Mexican cowboy the roundup was considered sort of a fiesta. They rode off in a circular formation as directed by Ahumada, laughing and whooping and twirling their ropes in the wildest excitement. Yet, when a day's work was done, the end results were satisfying, and a huge herd of cattle had been brought out of the hills.

There was also a slate of cooks and cooks' helpers on the roundups. It was their job to man the chuck wagons and keep the fires burning late into the evening to heat large kettles of beans. When at last dark settled over the range, when the stars had come out, the last man had come in, and the last meal eaten, the Mexicans sang. One man would start by singing a well known Mexican ballad or perhaps a song made up for the occasion, and the rest would join in at various intervals as the mood struck them. By this time Ramon Ahumada would have spread his slicker on the ground and by the light of a candle, he would open up a game of monte that would last until the roundup was over—until the last marketable animal was herded away, which was usually to the freight yards in Tucson (after the railway came in 1880.) [5]

Because cattle rustling had become prevalent, Pima County devised a system of establishing cattle brands in 1887, and eventually Noah owned a number of brands, each one used by himself and his different business partners. He held the JNB with John Bogan; the BXP with George Pusch; the NXA with brother Allan. With son, Nonie, he held the NCB brand and the 76 with his wife, Amy, as well as several others brands with different ranchers throughout the years. [6]

Many years later (after Noah's death), the ranch became the Arivaca Land and Cattle Company and these brands were merged into one. At that time, shares in the new cattle company were distributed to the various partners with one share of stock equaling three head of cattle bearing the partner's brand. In this way Ramon Ahumada, who often received cattle in payment for his services, became a major shareholder in the conglomerate.

Among other things, Ahumada's skillful management of the ranch allowed Noah to branch out into other ventures. One such business was a cold storage and ice plant in Tucson, the first of its kind. Noah owned half of the business, while partners George Pusch and John Zellweger each owned a quarter. Thus, when the devastating droughts came in the late 1890s, Noah was able to keep his ranch solvent by supporting it with off-the-ranch income, while less fortunate men on neighboring ranchers were totally wiped out during the dry years.

While Noah was establishing his ranch, don Pedro was setting up the Buenos Aries Ranch close to the Mexican border. Of this Mamie said:

"In 1881 my brother-in-law (don Pedro) took up a ranch on the 'Abra.' All through the summer the winds blew so distractingly there, that we named the ranch 'Buenos Aires' (good winds). Now, (in 1902) Buenos Aires is a post office of good standing and a customs port of entry. So, you see how names given unthinkingly, or in sport, became landmarks and towns." [7]

Long before establishing Buenos Aires (originally spelled Buenos Ayres), don Pedro had been ranching in southern Arizona. Besides raising horses and cattle, he also owned several herds of sheep and managed sheep for others. In the years following Epifanio's death, don Pedro had prospered. Yet, he had never forgotten his elder brother. As children he and Epifanio had been inseparable; as adults they were business partners. When elected to the Pima County Board of Supervisors, don Pedro requested a mountain in the Baboquivari range be named Aguirre Peak in honor of Epifanio. For, in don Pedro's eyes, his elder brother had been as steadfast and true as the beautiful mountain peak." [8]

Don Pedro's ranch house was built on a hill with a panoramic view of the surrounding countryside. It was no accident that the front of don Pedro's house faced his fields and gardens; he had constructed it in such a way that he might use a spyglass to oversee his property—to make sure his employees were working.

Don Pedro's ranch buildings were erected very near La Posta de Aguirre, the stage stop Epifanio was approaching when ambushed. Approximately six miles north of the Arizona-

Mexican border, this was also the site of Providence Wells Post Office in 1869. Indalecio Aguirre became postmaster of Providence Wells Post Office in 1878, which, according to postal records, was located in "a small hovel where Mexicans took care of mules."[9] Under don Pedro's supervision, this site (well inside the boundaries of Arizona), became the official port of entry into US from the Altar district of Sonora. (Sasabe, previously known to the Aguirre family as Mezquite, is now the official port of entry.)

In the early 1880s, don Pedro assigned his workers to build a lake at Buenos Aires.[10] The ranch buildings have disappeared, but the lake's retaining walls, now badly worn by wind and rain, are still visible. Once these walls held a body of water, measuring one mile long by three-quarters of a mile wide. It was a pretty little lake, watering thirsty cattle and sheep, irrigating fields of corn and beans and entertaining don Pedro's many guests, who came to bathe or skim across the water in a sail boat.

Don Pedro liked to entertain. One midnight in 1886, a Tucson pleasure party boarded one of his coaches, and set off for the Buenos Aires Ranch. Don Pedro rode in the stage with his guests: six other men and four ladies. "It was a pleasant drive out during the early morning hours," said a reporter from the *Arizona Citizen*.[11] "At four o'clock in the morning when Bowley's station was reached, everyone had a good appetite and enjoyed a sumptuous breakfast. A rest of four hours was taken, and the journey down the valley was then leisurely resumed and Mr. Aguirre's ranch was reached by four o'clock on Friday afternoon." After a long, but enjoyable drive, don Pedro eagerly showed his guests around the ranch, telling them of past adventures and how he had seen Mexican wolves and bears roaming these grasslands. Typical of the stories his guests may have been told is this one which appeared in *The Arizona Daily Star*.[12]

"One of Aguirre's horses became mired in the mud in the 'tulies' about a mile from the San Xavier Mission. The Papagos, on discovering it, pulled it out, and in the process choked the animal to death. When found by Aguirre's vaqueros, the Papago were busily engaged in carving the animal for distribution. The vaqueros raised a row about it, but it was too late. The Papago acquired fresh meat, and Aguirres lost a good horse."

One of the regular visitors to the ranches in Arivaca was

Mamie's brother, Allan. Mamie was particularly proud of her youngest sibling for his sunny disposition was taking him to new heights, socially—everyone who knew him liked him. After he arrived in Arizona, he had been employed by the government, surveying the Gila and Santa Cruz valleys. Then he spent three years as an Indian agent at Fort Apache and San Carlos. [13]

He was already taking an active interest in politics in 1881, when he married his Westport sweetheart, Minnie Chouteau, the granddaughter of the famed Pierre Chouteau, the founder of St. Louis, Missouri. Minnie and Allan encountered grief early in their marriage when their first son, Joab Pierre Bernard, died at four months of age. They buried him in Tucson's first Cemetery where he shared a headstone with Mamie's Butchie. Yet, brighter days were ahead for the young couple who were soon blessed with two more sons: Fritz and Allan Jr.

Allan built a large home in Tucson, at 428 South Third Avenue, only a stone's throw from Noah's, but he and his family always considered Las Ruinas Ranch their second home. This was especially true of Allan Jr. who in 1906 was living fulltime on the ranch at Arivaca with his wife and little ones. [14]

Mamie had good reason to be pleased with her brothers; they added so much happiness to her life. She especially enjoyed Allan's sense of humor and whenever he dropped in for a visit there was sure to be laughter. One of Allan's stories appeared in *The Arizona Republic.* [15] It was called "The Twenty-dollar Bet," and Allan told it this way:

> "Fred (Maish) and Pete (Kitchen), two old cronies, were playing seven-up one afternoon in the Palace Hotel for twenty dollars a corner. The game progressed for some time with intermittent arguments of one kind or another. Finally the players differed on the question of which one knew the most about religion. Maish eventually became riled and laid down the gage of battle. 'Why I'll bet you twenty-dollars,' he said to Kitchen, 'that you can't repeat the Lord's Prayer.'
>
> " 'Done,' Pete replied, and posted his bet, a twenty-dollar gold piece.
>
> " 'All right, go ahead,' the challenger said.

"Kitchener cleared his throat and began. 'Now I lay me down to sleep,' he intoned and was about to proceed when his partner interrupted and pushed the double eagles to Pete's side of the table.

"'You win,' Maish said. 'Take the money, but I'll be damned if I thought you knew it!' "

The coming of the railway to Tucson was another highlight in Mamie's life. Her old friend, Bob Leatherwood, was mayor of Tucson in 1880, so he was in charge of the gala event welcoming the first locomotive into town on March 20th of that year. Of course Mamie was in attendance to take in everything from the ribbon cutting to a banquet for the Tucson socialites. She wore her best dress, and watched as the first train entered Tucson; she listened as the Sixth Cavalry Band played rousing music and a small battery of cannons boomed out a welcoming salute. Then dignitaries mounted the bunting-draped platform to give speeches—all the top men from Central Pacific, Southern Pacific and Western Union were on hand to be greeted by Mayor Leatherwood, Will Oury, Charles Drake and Estevan Ochoa (Epifanio's second cousin). [16] Most of the men speaking that day were friends of the Bernard family.

The irony of the situation was that, although everyone in Tucson welcomed the first black, steam-belching locomotive, few realized it would bring catastrophe to the old established businesses. As Tucson residents began to buy the cheap goods, brought in by rail, local firms lost their customers. Tully and Ochoa, whose large store opened in 1868, were forced out of business. Safford, Hudson & Company and William Zeckendorf went bankrupt, as did many others. Another era had passed, and with its passing the older shops—the ones Mamie patronized—closed their doors, and it troubled Mamie to see her friends lose their life's savings.

Definitely Will Oury recognized the ill wind stirring as he rose to his feet at the big celebration and said, "The pioneers of Arizona have spent the best years of their life in preparing the way for the progress that we now see consummated; our life and death struggle with the ruthless Apache to retain a foothold upon a land of our adoption, running through many dark years, is now a thing of the past—our mission is ended today.

"Our last request is that you avoid trampling in the dust the few remaining monuments of the first American settlements in Arizona." [17]

As mentioned earlier, Mamie's sister, Jesse, came west with Allan in 1876. Jesse was the girl who had fallen head over heels in love with a young man named Louis, in Missouri. However, her parents had disapproved of the courtship and Louis went on his way—without her. So she had come to Arizona, and at twenty-six was nearing old-maid status when she accepted a marriage proposal from a rather charming gambler.

The groom was Thadeus D. Byrne, and shortly after the wedding Jesse and Thadeus settled in Charleston, Arizona, one of the roughest, toughest spots in Arizona. A ghost town now, Charleston was a milling town on the San Pedro River in 1876. It processed silver ore from the Tombstone area because Tombstone lacked water to process the minerals herself. Some old timers described Charleston as "a town that poured forth bars of silver bullion under a haze of gun smoke." Others said it was "a hangout for possibly the finest collection of stage robbers, murderers, and bad men in Arizona Territory." [18]

A friend of Mamie's, Mary Wood, who moved to Charleston in 1880, was more generously inclined, saying, "If you came to Charleston looking for trouble, there were plenty of citizens who would gladly supply you with any amount of it, but the honest, law-abiding citizen went his way with no greater hazard than he faces in any large city."

To be sure, Charleston did have some redeeming features. For one thing it possessed a schoolhouse at the west edge of town, and Jesse is thought to have been one of the teachers, but the days she spent in Charleston were not happy ones. Thadeus was rumored to be somewhat of a dandy who enjoyed the company of other women. At any rate, Jesse's son, Samuel Hughes Byrne, was born on July 1, 1885, and as Samuel remarked in later years, he only remembered seeing his father twice because, "Mother took me to Arivaca to live with Uncle Noah when I was two and a half years old." [19]

Since divorce was frowned upon, Jesse told everyone she was a widow and, for the next two years, she taught school at Ora Blanco, a small mining town, six miles east of Noah's ranch. It certainly took a great deal of courage for a woman to ride horseback to and from the ranch everyday. Trees were thick and chasms deep and could conceal any number of ruffians, but like Mamie and her mother, she had what it took to face adversity.

There were definitely days when Jesse was uneasy, if not actually terrified when riding to school alone. Indian attacks had been on the rise since 1882, when Apaches left the San Carlos Reservation. Later, they raided Bear Valley (near Ora Blanco), killing a rancher. To protect themselves the men of Arivaca formed a volunteer home guard. Pedro Aguirre was elected captain, and Noah, lieutenant. Arms and ammunition were supplied by the government, so Noah and Pedro picked up Arivaca'a quota in Tucson and brought the arms back to town by stage. [20]

During one twelve month period over a hundred men, women and children were killed by Geronimo's Apaches, so Tucson citizens appealed to Governor Zulich to do something about the terrible state of affairs. [21] On one occasion, in 1886, the Indians made a raid on Martinez Ranch close to Tucson, capturing a boy in the process. As soon as the news of the attack reached Mamie's brother-in-law, Mariano Samaniego, he gathered together thirteen men, all Mexicans, except one, and started in hot pursuit.

Samaniego had been wounded twice and lost a brother in Indians raids. However, in this encounter he escaped injury and, after a ride of four and a half hours with a running fight, the boy was recovered. At Martinez Ranch, Samaniego's reorganized the men. Then, with an additional six men, the posse pursued the Indians and overtook them just as they were making a second raid on an Italian family's ranch. Fortunately, the posse arrived in the nick of time, saved the family and recovered twenty head of previously stolen livestock. [22]

Later Mamie's son, Pedro, was pictured with the young lad who had been rescued. It is not known whether Pedro rode in pursuit of the Indians that day, but we assume he did. Young Pedro had a personal vendetta—Indians had killed his father.

Pedro was only six and a half when Epifanio died, but he idolized his father and knew Epifanio had been very proud of him. Mamie repeatedly told Pedro of his christening day when his father held him up in front of a large crowd in Mesilla, and the story served to cement a spiritual, father-son bond that remained with Pedro the rest of his life.

Pedro also remembered his father, riding horseback, the

reins held in his teeth, pistols blazing in both hands. His father's murder, followed by Butchie's death had traumatized Pedro. Yet, similar to his mother, he had practiced putting on a brave face and always appeared composed. So, no one suspected that depression was growing inside him like a noxious weed—waiting to snuff out his inherent cheerfulness, even as he wrote the following letter from the Buenos Aires Ranch on Sept. 11, 1886.[23]

> Dear Mama:
>   We are getting along fine. Uncle Pedro is going to town and will be away several days. There is nothing new here. I enclose a letter from doña Ma Antonio that Uncle Pedro forgot to send you in the letters he sent the girls some time ago.
>   Well, I will close. We are well.
> Saludes a todas las muchachas y muchachos.
>   Your son, Pedro

As a single parent, Mamie was extremely conscientious, doing all she could to keep her two remaining sons safe and happy. She usually kept Stephen with her, but Pedro preferred to live with Uncle Pedro; he enjoyed being with his Spanish-speaking cousins as well as riding the range with don Pedro's feisty vaqueros.

However, Mamie wanted Pedro to have the best education possible and, with this in mind, she sent him to Kansas to finish his schooling. Following graduation at the University of Kansas, he went to Mexico where he worked as an assayer for the Cananea mining district in Sonora, at the Democrata Mine. But Pedro was a sensitive young man. Often alone, he spent hours deep in thought—anxious and brooding. In his mind, there had always been the question of where he belonged; he spoke fluent Spanish, yet he never completely blended in with his Mexican peers. On the surface he bore an air of confidence, but inside the emotional storm which had been brewing for years was coming to a head.

Whether Pedro's nervous breakdown could be attributed to his father and brother's untimely death, or the stress of being pulled between two cultures, Mamie had no way of knowing. But in any event, he was very ill in 1887, when she sent Stephen to fetch him home from Mexico. [24] Brokenhearted, Mamie prayed for her son's immediate recovery, but healing is a slow process and it would take several years for her prayers to be answered.

It was comforting for Mamie to know that Noah, Allan and Jesse were on hand to support her whenever she was faced with troubles.

Sometime after Joab's death in 1879, their mother decided to move to Arizona. Accompanying Arabella to the Southwest was one of the family's former slaves and, although slavery had long since been abolished, this elderly black man chose to spend his remaining years with the family he loved.

Mamie had inherited many of Arabella's characteristics and the similarity was more evident as time went on. Both women were born organizers, both were resourceful and industrious, but now it was Mamie's turn to take care of her mother, to schedule appointments and take her mother to church.

For Mamie the 1880s represented a time of heavy responsibilities—ten years when she was torn between two generations, when two sons and a mother constantly made demands on her time and energy. Yet she bore her lot as she felt God expected her to do, with patience and a cheerful heart.

Chapter Nineteen—Ensenada

If there was one thing Mamie thoroughly enjoyed, it was having her sister, Jesse, close at hand. Both were teachers and, at the end of a school week, they could compare notes over a cup of tea, joke about their students' antics and laud their achievements. Classes were large; discipline was sometimes a problem and, similar to today's teachers, they relished the thought of a school break when they had time to travel. Before the advent of the railway, their greatest pleasure came from traveling in a horse drawn vehicle, but now, with the coming of the train to Tucson, they could go to exciting new places.

On one such school break, Jesse joined Mamie on a very special vacation to Ensenada on the Baja Peninsula of Mexico. Here is a condensed version of the trip as taken from Mamie's personal journals.

"To begin at the beginning, Sis and I started from San Diego for Tia Juana (by train, January 4, 1889 at 5 p.m.), accompanied by two valises, a roll of blankets and a lunch basket. As it soon grew dark we saw very little of the country between San Diego and Tia Juana. We caught glimpses of low salt marshes between San Diego and National City, then left the coast and were among hilly farmland.

"Finally at 7 p.m. and pitch dark, we arrived at Tia Juana where Colonel Garza was waiting for us. He, with his men carrying our traps, took us to the Tia Juana Hotel.

"The air was so different from San Diego—there was a delicious herb smell, and it seemed more like the month of May instead of January. It made me feel as if we were going to some quiet farm house rather than a hotel. The "hotel" we found to be a square frame house, built in the straight up-and-down board style—a hotel where one can hear the next door neighbor turn over in bed or snore. A hall runs through the center (of the building), with four rooms on each side, both upstairs and down. We had supper and adjourned to the parlor where there was a fire which was quite pleasant." (Note: It rained during the night making travel impossible, which meant the travelers had to lay over an extra day in Tia Juana.)

Mamie goes on to say, "After lunch the gallant Colonel came to take us for a walk across the line into Mexico to see the town and Custom House. We went to the Custom House first and inspected the offices and stables where we saw the carriage and a stout pair of horses which we were to use the next day. In one room there were six sewing machines which had been captured on their way to Ensenada. Now fancy anyone trying to smuggle one sewing machine across the line, over a trail, much less six. Whoever that smuggler was, he should have been allowed to go on with his machines. The very audacity of the situation ought to have filled the guards with admiration. There were half a dozen chairs, also a trunk and several other things too bulky to be smuggled over the line. We went into Colonel Garza's office and were shown the seals or official stamps and other things for the general undoing of smugglers.

"We came back over the line in time to see the afternoon train discharge its load of passengers, many of whom were sightseers and came out just to go over into Mexico. They hurried over, in groups of twos and threes, all eager to see the 'line.' The Colonel told us that, some days, their time was taken up showing the Customs House to visitors, all of whom asked for the impression of his official stamp on their handkerchiefs. He gave Sis two impressions on paper. Finally we arrived at the hotel gate, and the Colonel left us. But we were not yet satisfied, so we continued to walk, going out on the street and walking toward the ocean.

"Now to what side that is, as regards to a compass, I am utterly ignorant for I lost my bearings completely the night we arrived, and according to my idea of things the sun neither rose or set in the right place. In our walk among the fields we passed some sign posts with such imposing inscriptions on them, such as 'New York Avenue,' and 'New Orleans Avenue,' etc., showing a very impartial state of mind on the part the town planners—as if they were on both sides of the Mason and Dixie's Line in their sympathies.

"There is an immense frame building opposite the Tia Juana Hotel which is in reality another hotel which looks much like a box with windows, but the windows are broken, the floor rotting, the paper hangs from the upstairs wall in sad festoons, and there is a dejected air about it which is forlorn in the extreme. It is a monument of the shiftlessness of the booming times, for it is built on leased ground which someone has a lien upon. The lumber was not paid for, so the lumber merchant has a lien on it; the carpenters and paperhangers were not paid, so they too have a lien on it. So, taking all these things into consideration, it is a blessing the hotel doesn't topple over and crush the Tia Juana Hotel across the street—with so many people 'liening' on it.

"However, (the vacant hotel) has a lovely old garden attached to it with lovely shade trees and flowers, but there is such a rank, gone-to-waste air about it that it saddens one to see it. (Note: two years later, in 1891, a flood washed that hotel and most of the Tia Juana Hotel away.)

"When we came out of the garden it was near sunset. The air was soft and sweet with the smell of new grass. A field lark was balancing on the top of a pepper tree, singing its little heart out, and we could hear distinctly the boom of breakers six miles away. It made one think of a May morning after a shower, when everything is sweet and wholesome, and only man is vile—for the only man we saw was carrying beer bottles from a nearby store.

"That night we retired early, for we had to start at eight o'clock sharp the next morning."

(Note: The tourists left at ten o'clock the next day. The driver and Colonel Garza took the front seat of the carriage, while Mamie and Jesse sat in back. The carriage was so heavily loaded with valises and packages that the passengers literally had to sit with their knees under their chin. A guard, wearing a red shirt, accompanied the carriage on horseback.)

"We were stopped about every five minutes for a last word with someone," Mamie continued, " and people seemed to fall in line and come on with us until we had quite a crowd by the time we came to the last house. All had messages to give to the Colonel—or something more substantial. One man came running, out of breath, and handed us four bottles of wine which was stowed away under the valises. Another man brought cigarettes and matches.

"At last we were ready to start, and it was eleven o'clock. We came by the ranch of Mr. Aguellar, owner of the Tia Juana

Valley, and then three gentlemen in covered carriages joined us, and we came on together as "compañeros de viaje" traveling along the river bed awhile before coming up a hill to open countryside. The real name of the valley is the Tijuana which in Indian dialect means 'little turtle.' There were so many turtles in those parts that the name was given to that valley. So, farewell to the romantic associations with the name Tia Juana meaning 'Aunt Jane.'

"The beauty and fertility of the valley is undisputed and great fields of wheat and barley were on both sides as we traveled along. Here and there were good substantial houses with nice gardens that had a thrifty look about them, which was good to see.

"Later we passed the ruins of a three hundred year-old Jesuit Mission. Think of it, and you will feel young, even at sixty.

"I don't know how long nor wide that valley is, but I know it was well into one o'clock when we commenced to climb a hill. This led to another valley, equally fine, but not so well cultivated. After we passed that hill we lost sight of the Tia Juana River, but came upon another small stream. This land was the beginning of the International Company of Mexico, and the houses had a 'squatter-look,' with small cultivated patches of ground."

"As it was past noon by the sun, and the horses were a little blown from climbing the hill, we concluded to stop to have lunch. The Colonel had been carrying a red cover, and this we spread on the ground in the shade of the carriage. The signal for lunch brought out a basket from our carriage and another from our compañeros. Between them all, we had a most delightful lunch including one of the tenderest roast chickens I have ever eaten.

"The gentlemen tasted some of the wine and pronounced it good. So our first meal on the road was a success. After lunch our compañeros very kindly offered to take some of our baggage which was a relief. So when we started my knees were in a more comfortable position."

"We soon came to a lovely clear stream which we crossed and then we were in the Carrizo Valley which is narrower than the Tia Juana, but very lovely. There we saw several families, all glad to see the Colonel who seems to be a favorite. One couple stood at the roadside waiting for us, the woman wearing a freshly ironed calico dress and a man's hat. She had a little basket full of long slender leaves which she told me were greens and very good to eat. The man had a complaint to make about some sheep that came to his part of the ranch and ate everything up. He wanted it stopped, and the Colonel agreed it should stop. The woman was an Indian; evidently the man was not. She stood there with her broad good-natured face smiling up at us, the picture of content.

"Two young men wore ridiculously tall hats and stood off a little distance, but had nothing to say. At another place they had killed a beef, and the meat was hanging all over the 'enramada' in front of the house, the owners thereof coming out to shake hands and have a few words with the Colonel.

"We literally crawled out of this valley, the hill was so steep and rutted. We ladies insisted on walking up the hill. It was truly awful to see the carriage; it came so close to turning over on its side, and I shuddered to think what it would be like going down the other side. So, we (Jesse and I) took our time going up, gathering flowers and leaves from the bushes along the way and altogether enjoyed our walk. At the top of the hill we again mounted, settling ourselves for a longish ride (with the Colonel telling some amusing stories en route) before we reached Los Palmas, the stopping place for the night.

"At Los Palmas we found another hotel, built on the severely simple style of a 'goods box,' again two stories high, but this one is varied by having three long rooms crossways and four small ones, the other way, down stairs. Upstairs, the old original goods box is adhered to, with thin walls which gives one the delightful sensation of being all in one room, only behind curtains. One can't feel lonely or timid, for you can hear your neighbor breathe.

"We had a good supper and retired to a warm little room upstairs where we slept undisturbed until morning. At six o'clock a horn was blown, somewhere in front of the house, which was the signal to get up. We dressed, had our breakfast and asked for our bill and were told we were their guests because we were Colonel Garza's guests, and he theirs. So much for traveling in good company!" (Note: Day two followed a similar pattern as the previous day with the highlight of the day being Burro Cañon.)

"We rode along open fields for miles and then came to Burro Cañon and here words fail me for it was lovely beyond expression. The branches of great oak trees almost meet overhead in some places. A lovely clear stream runs in and out among the trees and rocks, then falls over the roots of a tree into a natural basin. From there it goes under a shady green bank where it is lost to sight for a while. And when it comes out further down it is much broader, leaping over rocks and making such a noise that we could scarcely believe it was the same quiet little stream we had seen earlier.

"This valley is watered by the Guadalupe, which they tell me is a large stream all year round. In this valley are the Flower Brothers' Ranches. They are beautiful pieces of land, in a high state of cultivation. There is no irrigation needed in this valley, and crops never fail. We stopped at the first ranch we came to and took down our lunch baskets. Mr. Flower gave us permission to use the kitchen stove to make tea and coffee. Sis and I, taking possession of the kitchen, soon had tea and coffee made and were ready for lunch. We did full justice to the edibles which were added to by Mr. Flower bringing fresh butter and milk. Our compañeros contributed to the feast with some broiled lamb ribs, cooked on a stick over the coals and savory as only meat cooked in such a way can be.

"The house is a curiosity. It looks so very old and time-worn, the floors are worn until the boards shine in places and have dents in them, as if generations of feet, 'long since resting with sandals loose, and on the other side,' had walked or danced on them. The steps are also worn with deep grooves running down the middle and, being slippery, makes walking on them a matter of some care. The house is adobe, thick walls and a flat roof. The kitchen, built of lumber, was evidently an afterthought. In the yard are immense banana trees, their leaves drooping and leaves all torn in the manner of banana trees generally. A lovely orange tree is growing in front of the door, full of fruit which we imagine were counted, as the owner has the reputation for being a little near. Nevertheless, the Colonel picked two for us and they were delicious after the manner of all 'stolen fruit.'

"After lunch, rested and refreshed, we came on again, traveling through a field where they were plowing with four horses hitched to a patent plow that plowed, sowed and harrowed all at once. Further along we passed another old ruin, a mission on a slight hill, and we could see how the land had been laid off into gardens and fields. Some old pear and apricot trees, still alive, bloom and bear fruit in its season and are everlasting monuments to the long dead priests who toiled, prayed—and perhaps persecuted the poor Aztec, trying to show them the beauty of holiness by roasting their feet, breaking their bones and such gentle measures—all in the hope of making them Christians and, at the same time, discovering the secret hiding places of their treasures. But they must have been brave, those old priests, to come to this faraway land. How they must have enjoyed looking over this beautiful valley and thinking it was theirs in the name of the church.

"We soon came to where Mr. Fenochini is starting a military station for the custom house guards with Colonel Garza in command. It is what the sign on the house says, a 'Gendarmerie Fiscal Zone 30 & C.' I cannot say just what that means. I only know that it is the general rendezvous of the custom guard house, and Colonel Garza will have his headquarters there when it is finished. The house is a two-story panel with a one story 'L' and this 'L' has a good wide porch in front of it. They have a garden started, a well dug, stables put up and in fact everything comfortable. There we stopped for an hour while the Colonel attended some business. When we left the 'gendarmería' it was growing late, and we hurried along through wheat and barley fields, crossing the river once in awhile, passing ranches and wild looking country.

"The sun was setting by the time we came to another divide, and as we topped the hill it was dark. But the moon shone so brightly it did not stay dark long. We rode along another divide and this time kept going, down, down, down with the brake on and the horses holding back the best they could. It felt like we must be going through the earth's crust, for it seemed we would never get to the bottom of that hill.

"Then all at once there was the ocean before us and we were riding along through Sauzal de Camanche and over the beach admiring the lovely shiny waves that looked like silver. The sea seemed high, and the waves broke so near it seemed the spray would reach us. Again we went inland among high hills that shut off our view of the ocean. Then down again and there they were—the lights of Ensenada and the bay shining below us. It was eight o'clock. We were tired and presented anything but an attractive appearance when we walked into the well lighted sitting room at the Iturbide Hotel. My veil and hair was awry, and our eyes were blinking in the bright lights like owls in the daytime. But we were soon in our own pleasant room, tired and sleepy, but very much delighted with our trip overland to Ensenada."

After the sisters returned from their vacation, they settled into their regular routines, teaching school during the week and, on weekends taking their aging mother to church when she felt well enough to accompany them.

In early 1890, Noah and Amy built their dream home in Tucson on 47th South Fourth Street. It was styled after the Westport mansions the couple had admired as children. A beautiful structure with distinctive southern charm, it still stands today. Restored to its former grandeur, it boasts a massive central hall for receiving guests, a large dining room, two spacious parlors and three fireplaces each with mirrors inset above sculptured hardwood mantels. Shortly after the family moved to Tucson, Noah and Amy were blessed with two additional children: William, born in 1891 and Amy, born in 1896.

Moving into Tucson didn't mean Noah had given up ranching. Quite the opposite; he kept his Arivaca holdings and the whole family returned to Las Ruinas Ranch on week-ends and holidays.

Jesse and her son, Samuel, who had been living on the ranch, moved their belongings to Tucson, too, and Jesse began teaching in San Xavier where she taught for the next nine years. Samuel went to school at San Xavier, but as he said, "most weekends Mother and I spent in Tucson, a distance of ten miles by horse and buggy. Summer vacations were always spent at Uncle Noah's Arivaca ranch." Samuel recalled how everyone in those days called the ranch "Las Ruinas," and went on to say that one day a sword was found among the ruins. "It was an old sword of pure Damask steel which could be bent until both ends touched. Yet, it came back perfectly straight after such a test." Etched on the sword was the inscription 'Para Mi Rey' (for my King)."

In 1891, Mamie proceeded with a claim against the Department of Indian Affairs for losses Epifanio had incurred by "reason of depredations committed by the Apache Indians." The seventeen-hundred dollars she was later awarded did nothing to compensate for the loss of her husband, but it did help her sons with current expenses.

At this time, son Pedro was in San Diego, California, and Stephen, who had previously graduated from Tucson High School, was living in Tombstone. Stephen was very athletic, playing and coaching baseball in Tucson, before going to Lawrence, Kansas, (Westport's old rival town) where he completed a business course at Lawrence College. Not long after his return to Arizona, Stephen brought home a "proper" young lady by the name of Miss Willie Sneed. On February 4, 1892, the young couple were married, and on November 11, 1893 they presented Mamie with her first grandchild. Little Stephen Epifanio Aguirre quickly won his grandmother's affection, as did his brother, Ben Sneed Aguirre, born in 1895; his little sister, Helen, born in Nogales, Arizona, in 1901, and younger brother, William Munro Aguirre, who was born in Naco, Arizona, in 1904.

Another happy event, during this time period, was Mamie's appointment to the University of Arizona, as head of the Spanish Language Department. This was a distinction which entitled her to be posthumously named "the first woman professor in the University of Arizona." On October 6, 1896, the *Tucson Daily Citizen* had this to report:

Spanish in the University

The faculty of the University has received an addition by the employment of Mrs. Aguirre, who will give instruction in Spanish. A better selection for this department could not possibly have been made. Mrs. Aguirre is a lady of exceptional talent, and educated both in Spanish and English to a degree which is a perfect guarantee of the excellent service she will render. The constant watchfulness of those having the university in charge will secure for it every advantage necessary to its perfection as the leading educational institute of the Southwest."

At the time of Mamie's appointment, Mariano Samaniego, a longtime advocate for advanced education in Arizona, was a member of the Board of Regents and Treasurer of Regents at the University of Arizona. Realizing Mamie's capabilities, he added his personal recommendation and, in her new role, Mamie quickly became known by students and staff as "the cheerful little professor with ringlets." [1]

While Mamie was still teaching in the University, two sad events occurred. Arabella, who had come west to be with her children, died at Noah's home on November 12, 1899, at the age of eighty-four. Four months later, on March 13, 1900, Noah's wife died. Amy's death was particularly tragic in that her children were still very young: Nonie was fourteen; Ned, eleven; William, nine; while little Amy was only four years old. It was an extremely difficult time for Noah, but thankfully, his sisters were on hand to help him care for his children.

Mamie was already living in his home. And, after resigning her teaching position in San Xavier, sister Jesse, who had been spending week-ends with Noah's family, moved in full-time. At first, Jesse took on the housekeeping duties and kept an eye on Amy, the preschooler, while Mamie was teaching classes at the University, but no sooner had the extended family settled into their new routine when it became apparent Jesse had serious health problems.

A visit to the doctor confirmed Mamie's worse fears; "Sis" had developed a potentially fatal kidney disorder—Bright's disease.

Chapter Twenty—The Final Years

Two years had elapsed, and on May 6, 1902, Mamie looked worried as she gazed out of the front parlor's bay window. Jesse was very ill. Noah had taken her to California by train to consult a specialist, and Mamie was home, alone. Noah's children, Ned, Willie and Amy were in school, while sixteen year-old Nonie was out at Las Ruinas Ranch—partying, Mamie suspected, and the young scamp would get a tongue-lashing when she caught up with him.

The sight of heat waves rippling off the wall of a building across the street caused Mamie's frown to deepen. Summer was about to descend on Tucson. Already the tall ocotillo in the front yard had dropped its leaves, and the yellow cactus blossoms were withering. Soon the oppressive heat would smother the town and much of the landscape would revert to thorns and drifting sand.

Mamie hated to see the flowers go, to feel spring turn to summer. One day she would avoid the heat, spend her summers on the beach in California where a cool ocean breeze would freshen the air around her. Then in the fall she would return to her beloved Tucson to enjoy the lovely warm winters, but that was a dream she would never be able to realize at present—not with Jesse so ill and Noah relying on her to look after the children.

As she stood pondering these thoughts, an automobile turned the corner and came chugging past the house, the dust from its wheels rising in a reddish haze. The car was another thing Mamie hated to see: those noisy, new contraptions displacing the lovely jingle of horse and buggy traffic. Changes—they had come so fast to Arizona, but then her whole life had been one of change. "Amazing," she mused, "how happy, how tragic, how very unpredictable life's journey can be!"

The automobile disappeared from sight, and she brightened as a more pleasant thought crossed her mind. For some time now, friends had been begging her to write a book—and so she should. After all, she had lived through an era with events like none other: the Civil War, Apache raids and five times she had made the long journey over the Santa Fe Trail. What strange times! she thought. *Yes, she really must finish writing her memoirs and have them published.*

With new determination, she turned from the window and began rummaging through a stack of papers on her desk. First things first, she decided as she found a writing tablet, drew up a chair and sat down. She would begin by writing to son Pedro, who was living in the border town of Nogales; she would ask him to return the papers she had written last November for the Federation of Women's Clubs. She felt a flush of pride, remembering how her story had been read aloud at the Women's Conference in Foresters' Hall in Phoenix and, afterward, the many compliments she had received. [1] She had savored the recognition and proudly sent the papers to her eldest son, hoping he, too, would read them and think them important.

Dipping her pen in an inkwell, she began to write.

May 5, 1902

"My own dear Pedro: Please bundle up all those papers of mine and send them to me. I am going to go over all of them this summer while I'm at the ranch and arrange them, so they can be published some day. I have several here to add to them. They may be valuable one of these days, so please attend to this before you leave. None (Noah) is in California now with Sis. Nonie is having a good time I'm sure.

I hope you are all well, now. I had such a scare about little Helen (Stephen's baby). I wish I had her here with me. Pedro dear, do let me hear from you. Can't you imagine how anxious I feel? With love, I'm your own mama...M.B. Aguirre. [2]

With Jesse's illness paramount in her mind, it never occurred to Mamie that Pedro was keeping a secret, and the announcement of his wedding the following month was completely unexpected. Pedro had not only recovered from his illness, but gained a deeper appreciation for those he loved. His marriage to Lucy Linder Catlett, a widow with two small daughters, took place in Bisbee, Arizona on June 25, 1902. If the wedding was a surprise, it was a pleasant one and, from that time on, Mamie affectionately referred to Pedro's wife as "my darling daughter, Lucy."

Pedro brought Lucy and her girls to Tucson, where they lived at 737 North Stone Avenue. Lucy's daughters, Hattie and Edith, adored Pedro and happily accepted "Aguirre" as their surname. Years later, they often referred to the terrible loss they suffered when Pedro died. They loved Mamie, too, calling her "Aunt Mame," and sometimes Mamie took care of the two girls while Lucy traveled with her new husband.

At other times, Mamie would be invited for dinner and, on one occasion when food was spilled, Lucy recalled Mamie scolding her for mopping the floor. "You should not be scrubbing floors," Mamie had said. "We can hire a maid to mop the floor!"

Lucy had not appreciated Mamie's remark which she chalked up to Southern arrogance. Yet, there was reason for Mamie to be genuinely concerned; Lucy had just miscarried Pedro's first child. [3]

Regardless of how she was perceived by her daughter-in-law, Mamie thought a great deal of Lucy and enjoyed her company, although there was seldom time to visit. Jesse was growing weaker by the day, so most of Mamie's time was spent at her sister's bedside, fetching and carrying—with night vigilance growing longer and more taxing as the disease progressed. Then on the evening of July 29, 1902, Jesse died. This tribute appeared in the *Arizona Daily Star*:

> Mrs. J.G. Burns (Byrne) passed away at 10 o'clock last night at the home of N. W. Bernard on South Fourth Avenue after a lengthy illness. The deceased had been suffering for some time from Bright's disease. Mrs. Burns (Byrne) was well known to this city, and her death will be a source of general sorrow to many. She was one of the pioneer teachers in Pima county and did much toward bringing the schools up to their present high standard.

Jesse was buried in Tucson. She had been more than a sister to Mamie; she had been one of Mamie's dearest friends.

At times Jesse's divorced status had troubled Mamie. She was honest to the core, and falsely reporting Jesse as a widow went against her principles. Yet, a widow could teach school, whereas a divorcee could not, and since Jesse needed a job, she could never admit to having been divorced.

After Jesse's death, Mamie expressed her feelings in a poem she pasted in her scrap book, *Loss*, written by Mary Cleaver.

> One heart, one heart the less!
> When I name the names of my friends—
> One love that was born to bless
> In a mirage of falsehood ends.
> The sunshine seems the same,
> And the opal tints the sea,
> And the goldenrod's yellow flame,
> Yet something had gone from me.

Mamie spent the summer of 1902 at Las Ruinas Ranch, as she planned. It had been her intention to sort through her papers that summer, reshape her memoirs into a book worthy of publishing. Unfortunately her book never went to print as once again, she set her dreams aside in order to help her family.

Summer was beautiful that year on the ranch, and Mamie accompanied Noah's children on a picnic to Bear Valley, where John Bogan, one of Noah's business partners, managed the Bear Valley ranch east of Arivaca. Picnics were always special family events, and this one added a little sunshine in Noah's children's lives following the death of their mother, their grandmother and Aunt Jesse. The family carried a camera along and Mamie treasured the photos that were taken that day. She especially liked the photo of young Ned, seated on top of a huge mushroom-shaped rock. Ned was a sensitive, kindhearted boy who had easily won a place in her heart.

Among the visitors to the ranch that summer was Bob Leatherwood, the Mayor of Tucson, and speculations grew that he had come especially to visit Mamie. Mamie and Bob were the same age, had similar backgrounds and shared Civil War experiences. At age fifteen, Bob had joined the Confederate army in defense of what he believed was the right cause. [4]

Similar to other young Southerners, he left the war zone when opportunity presented itself and struck out for Arizona, bringing with him his Confederate military cap and uniform which he proudly wore on special occasions.

After he arrived in Tucson, Bob busied himself in various enterprises and served the public as Pima County Sheriff and County Treasurer. He also joined the Arizona Rangers, took his turn as captain and led a charge against Geronimo in 1876. Twice Bob was elected to the Arizona Legislature. As previously mentioned, Bob was Tucson's mayor when the Southern Pacific's locomotive made its initial run into Tucson. With his Southern charm and leadership ability, he proved himself a competent host for what was later termed "the event of the century." [5]

Bob Leatherwood spent many of his summers on Las Ruinas Ranch from 1894 onward, [6] helping with ranch chores and engaging in some lively discussions. He had a quick wit and a keen sense of humor. Yet, when in a serious mood, he would reflect on the fate of the South and Southern rebels, such as Jesse James and Cole Younger, who had put up such strong resistance to the Union, long after the cause was lost.

Jesse James had been shot and killed by one of his own men in 1883, while Cole Younger was captured in 1876 and sentenced to life imprisonment. Twenty-six years later, Cole was released and returned to Lees Summit, Missouri, the place where he was born. [7] Then began an uphill battle as he tried to fit into a world which had gone on without him. He worked as a laborer without success, before joining a carnival in which he appeared as a sideshow attraction. Called "Cole Younger's Coliseum," the sideshow was sponsored by Lew Nichols Carnival Company and was a favorite attraction which toured six states—Arizona, New Mexico, Oklahoma, Arkansas, Kentucky and Texas.

To help with Cole's rehabilitation, his former school teacher, Stephen Elkins, then a distinguished US Senator, sent the ex-convict a hundred dollars. It was the least Elkins could do for the man who had saved his life so many years before. [8]

Elkins still corresponded with Mamie, and in his letters he recalled the "good old days" when he traveled with the Aguirre mule train.

One of his letters, written on government stationery, reads as follows:

Senate of the United States,
Washington D.C.
Elkins, W. Va., July 3rd, 1903

Dear Mame [9]

I had seen the article you enclosed, but thanks for sending it. I am so glad you are feeling better and hope you will return this fall to St. Louis. I am very glad you ... (illegible), but I am sorry to hear about Dory Jones—poor Dory. He deserves better things, for he is a good fellow. I was so happy to hear from Mrs. Jones and what you say about her. Do give her my love when you write. Does she need anything? I have a notion to send her a hundred dollars. [10] I believe I will anyway. She is such a lovely good woman. As you say, how happy we all were away back in the '60s in old Mesilla. Glad you saw Ada. Hope Juanita has a good husband. I sent Agnes and another niece to Europe this summer. I am sure they are having a good time.

I have good news from Hallie (wife) and Katharine (daughter). Both are very well, and Hallie is improving and in fine spirits. I think she will return home in September. I will tell her about your letter. I wish you were here. The place never looked so beautiful.

I am kept hard at work. Sallie is here with her children, and Elizabeth comes in August. Don't ever tell your age again; you will pass for ten years younger. Hereafter say you are fifty. With love to all the children.

I am sincerely yours, S. B. Elkins

It pleased Mamie to see that Stephen had never forgotten his old friends, especially Dory (Theodore Robert Jones) who miraculously survived the snowstorm on the Santa Fe Trail. In October 1876, Dory married Harriet Baker Boone, a descendant of Daniel Boone, and made his home in Pueblo, Colorado, where he lived to the ripe old age of eighty.

Besides keeping in touch with friends and family, Mamie pursued other interests. She was active in the Methodist Episcopal Church, the Women's Library Club and was a founding member of the Tucson Women's Club.

When the Society of Arizona Pioneers was organized in 1884, women were not allowed to join, and this annoyed Mamie. Life in the west had not been easy for pioneer women. They had worked along side men and done their share to bring law, order and education to Arizona. They had raised money to build churches and schools, and established benevolent societies. *Why were pioneer women not allowed to join the Pioneer Society? It wasn't fair!*

Mamie was so incensed that she lobbied to form a club for pioneer women. The end result was the Ladies' Auxiliary of The Arizona Pioneers, and when the women held their first meeting in 1902, Mamie's old neighbor, Larcena Pennington Page Scott, was the club's first president while Mamie was the first vice-president. [11]

Besides attending to what she referred to as her social duties, Mamie also enjoyed several interesting hobbies. One was collecting and displaying Apache baskets. [12] Credited as an authority on native culture, Mamie was commissioned to take an exhibit of native baskets to the World's Fair in St. Louis in 1903. Her nephew, Allan Bernard, was one of her traveling companions on this trip and, while at the World's Fair, young Allan met Agnes McDermott—the girl of his dreams. Romantic by nature, Mamie enjoyed the young couple's exuberance and, shortly after the fun-filled days at the fair, they exchanged wedding vows and took up residence on Las Ruinas Ranch.

This particular fair celebrated the centennial of the Louisiana Purchase, and on May 16th, 1903, Mamie became an Honorary Member of the Louisiana Purchase Exposition and was presented with a scroll by Governor Alexander Brodie. [13]

Another milestone was reached when son Stephen, who was working for Green Gold-Silver Company based out of Chihuahua, moved to San Francisco and Mamie was able to travel to California to visit Stephen, Willie, and the four grandchildren. On July 1, 1905, son Pedro escorted her to the railway station, and *The Arizona Daily Star*, reported that "Mr.Aguirre will see his mother, Mrs. Mary B. Aguirre, off for San Francisco tonight and will return to La Brisco (Sonora, Mexico), tomorrow."

It was during the time Stephen was living in San Francisco that Mamie realized a dream. The family was able to acquire a charming little cabin on the beach, called "Idle a Wyle," at

La Junta, California. How Mamie loved staying at the cabin, especially since it brought such wonderful relief from the heat of an Arizona summer.

However, the spring of 1906 brought dreadful news from California. A devastating earthquake rocked San Francisco. The papers were full of it, and Mamie worried until she heard Stephen had escaped unharmed. On May 3, 1906, Stephen's name appeared in *The Daily Star*. [14] The article was entitled, "Tucson Man Lost Socks."

> "Stephen Aguirre, purchasing agent for the Green-Gold Silver Company, arrived over the Southern Pacific from San Francisco.
>
> "With his family, he was living in San Francisco when the earthquake occurred, followed by the fire that devastated almost the whole city. Fortunately, they resided in a part of the city that was not touched by fire, and very little damage was done to their residence by the earthquake.
>
> "'No,' said Aguirre, 'You can say for me that I did not lose everything. However, I regret the fact that I am short one package of laundry. This was sent to the wash shop the day before the earthquake and, as the laundry burned, I lost my socks, handkerchiefs and a few collars'."

Mamie was delighted to hear that Stephen and his family had survived the earthquake without major losses. She was also pleased to discover the trains would be running to California on schedule since she had made plans to spend the summer at the coast—just as she had the previous year. For several months, Mamie had planned for this excursion. She would be traveling on the Southern Pacific in a luxurious Pullman, a coach much nicer than anything she had ridden in before, then spending the summer by the sea, in cool comfort. For all intents and purposes, the California vacation was a dream come true—a dream with a nightmarish ending.

Chapter Twenty-one—A Painful Ending

Life often presents itself with contradictions. The best of times may also present the worst experiences. And so it was with Mamie—the early 1900s which presented her with the most amazing conveniences, also brought tragedy.

In May 1906, after once again saying good-bye to Pedro, she boarded the train and, as the engine gained full throttle, she thought of the many pleasant trips she had taken by rail. Her first recollection was traveling with her parents on the B & O Railway, fifty years before. Later, as a young bride, she toured the eastern cities with Epifanio and, later still, she rode in a coach as her little ones marveled at the sound of the engine's high pitched whistle and shunting passenger cars. She had been a traveler all her life, yet, none of those early trains were nearly as comfortable as this one. Enjoying the train's rocking motion, she sank back in her seat and thought of the peaceful days ahead, imagining how she would watch gigantic waves roll onto a sandy beach, and how she would listen to the hoot of ships and the chuckling of seagulls.

What other plans Mamie had never materialized, for on May 9, 1906, while traveling near San Jose, California, the train jumped the tracks. *The Arizona Daily Star* gave this account of the train wreck. The reporter did not mention Mamie by name, because her injuries were not considered serious.

Arizona Daily Star: May 10th, 1906: Tucsonians In A Coast Wreck

"San Jose, May 9—A serious wreck occurred at Eden-vale, seven miles south of this city at 7:10 this morning when the Overland Limited due here at 7:25 was ditched.

"One man was killed, one Chinaman fatally injured, thirty or forty Chinese and passengers, more or less, injured and the fireman, M. Stone of this city, suffered injury to his right leg so severely that it has since been amputated. The accident was due to a truck under the car behind the baggage car jump-ing the track and striking the switch as the train was making a speed of fifty miles an hour. The baggage and mail car and one Pullman were telescoped and piled in a heap and, of the nine cars, only the last was undamaged.

"Engineer William Brown was hurled from the cab, but he struck the earth in a mud hole and was uninjured. The car behind the tender, contained twenty-one Chinese prisoners under guard of the United States Marshall B.F. Daniels and the deputies who were conveying them from Tucson for deportation. Nearly everyone of them was injured, several seriously and one fatally. A relief train conveyed the injured to this city where they are being cared for."

In pain, but cheerful as ever, Mamie sent this letter to her daughter-in-law from her hospital bed in San Jose, California. She was weak and her arm was too sore to write, yet physical discomfort would not stop her from saying what needed to be said. [1]

May 20, 1906
My dear daughter Lucy:-
I have not been able to write yet after the grand shake up, so Nora is writing for me. I am now sitting up in the rocking chair this afternoon, and am very comfortable. I want to know how you are and whether you are going away on the 20th or not, or what you are going to do? I have been so weak I could not blow my nose. It seems like it struck that way.

You wanted to know about the wreck. Well, it was awful! The diner went off the track and most people were in the diner, and they were all thrown helter-skelter, pell-mell. The car I was in was thrown off the track, turned on its side, and I was shaken up generally. My right arm was hurt and bruised, and I can not use it yet. A woman was thrown right on to me and dug right in my abdomen, right on the pelvic bone, and nearly killed me. The soreness is pretty much all gone now.

I have taken a bad cold, have had an awful cough which nearly exhausted me. I have coughed until I was so weak I could not cough any longer. The doctor has got the upper hand of the cough now, and I do not cough nearly so much. I have a fine appetite. For instance I had a squab, green peas, potatoes and gravy, bread, butter, a cup of tea and a dish of strawberries for my dinner, and enjoyed every bite of it. Dr. Holbrook is so kind and good to me. None (Noah) came Friday, which was a surprise. It was so cold he had to put on his heavy underwear.

Write soon, with lots of love, your mother

per. N.T.

A postscript from her caregiver, Nora, reads: My dear, the above is as Mrs. Aguirre dictated, and it is the first time she has wanted to write or could collect her thoughts. She described the dinner exactly as I have written, and when you write do not let her know how ill she is. She thinks Mr. Bernard just happened to be on his way to the city. <u>Monday morning</u>: She seems just about the same. She has a bad cough all right. Nora

May 24, 1906: Two weeks have elapsed since the dreadful train wreck and Noah sits at his sister's bedside. Glancing out of the hospital window, he notices that the morning had broken, and a mist spreads an ominous grayness over the San Jose Valley. An automobile rumbles along on the street, emitting a plume of smoke which blends with the mist.

"I believe Doctor Holbrook is on his way to the hospital, Mamie," Noah says, attempting to sound cheerful. "Yes, here he comes in his new roadster." Noah rises in his chair to peer out, then glances back at the patient. Mamie's cough has worsened; her breathing has a hollow ring and sounds much like Jesse's just before the end.

Please God, not our dear Mamie, too! Losing another sister is more than Noah is prepared to endure. Yet, how can he deny what he is seeing: Mamie's eyes are ringed with dark shadows and her cheeks are hollow. As he watches, her lips twitch into a smile and he feels more hopeful. "Feeling better, Mamie?"

She flickers another smile. "I fancy I can hear the wagons, None."

"A car Mamie…that was a car, not a wagon. The doctor is on his way."

She coughs, a soft raspy sound, revealing the effort it takes to breathe and speak at the same time. "It's the freight wagons; they're loaded and ready to leave. I must go with them."

A chill sweeps over Noah. "Mamie, you've been dreaming! There are no freight wagons." She is trying to tell him something, and he bends low to hear her voice.

"He's here, None. He's come for me. Two white horses..." She is still smiling as her words break into another cough. "Mine has white ribbons flowing from its bridle. Oh how tall he looks, my darling Epifanio..."

"Mamie!" Even as Noah speaks he hears the gurgling of lungs filling with fluid—the sound of death. "Mamie!" A rustle from something behind makes him turn. Earlier, he had opened the window, hoping the fresh air would ease Mamie's breathing. So heavy is the morning air, no breeze is blowing; yet the curtains move as if someone has touched them in passing. Rubbing his eyes, Noah gazes out the window, then rubs them again. In the mist, he sees shapes, perhaps two white horses and, beyond them, ten huge mounds swaying like large wagons in clouds of dust. "A mirage," he reasons. "Folks see strange things in a mirage, especially when they're distressed."

Yet, how can he explain the sense of peace he feels as he turns to the motionless form in the bed. [2]

When Mamie died May 24, 1906, Noah was at her side. She was not yet sixty-two years of age. What a life she lived! What a legacy of cheerfulness, hope and determination she left for those wise enough to travel in her footprints!

Arizona Daily Citizen, Tucson, Arizona, May 24, 1906

"Mrs. Mary B. Aguirre, of this city, one of the pioneer women of the Southwest, and one of the chief factors in the establishment of the excellent public school system in this city, died this morning in San Jose, California. At her bedside when she passed away was her brother, N. W. Bernard.

"Death was due to injuries sustained in the wreck of a Southern Pacific train near San Jose on May 10 (sic). This was the train carrying the Chinese whom United States, Marshall Daniels was taking to San Francisco for deportation.

"No woman in the Southwest was better known than Mrs. Aguirre. She was a recognized authority on the history of New Mexico, Arizona and Sonora. She had traveled considerably and contributed many papers on Southwest history at meetings of pioneers.

"Mrs. Aguirre had not been in very good health for some time. Nevertheless, while she was rather delicate, she was able to travel alone, and was en route to San Jose to spend the summer when she sustained the injuries which caused her death.

"In a letter to her son Pedro, Mrs. Aguirre, describing the wreck, stated she was in one of the Pullmans. The car left the track and turned over on its side. Mrs. Aguirre was hurled against a seat. As she fell another woman fell on top of her. Mrs. Aguirre sustained internal injuries and her right arm was rendered useless.

"As soon as it was learned that Mrs. Aguirre had been injured, her brother N. W. Bernard left for San Jose and was with his sister continually until the time of her death. In a letter to Pedro Aguirre, soon after the accident, Mr. Bernard stated that Mrs. Aguirre's condition was very critical. San Jose physicians stated that Mrs. Aguirre must have complete rest and must not be excited in anyway. Pedro Aguirre intended to go to San Jose, but was advised not to, as it was feared his presence would have excited his mother. Mr. Aguirre was at the time in Sonora. He is connected with Black Mining Company at Cerro Prieto and had just returned from Durango and Sinoloa, where he had been to procure laborers to work in the mines. Late yesterday afternoon, he received a telegram from San Jose which seemed to indicate that Mrs. Aguirre was improving. This forenoon, however, a telegram came stating that Mrs. Aguirre had died at six o'clock this morning.

"Messages were immediately sent to the other son, Stephen Aguirre, who is with Green Gold-Silver Company in Chihuahua, and to Hon. A. C. Bernard, a brother. Mr. Bernard was in La Brisca at the time.

"It is expected that N. W. Bernard will arrive home on Saturday morning with the remains. Until then no funeral arrangements will be made.

"Mrs. Aguirre was, for a number of years, a teacher in the public schools and also in the University.

She took a great interest in the public school system and aided greatly in its establishment."

Arizona Daily Star—Tucson, Arizona, Friday, May 26, 1906
"Death of Mrs. Aguirre: The sad intelligence was received yesterday morning of Mrs. Mary B. Aguirre's death at San Jose resulting from injuries received by her in the wreck of a Southern Pacific train on the tenth (note: the accident occurred on the ninth), which was at the time noted in the Star as carrying Marshall Ben Daniels and a number of Chinese. The deceased was in a Pullman and received fatal internal injuries. As soon as word was received here of her misfortune, N. W. Bernard, her brother, left immediately for San Jose. He was near her bedside when she passed away.

"The intelligence of her death was the cause of general expressions of regret as the deceased was well known by all of our old-time citizens and was much beloved by all who enjoyed her acquaintance.

"Mrs. Aguirre was one of the pioneer women of New Mexico and Arizona, coming to Las Cruces on the Rio Grande in 1863 with her husband, Epifanio Aguirre, from Westport, Missouri, the place of her home. This was the year previous to the territorial organization of Arizona. Her husband was a native of New Mexico, where he was a large freight contractor, having done extensive freighting from the end of the railroad to Arizona and New Mexico. He was counted one of the brightest businessmen in the Southwest. The father of the deceased woman was connected with Aguirre in the business and in this way he became acquainted with his future bride.

"In 1868 (s.b. 1870) her husband, returning from a visit to his brother Pedro in Altar, Sonora, was killed by the Apaches near Sasabe, 65 miles south of Tucson, leaving a wife and two sons, Pedro and Stephen, to mourn his loss. Mrs. Aguirre came to the Territory…and took charge of the public school at Tres Álamos on the San Pedro thirty miles east of the city. She taught the first public school at that place. Owing to the frequency of the Apache raids on the San Pedro her brother, N. W. Bernard, insisted on her coming to Tucson, where she became one of the most efficient teachers for several years. Later she became one of the corps of teachers of the preparatory department of the University. She was there for several years as teacher of Spanish. She leaves to survive her, Pedro and Steve Aguirre and two brothers, N. W. Bernard and Allan C. Bernard. Don Pedro Aguirre, her brother-in-law, is one of the leading stockmen of this county located at Buenos Ayres. Don Pedro's sister, Mrs. M. Samaniego, lives in the city. Steve Aguirre is in Chihuahua; Allan Bernard is in La Brisca and Pedro Aguirre is in the city. N. W. Bernard is accompanying the remains to Tucson.

"The date of the interment will be announced later. The remains will arrive tomorrow morning."

Arizona Daily Star, Tucson Arizona, May 29, 1906

Funeral Notice: "Mary Aguirre died on May 24,1906 in San Jose, California of injuries received in a Southern Pacific train wreck on May 9, 1906. Her brother, N. W. Bernard (Noah Worthington Bernard) accompanied the remains to Tucson for burial. The funeral was held, Monday, May 28, 1906, at the home of N. W. Bernard, 417 South Fourth Street.

Epilogue

As unexpected as Mamie's death had been, perhaps more shocking was the deaths of seven other family members—all within the following year. They were Mamie's son Pedro; her brother, Noah; brothers-in-law, Mariano Samaniego, don Pedro and don Yjinio, as well as don Yjinio's wife, Sarah, and Mamie's Cousin William, her father's business partner.

Don Pedro's death was the least surprising; he had been a diabetic for several years. Unable to care for himself, Dolores (Lola) Samaniego took him into her home until his passing on February 21, 1907. He was seventy-one years old. Sidney DeLong wrote this tribute on behalf of the Society of Arizona Pioneers:

> Pedro Aguirre has always been known as a man of honor, whose word was undoubted and his acts of charity to the poor and unfortunate have been extensive, but never came to light from him; his praise did not come from self, but his good acts spoke for him."

Don Pedro's body was taken from the Samaniego residence (now one of Tucson's downtown cafés) to the Roman Catholic Cathedral where a funeral service was performed. His two eldest daughters inherited the major portion of the Buenos Aires Ranch, before selling it to La Osa Cattle Company on January 29, 1909, for six-thousand dollars.

Noah's death on February 23, 1907, a month after don Pedro's, shook the community to its foundations, and his funeral procession was said to be the largest Tucson had ever seen. *The Tucson Citizen* reported that "Carriages extended for almost a mile as they followed the funeral conveyance," while a second report read:

> "News of the death of Mr. Bernard spread rapidly downtown, and it caused a distinct shock to his many friends. He was one of the leading citizens in this town, and it is realized that in his death Tucson suffers a distinct loss. Mr. Bernard was taken ill last Sunday. He had not been feeling well for several months

and seemed to be gradually losing strength. When physicians were called to attend him last Sunday they found he was suffering from an attack of peritonitis. He continued to grow worse. An operation was resorted to as a last resort, but the patient's condition was so weakened he sank gradually to his death. He was unconscious most of yesterday and today. The end came peacefully today, shortly after noon. It was realized yesterday that his chances of recovery were very slight. Mr. Bernard was, without doubt, one of the foremost citizens of Tucson. He was the owner of a large cattle ranch and mining properties in the Oro Blanco district and one of the stockholders in the Tucson Ice Company."

Another tribute to Noah stated:

"One of Arizona's leading pioneers (Noah Bernard), was a man of more than ordinary integrity, character and ability, and was much esteemed by all who knew him on account of his attractive qualities. He did as much as any citizen of his day and generation for developing the material interests of this section of Arizona in which he lived. He was active in the building of educational institutes and gave freely of his income for the same. As a public servant, he made a record which was always above suspicion and reproach and rendered valuable service to the territories of which he was a member. He was a shining example of the great principles for which we stand. As a citizen of Tucson, he was honored, beloved and respected by all who came to know his work, and the Star (with the people of Tucson) says as a benediction to this honored man: Requisat in peace."

Noah didn't leave a written will. While in bed and waiting to be taken to St. Mary's Hospital on Friday the 22, 1907, he made his last wishes known to son Nonie and brother Allan and his long-time friend, George Pusch. He asked them to ensure his enterprises were continued—especially the Las Ruinas Ranch.

Here is a condensed version of Noah's nuncupative will:

"I desire that all my real and personal property, including ranches and all interests in cattle and horses and brands and also my interest in Tucson Ice and Cold Storage Company, shall, at my death, go to and be equally divided, between my four children, Noah C. Bernard, Edwin P. Bernard, Wm. R. Bernard and Amy Belle Bernard...that the same (property) shall remain in tact and should not be sold, divided until the said children should become of age."

In this way, Las Ruinas Ranch was restructured and the

ranch became the Arivaca Land and Cattle Company under new management. Young Nonie Bernard became the superintendent of the cattle company, while various other shareholders owned stock in the company. In 1917 when Amy turned twenty-one, the shares of the Arivaca Cattle Company were divided among the four children. However, by 1917 ranching had changed in Arizona, and the old style of ranching was no longer feasible. Homesteaders were stringing barbed wire across land that had once been open range. So, Noah's children simply sold their respective shares in the ranch and moved to California.

Both of Mamie's brothers were civic minded, helping to put in place the legislation that governs Arizona today. At one time, Noah was the Supervisor of Pima County as well as Arizona's Territorial Representative to the 1895 Legislative Assembly. In 1901 and 1903, he was Tucson's representative in the 21st and 22nd Legislative Assembly and, in 1905, he was a member of the Legislative Council for the Pima County and Santa Cruz Counties.

Allan, who had been a mule skinner when first coming to Arizona, was also a surveyor, defining the Gila and Santa Cruz River Valleys in 1877. Later, he was the clerk at the Indian camps of San Carlos and Fort Apache and served as an interpreter at the time of the Geronimo uprising. He was also a cattleman, miner and was one of the founders of the Elks Lodge in Tucson. In public office, he served as sheriff of Pima County, Clerk of the United States District Court, was a member of the Territorial Legislature and the Tucson City Council, serving as Mayor on several occasions, before moving to Phoenix where he was the Superintendent of the Motor Vehicle Division of the Highway Department, a position he held until 1930, when he suffered a sudden, fatal heart attack.

Perhaps the most shocking event of 1907 was the death of Mamie's son, Pedro, on August 2nd. Again *The Tucson Citizen* was on hand to give a report:

"News was received late yesterday afternoon, conveying intelligence of the sudden death, in Nogales, of Pedro J. Aguirre.

"Mr. Aguirre has been taking lunch about two o'clock with Frank Duffy, a prominent attorney in Nogales. They left the restaurant, but before they had gone half a block from the place, Mr. Aguirre suddenly uttered a sharp cry, threw up his hands and dropped on his face upon the sidewalk—dead. The cause of death was heart trouble.

"Pedro was one of the best known men in Southern Arizona. He was born in Westport, Missouri, forty-four years ago and came to this city with his parents when he was six years of age. He had resided in Tucson, and was one of the most popular residents of this city."

Yet, Pedro's story didn't end on a dusty sidewalk in Nogales. Besides his wife and two stepdaughters, Pedro left someone else—an unborn son. Six months after his death, Pedro's wife, Lucy Linder Aguirre, gave birth to a bouncing baby boy. Lucy named the little fellow, Pedro Joab Aguirre. Known to his friends as Pete, he grew up to be a man his father and Mamie would be proud to call their own. As a very young child he moved with his mother to Mexicali, Baja California, Mexico. He became a successful and well respected businessman and like his father, Pedro, and his grandfather, Epifanio, he spent his entire life, living and working on both sides of the US-Mexican border. As a result, his life adds both richness and continuity to Mamie's story.

He and his wife Rowene, raised three daughters: Jean, Andra and Rowene. All three daughters plus some of Mamie's great-great-grandchildren were present in October 1983, to see their ancestor, Mary (Mamie) Bier Aguirre inducted into the Arizona Women's Hall of Fame, where Mamie was recognized for her achievements in the field of education. Epifanio's grandnephew, Yginio Aguirre, was also present at the induction service. Deeply moved by this event, Rowene Aguirre Medina recalls how honored she was to accompany Yginio to the stage to accept her great-grandmother's award. It was indeed fitting that Yginio was on hand to represent the Aguirre family, giving Mamie the same support posthumously as the family had done throughout her life.

As for Stephen, Mamie's youngest son; he was killed in a car accident in 1926, in Deming, New Mexico.

Mamie's descendants continue to thrive, or as Mamie so aptly put it, "The old order changes, giving place to new, and God reveals himself to us in many ways." Mamie's great-great-great grandchildren have been baptized in the same long, white christening gown Mamie's baby wore in Mesilla in 1864. And hundreds of visitors (including myself), have been served from the beautiful silver tea service—a wedding gift to Mamie from Epifanio—the symbol of young lovers who set out on "a journey of the heart," many years ago.

Author's Notes

As I write the final pages of Mamie's story, I am here, alone, in a little cabin on the ranch which was once called Las Ruinas, and I can readily see why this country was so well loved. It is a beautiful place, this ranch, which chiseled itself so firmly into the hearts of the Aguirre-Bernard families. The sun is beginning to set; a rustle of leaves tells me the quail are scurrying to their roosting place for the night. I count fourteen of them, their black tasseled heads nodding as they toddle along, visiting in small chirps—just as quail did in Mamie's day. A whir of feathers, and a flock of doves make patchy outlines in the darkening sky, and then crickets begin to sing their long soothing melody.

I reflect on my visit to Arivaca's charming old schoolhouse in which Mamie taught. It is still in excellent condition and, due to the efforts of the late Fred Noon, records are now in place, proving Arivaca School District No. 5 was established on April 8, 1879. This, along with 1879 records of payment to teachers, proves beyond a doubt that Arivaca School is the oldest standing school in Arizona.

It gives one quite a thrill to stand in the schoolhouse and picture Mamie in front of a roomful of Spanish-speaking children, doing what she loved to do best—teach school.

If it can be said that time has not much altered the schoolhouse in Arivaca, then it certainly holds true for the little town itself. Cattle, chickens and the occasional pig still wander down Arivaca's main street. Neighbors still visit in the shade of the half dozen business establishments. Such is little Arivaca! The closing of nearby mines have halted Arivaca's growth and, much like a western movie prop, the town seems caught in a time warp. It has never been sophisticated, nor does it pretend to be. Quite simply, it is what it was in Noah's day—a diamond in the rough.

The building which housed Noah's store and post office is also still intact. It is made of strong adobe bricks and, today, houses a feed store. It has been re-roofed, but the original log rafters can still be seen—the vigas securely placed by Mexican workers over a century ago, are as solid as ever.

As for Las Ruinas Ranch, it is still a place where shade trees and deep cañons muffle the sound of the outside world, where an indescribable peace fills the soul—Las Ruinas is where Mamie spent so many happy days. I picture her watching the sunset, just as I am doing, enjoying the sight of a pink and yellow sky turn to starlight. I imagine her lighting a lamp, sitting down at a table and pasting her favorite poetry in that priceless black album, reading over each poem, letting the words weave precious memories of days gone by—the sadness and gladness of a life, blending together, to reflect the life story of a Southern Belle who met formidable challenges with a cheerful heart.

Additional note:

Westport, the town so well loved by the Bernard family, is no more. Among the few remaining mementoes is Westport Road (formerly Main Street) and the Westport Museum, housed in the old Harris-Kearny Home, in the heart of Kansas City.

PRAYERS FROM A DEPARTING TRAIN

© Annette Gray

I've been a traveler all of my life
have gone where pioneers go;
have followed the treacherous Santa Fe Trail
to where parched desert sands blow.
I've seen herds of buffalo from a door,
of a mule-driven ambulance;
I've ridden horseback through dried sage
on a windblown Las Cruses ranch.
I've hurried by stage coach, used pony express,
felt the pain of Apache raids.
From the ox-driven cart, to a steam engine's start,
I have witnessed a whole era fade.
Some roads which I traveled have led straight up hill
to a view which is grand to behold.
And some of the journeys which started so well
have held stories too sad to be told.
I've smiled as I swayed in a Pullman's new car
on the Southern Pacific Railways,
never dreaming a modern conveyance like this,
would summon an end to my days.
I am done now, they say; this train carries me away
to Tucson's quiet graveyard to rest,
where both kin and friend will mourn my life's end
and remember my place in the West.
God be with you my sons who are traveling behind,
Life's cares may frequent your road.
'Tis a mother who leaves from earth's station today
who prays she has lightened your load.

General Information

1. All poems collected by Mary Aguirre are currently held in family collections in Arizona, New Mexico and California.

2. The author's personal collection of notes , in Canada, are based on events documented by the Aguirre family and memoirs prepared by Pedro (Pete) Joab Aguirre henceforth cited as Aguirre ms.

3. For other articles written by Mary (Mamie) Bier Aguirre, see also "Indian Traditions of the Creation and Flood" and "Some Arizona Local Names." These can be found in the Arizona Historical Society Library/Archives, Tucson, Arizona.

Notes

Chapter 1—In The Beginning

[1] Mamie's parents, Joab Bernard (age 38) and Arabella Mather Bier (age 22), were married in 1838.

[2] Prior to Mamie's birth, her father had spent a good deal of time with his friend, President Tyler. One man, by the name of William McPherson, who wanted Joab to help him climb the political ladder, wrote this letter. It was addressed to the Reverend Joab Bernard and was found among Mamie's keepsakes.

> St. Louis, February 4, 1844
> Dear Sir:
>> "Should opportunity present, I should be pleased if you would speak of me to the President (President Tyler) in such terms as you may feel justified in doing, particularly as to my general standing and how you think my appointment would be received by all parties and also senators...
>> ...You are aware that I have not been identified with politics since coming to St. Louis, but as between Clay (presidential candidate from Virginia) and Van (Van Buren, US President 1841-45) I shall vote for the first.
>> We have no news of interest here, except that the good work is still going on in the Methodist Churches and souls are easily converted to God. (Aguirre ms.)

[3] Mamie's father had holdings in Kansas as early as 1855. At one time there was confusion as to Mamie's father's business role, due to the name he shared with his nephew, "Joab Mitchell Bernard."

It was finally agreed that Mamie's father managed the trading store in Westport, was appointed postmaster of St. Bernard and was a pastor in the Methodist Church. His nephew, also Joab Mitchell Bernard (Joe) did none of these things according to his family. The younger Joab worked for Epifanio in the freighting business and, as a respected rancher, he spent most of his adult life in New Mexico. (Aguirre ms.)

[4] WHMC-KC, *Kansas Historical Collections* VII, p. 442.

[5] *Encyclopaedia Britannica,* 24 vols. Edited by Walter Yust. 28th ed. (Wm. Benton, University of Chicago) 1960.

Chapter 2—A Narrow Escape

[1] K.A. Moore, *An Everlasting Possession* (Kansas City, Missouri: Westport Historical Society) 1965, p. 9

[2] O.G. Villard, *John Brown,* 1943, pp. 209-210.

[3] William Goff, *Old Westport,* Westport Historical Archival Collection, (Kansas City, Missouri: Westport Historical Society, 1977), pp. 1-3.

[4] *A History of Kansas, City Missouri* (http://www.kcmo.org/kcmo.nsf/web/history (2003).

[5] Census 1855, *Jackson County, Missouri,* (pop. 478 residents).

[6] Charles A. Hawley, *Kansas City Times,* Sept. 23, 1955.

[7] Main Street, Westport is now Westport Road, Kansas City.

[8] A house vacated by John Harris in 1854, is thought to have been the Bernard residence. Following Joab's death and Arabella's move to Tucson, this house (not to be confused with the larger Harris House) was demolished in 1898 to make room for John Beedy's Coal Yard. (Aguirre ms.)
Also Wm. Goff, *Old Westport,* p. 7.

[9] Aguirre ms. John Harris's sons-in-law, Charles Kearney and Wm. Bernard operated a store in the Metropolitan Building: Charles Kearney married Josephine Harris. Wm. Bernard married Susan Harris

[10] Colonel Boone's wife, Anne Reid Hamilton, was Cornelia Bernard's sister-in-law (Colonel Albert Boone was a grandson of the famous Daniel Boone.

[11] Carrie Westlake Whitney, *History of Kansas City, Missouri, 1808-1908* (S.J. Clarke Publishing Company, Chicago 1908) Vol. 1, p. 1.

[12] The grand old Harris mansion still stands; it is known today as the Harris-Kearney House Museum, in Kansas City.

[13] Carrie Westlake Whitney, *History of Kansas City, Missouri 1808-1908* (Chicago: S.J. Publishing Company, 1908), Vol. 1 p. 1.

[14] W. Goff, *Old Westport* (Kansas City: Westport Historical Society), p 15-18.

[15] Ibid., p. 48.

[16] Ibid., p. 15-18.

[17] Encyclopaedia Britannica, 24 vols. Wm. Benton, Edited by Walter Yust. 28th ed. (Chicago: University of Chicago, 1960), vol. 4. p. 266.

[18] Aguirre ms. Mamie's sister, Margaret, met her in St. Louis. It is believed Mamie's sister, Kate, may have remained in Baltimore to assist her aging grandparents.

Chapter 3-Trouble On The Border

[1] Richard Corley, D.D., *History of Lawrence, Kansas* (Lawrence: Lawrence Journal Press, 1895) Ch. I
[2] Ibid.
[3] Ibid.
[4] Ibid.
[5] Mamie visited members of the Jones family in New Mexico in 1864.
[6] Martha B. Caldwell, *Annals of Shawnee Methodist Mission* (Topeka: Kansas State Historic Society) p. 86-88.
[7] Ibid.
[8] Martha B. Caldwell, *Annals of Shawnee Methodist Mission*, pp. 86, 95.
[9] Ibid., p.62.
[10] Ibid.
[11] Missouri's Ordinance of Secession was passed by rump legislation in Neosho, Missouri, Oct. 31, 1861.
[12] Tyler, the former president of the US died January 18, 1862.
[13] Ken Burns, *The Civil War,* Ken Burns, and Burns, Ric. productions Films and WETA-TV 1990   (9 episodes)
[14] Ibid.

Chapter 4—A Confederate Flag

[1] Mamie B. Aguirre, "A Spanish Trader's Bride," *The Westport Historical Quarterly*, Dec. 1968,
vol. IV, #3. P.7. William Goff, *Old Westport* (Westport Historical Society) p.28. (Note: Albert Boone, owner of the Boone building was the grandson of Daniel Boone and a brother-in-law to Mamie's cousin, Cornelia (Bernard) Hamilton.
[2] *Kaleidoscope,* WHMC-KC pp. 9-13.
[3] Aguirre ms. Florence Price would later become Mamie's bridesmaid.
[4] William A. Goff, *Old Westport* (Kansas City: Westport Historical Society, 1977), p. 14.
[5] Frederick Daab, *Letters of Frederick Daab*, (WHMC-KC).
[6] Editorial, "Young German in Westport Gave Life For Freedom In Civil War," *Kansas City Times,* Sept. 23, 1955, Frederick Daab, one of the first to enlist in the Union army, was killed with General Lyon at Wilson Creek.
[7] William A. Goff, *Old Westport* (Kansas City: Westport Historical Society, 1977), p. 79.
[8] Adrienne Christopher, *The Life Of Stephen Benton Elkins*, (Kansas City , Missouri: Westport Historical Society, undated), p. 32.
[9] Homer Croy, *Cole Younger, Last Of The Great Outlaws* (Nebraska: University of Nebraska Press, 1999), p. 5.
[10] Ibid.
[11] *Dictionary of American Biography*. Edited by Allen Johnson. Dumas Malone. (New York: Charles Scriber's Sons) Vol. III, p. 83.

American National Biography. Edited by John A. Garraty. Mark C. Carnes. (New York: Oxford Press, 1999) Vol. 7, pp. 411-412.

[12] Homer Croy, Cole Younger, *Last Of The Great Outlaws* (Nebraska: University of Nebraska Press, 1999), pp. 8-15.

[13] Ibid.

[14] John A. Garraty and Mark C, Carnes, *American National Biography,* (New York: New York Oxford University Press, 1999), p. 413.

[15] The word "Secesh" was used during the Civil War to denote a person or policy favoring separatism.

[16] WHMC-KC, Kansas Historical Collections XIV pp. 206-207.

[17] William A. Goff, *Old Westport* (Kansas City: Westport Historical Society, 1977) p. 7.

[18] Aguirre ms.

Chapter 5—Romance

[1] K.A. Moore, *Enter The Jones Family*, (Kansas City: Westport Historical Society, 1965), Ch. 5, p. 22.

[2] *K.A. Moore, An Everlasting Possession,* (Kansas City: Westport Historical Society,) Ch. 3, p.17.

[3] Territory of Arizona, *Pima County Records*: Pedro Aguirre I (patriarch) received American citizenship Nov. 19, 1855.

Chapter 6—The Handsome Mexican

[1] Y. F. Aguirre, "The Last of the Dons," *Journal of Arizona History*, vol. 10 (1969) p. 243, copy in author's file (information also from family anecdotes)

[2] Aguirre ms. After the patriarch Pedro Aguirre's death, Indalecio and Santitos accompanied Epifanio, Mamie and Delores Aguirre to Altar, Mexico. Later, they made their home with Epifanio's brother, don Pedro in Arivaca, Arizona.

[3] Yginio F. Aguirre, *Echoes of the Conquistadors*, (Casa Grande: privately printed, 1994), pp. 31-32.

[4] Gadsden Purchase: a tract of 45,535 sq. miles now contained in New Mexico and Arizona was purchased for $10,000,000 from Mexico in 1853.

[5] *The New Mexican*, Feb. 16, 1866. (dissolution effective as of Nov. 20, 1865)

[6] Yginio F. Aguirre, *Echoes of the Conquistadors* (Casa Grande: privately printed 1994), p.42.

[7] K. A. Moore, *An Everlasting Possession* Ch. 3, p.17-18.

[8] *Kansas City Star*, Kansas, Missouri, Aug. 13, 1939, pp. 20-23.

[9] Ken Burns, *The Civil War*, Ken Burns and Burns, Ric. Productions Film and WETA-TV 1990 (9 episodes).

[10] Although Stephen Elkins was born in Ohio, both of his parents were born in Virginia.

Chapter 7—Parting

[1] Homer Croy, *Cole Younger, Last of the Great Outlaws* (Nebraska: University of Nebraska Press, 1999), p. 24.

[2] Martha B. Caldwell, *Annals of Shawnee Methodist Mission and Indian Manual Labor School* 2nd ed. (Topeka: Kansas State Historical Society, 1977), p. 113.

[3] *Encyclopaedia Britannica,* 24 vols. Edited by Walter Yust. 28th ed. (Chicago: London: Toronto: Wm. Benton, University of Chicago, 1960)

[4] The Union Hotel in Kansas City was located at 1409, Grand Avenue, Kansas City.

[5] Homer Croy, *Cole Younger, Last of the Great Outlaws,*(Nebraska : University of Nebraska Press), pp. 31-32.

[6] Neil Block, *Missouri Division - William T. Anderson Camp #1743, Huntsville, Missouri,* http://www.missouri-scv.org/html/camp 1743.htm (2001-02-01)

[7] Ibid.

[8] Richard Cordley, *A History of Lawrence, Kansas* (Kansas: Lawrence Journal Press, 1895), Ch.5.

Chapter 8—On The Santa Fe Trail

[1] Katharine Jones Moore, "The Odyssey of James Hamilton," *The Westport Historical Quarterly,* Vol. V. (1969) The Hamiltons moved back to Westport after the Civil War ended.

[2] "Ambulance" was a term used to describe a carriage designed especially for long-distance travel—a self-contained vehicle used by regular travelers as well as the injured and ill.

[3] Eighteen year-old Johnny Behan went to Prescott, Arizona, in 1863 and likely accompanied the same Aguirre mule train as the new Arizona Territorial Governor.

[4] Thought to be related to Pete Kitchen of the "Kitchen Ranch" (El Potrero) in Southern Arizona.

[5] K.A. Moore, "Enter The Jones Family," *Westport Historical Quarterly,* IV pp. 22-23.

[6] Marc Simmons, *The Old Trail To Santa Fe,* (Albuquerque, New Mexico: University of New Mexico Press , 1996), p. 91.

Chapter 9—A New Home

[1] Colonel Jones family, Samuel Jones, former postmaster of Westport.

[2] Adrienne Christopher, "The Life Of Stephen Benton Elkins" *Westport Historical Quarterly,* p. 30.

[3] *Wagon Tracks,* Vol. 5 November 1990, p. 13.

[4] Aguirre ms.

[5] Capt. George Todd was a bridge mason before joining Qauntrill's guerrillas. On Oct. 21, 1864, he was shot by snipers in the Battle of Westport, and was buried that same night in the Independence Cemetery.

Chapter 10—Life In New Mexico

[1] Note: The sutler (storekeeper) stocked his shelves with conveniences to sell to the Fort's soldiers.

[2] *Albuquerque Weekly News* (1897), also Yginio F. Aguirre, *Memories of Rancheros & Vaqueros of the Southwest* (Casa Grande: Aguirre, 2000), p. 52.

[3] Y. F. Aguirre, *Echoes of the Conquistadores* (Casa Grande: Aguirre, 1994) p. 43.

[4] *New Mexican.* Feb. 16, 1886 edition, Notice of dissolution, Nov. 20, 1865: The partnership heretofore existing between Epifanio Aguirre, Pedro Aguirre and Conrado Aguirre, has been dissolved by mutual consent. The settlement of all the business pertaining to the late firm will be made by Epifanio Aguirre. Las Cruces, New Mexico, Nov. 20. 1865.

[5] M. Caldwell, *Annals of Shawnee Methodist Mission* (Topeka: Kansas State Historical Society, 1977) p. 114.

[6] Kathleen Moore, "The Odyssey of James Hamilton," *Westport Historical Society,* Vol. V #3, Dec. 1969, p. 22.

[7] *Prescott Miner*, September 20, 1867.

Chapter 11—The Road To Altar

[1] R. A. Mulligan, "Apache Pass and Old Fort Bowie," *Smoke Signal*, #11 (Tucson: University of Arizona, 1979)

[2] Ibid.

[3] An enumeration by Charles Shibell gives Tucson's population as over 3,000 inhabitants in 1870.

Chapter 12—Death On The Trail

[1] Stopping stations were spaced roughly ten miles apart, depending on water supply. Taking into account the distance traveled, the Aguirre stage was about to make its sixth stop of the day when attacked near Posta Aguirre (approx. six miles north-east of present day Sasabe, Arizona).

[2] An unnamed passenger was also riding atop the stage when the ambush occurred.

[3] Aguirre ms. also *Prescott Miner* (Jan/1870) also *Weekly Arizonan* (Jan. 29/1870).

[4] As reported by Epifanio's great-nephew, Yginio Aguirre, who also states, "The death of don Epifanio marked the end of a man who gave his life to the development of the Southwest by bringing supplies to the territorial forts of the U.S. Government, and supplies and merchandise to the towns along the Santa Fe Trail and the towns in Northern Mexico. He was a fearless frontiersman and a great pioneer, respected by all."

[5] Arizona State, *Pima Court Records, Tucson.* (Probate of Will) Correction to the *Weekly Arizona* report: Epifanio Aguirre died January 16, 1870.

[6] Elizabeth R. Brownell, *They Lived In Tubac*, (Tucson: Westernlore Press, 1986), p. 54.

Chapter 13—The Aftermath

[1] In 1863 Maximilian accepted the Mexican Imperial crown from Napoleon of France. He served as the Imperial Emperor of Mexico until 1867, when the Mexican people rebelled against foreign intervention. At this time, Maximilian and other leaders of the French regime were put to death.

Chapter 14—Life In Missouri

[1] Katharine Jones, "Moore, The Odyssey of James Hamilton," *The Westport Historical Quarterly*, Vol. V, Dec. 1969, p. 31.

[2] Eleanor Bernard's personal files, Tucson, Arizona.

Chapter 15—Teaching On The Frontier

[1] *Territorial Governors: Biography of Anson Pacely Killen Safford*, copy in Arizona Historical Society Archives, Tucson, Arizona. (Safford served as Governor 1869-1877)

[2] *Arizona Miner*, Feb. 8, 1873, Prescott, Arizona.

[3] *Territorial Governors: Biography of Anson Pacely Killen Safford* p. 56.

[4] *Arizona Miner*, March 3, 1871, Prescott, Arizona.

[5] C. L. Sonnichsen, *Tucson, The Life And Times Of An American City*, (Norman: University of Oklahoma. Press, 1982), pp. 83-85.

[6] Ibid.

[7] M. B. Aguirre, personal manuscript, copy also found in Arizona Historical Society Archives, Tucson, Arizona.

[8] C. L. Sonnichsen, Tucson, *The Life And Times Of An American City*, (Norman: University of Oklahoma Press, 1987), pp. 87, 88.

[9] M. M. Rice, "Bob Leatherwood, Reminiscences of M.M. Rice," (Publisher unknown) Copy in Arizona Historical Society Library/Archives, Tucson.

[10] "In Memoriam, R. N. Leatherwood," by the Masonic Lodge of Tucson, copy in Arizona Historical Society Library/Archives, Tucson.

[11] King William was the nickname of German-born Otto Von Reichen-Bach. He came from an aristocratic family and was a professional gambler.

[12] "The Territorial Governor, Biography of Anson Pacely Killen Safford," Territorial Press Association of Arizona pp. 50-71.

[13] *Arizona Weekly Star*, Tucson, December 19, 1878. Previous to this, Governor Safford had caused quite an uproar in Arizona by granting himself a divorce from his first wife—a highly unethical move for a governor to make.

[14] Virginia Culin Roberta, *With Their own Blood,* (Fort Worth: Texas Christian University Press, 1992), p. 179.

[1] Mary Brier Aguirre, *Coincidence* (a condensed version from Aguirre ms.) A copy in Aguirre Family Collection, Arizona Historical Society, Tucson Arizona.

[2] Aguirre ms. Indalecio Aguirre lived in the Arivaca area most of his life, marrying Jesusita Cordova Rivera and raising seven children. A vacant house, believed to be his, sits just off Arivaca's main street, to the south. His sister, Santitos, also grew up on don Pedro's ranch, but later moved to El Paso. Four months prior to her death, she returned to Tucson where she died on, or about, Feb. 9, 1916, at the age of sixty-four. She chose to be buried in Arivaca's quiet little cemetery.

[3] Mary Kasulaitis, *A Canyon Named McCaffery*, self published. Arivaca. 2004, also *Arizona Republican*, January 26, 1915, p.2.

[4] *Arizona Citizen*, August 19, 1870. Don Pedro managed a large herd of sheep, purchased in California, which belonged to Lord and Williams.

[5] John and Lillian Theobald, *Arizona Territory Post Offices and Postmasters* (Phoenix, Arizona: Arizona Historical Foundation, 1961), p.83.

[6] Bernard Family Collection, Arizona Historical Society Library/Archives, Tucson, Arizona.

[7] Bernard L. Fontana, *Entrada, The Legacy of Spain and Mexico in the United States,* (Tucson: Southwest Parks and Museums Association), p. 98. William Hartmann, *Desert Heart: Chronicles of the Sonoran Desert*, (Tucson: Fisher Brooks, 1989) pp. 36-56.

[8] Bernard Family Collection, Arizona Historical Society Library/Archives, Tucson, Arizona.

Chapter 17—Cousin Johnny Meets Wyatt Earp

[1] *Weekly Arizona Miner*, Prescott, Arizona. Sept. 9, 1878.

[2] *Weekly Arizona Miner*, Jan. 3, 1879, "Albert Behan, one of Prescott's brightest youths, has been made more than happy by a present, from his father, of a nice horse and new saddle. Albert believes in training himself while young to the horse and chase, so that when he attains the age of manhood there is no mistake about his competency to perform the duties of the office of Sheriff of Yavapi, of which his father made the best officer we have ever had."

[3] *Weekly Arizona Miner*, September 28, 1878.

[4] Record of the Clerk of the District Court of Yavapai County, June 2, 1875, Clerk: William Wilkenson.

[5] Boyer, Glenn G., *I Married Wyatt Earp, The Recollections of Josephine Sarah Marcus Earp* (Tucson, The University of Arizona Press, Twelfth printing 1998) pp. 15-20.

[6] Postal Receipt Books for Tombstone, Sept 11, 1881 (#2298: from Josephine Behan to Mrs. Marcus of San Francisco)

[7] *Denver Republican*, May 22, 1882.

[8] Tax Records of Tombstone 1881. John Behan owned lot ten, block forty-nine on the northeast corner of Seventh and Safford Streets.

[9] *The Tombstone Epitaph*, Tombstone, Arizona. October 27, 1881.

[10] Ibid.

[11] Ibid.

[12] William Barclay Masterson, *Famous Gunfighters of the Western Frontier*, (Ruidoso, New Mexico: Frontier Book Company, 1959), p.35.

[13] *Leadville Daily Herald*, August 20, 1884, Leadville, Colorado.

[14] *The Tombstone Nugget*, Oct. 27, 1881, reprinted Oct. 30, 1881, by the *Tucson Weekly Star*.

[15] Glenn G. Boyer, *I Married Wyatt Earp, The Recollections of Josephine Sarah Marcus*, (Tucson, Arizona: University of Arizona Press 1998), p.242.

[16] *The Tucson Citizen*, May 11, 1889. Tucson, Arizona (obituary)

[17] Albert Franklin Banta, "Tribute to John Harris Behan," Prescott Historical Society Archives, Prescott, Arizona.

[18] John and Lillian Theobald, *Arizona Territory Post Offices & Postmasters*, Phoenix: The Arizona Historical Foundation, 1961), p.50.

Chapter 18—Life Goes On

[1] Y. F. Aguirre. Oral history, 2003.

[2] *Pima County school records*, 1884. Arivaca School District #5 was established April 9. Incomplete school records show that Mrs. Aguirre was Arivaca's first teacher in 1879, and Mary B. Aguirre received eighty dollars for teaching school in Arivaca from Nov. 3. to Nov. 29, 1884.

[3] Dane Coolidge, *California Cowboys*, (Tucson, Arizona: University of Arizona Press, 1985), pp. 56-77.

[4] Ibid. (Ramon Ahumada and his beautiful dark-eyed wife were known as hospitable and good-hearted. Noah's second son, Edwin (Ned), nominated Ramon to the Cowboy Hall where his portrait hangs today.)

[5] Dane Coolidge, *California Cowboys*, (Tucson : University of Arizona Press, 1985), p. 71.

[6] Fred C. Noon, "Ramon Ahumada 1868 - 1926," *Arizona Cattlelog*, copy Arivaca Public Library, Arivaca, Arizona.

[7] Aguirre ms. Written for the Cosmos Club in 1902 by Mary Aguirre. Copies can also be found in the Arizona Historical Society, Tucson, Arizona.

[8] Will C. Barnes, *Arizona Place Names*, (Tucson: University of Arizona Press, 1988), pp. 12-13.

[9] Yginio F. Aguirre, oral history. Also John and Lillian Theobald, *Arizona Territory Post Offices & Postmasters* pp. 122, 153,171, Also Will C. Barnes, *Arizona Place Names* pp. 66, 392.

10 Similar to don Pedro's ranch buildings, the Buenos Aires (Ayres) Lake has long disappeared. The Buenos Aires National Wildlife Refuge has taken over the ranch and a modern information center overlooks the dry lake bed.

[11] *Arizona Citizen*, July 24, 1886.

[12] *Arizona Daily Star*, April 8, 1884.

[13] Allan Bernard, who came to Arizona in 1876 (as a seventeen year-old), made quite a name for himself before he died July 4, 1930. His life's story, which would fill several books, was full of challenges. This tribute was given by a fellow Elk. "The life of 'Al' Bernard was so honorable in its purpose and so far reaching in its effects that it has become an integral part of the history of Tucson. Mule skinner, surveyor, clerk, Indian trader, cattleman, miner, Indian Scout,

legislator and member for several years of the Tucson City Council, he devoted his life to public service.

"...He served as sheriff of Pima County, Clerk of the United States District Court of Tucson, was a member of the Territorial Legislature and of the City Council, and as Mayor on several occasions. He served as Tiler in the 385 Lodge and was truly an outstanding Brother."

The editor of the Arizona Star described Allan as a man "who, when encountering others going the same way, hails them heartily and proposes a song to lighten the burdens, a story to relieve the stones and brambles."

[14] Phil Clarke, "First Visit To Arivaca," personal files of Fred Noon, also found in Arizona Historical Society, Tucson, Library/Archives.

[15] Editor, "Al Bernard, Tells How Old-timer Repeated Lord's Prayer, Won $20.00 Bet." *Arizona Republic,* April 10, 1929.

[16] C. L. Sonnichsen, *Tucson, The Life And Times Of An American City,* (Norman: University of Oklahoma Press 1982), pp. 102-107.

[17] Ibid.

[18] John and Lillian Theobald, *Arizona Territory Post Offices & Postmasters,* (Phoenix: Arizona Historical Foundation, 1961), p. 91.

[19] Arizona Pioneers' Historical Society, biographical sketch of Samuel Hughes Byrne.

[20] *Arizona Daily Star*, Jan. 14, 1882.

[21] Douglas D. Martin, *An Arizona Chronology, The Territorial Years 1846—1912* (Tucson: University Press, 1963).

[22] Yginio Aguirre, *Echoes of The Conquistadores,* (Casa Grande, Arizona: privately printed, 1994), p. 46

[23] Aguirre ms.

[24] *Phoenix Herald*, January 1887.

Chapter 19—Ensenada

[1] K.A. Moore, "Some Bernards," *An Everlasting Possession,* (Kansas City: privately printed, 1965), p. 20.

Chapter 20—The Final Years

[1] Aguirre ms. also found in the archives of Westport and Arizona Historical Societies.

[2] Aguirre ms. Pedro Joab Aguirre and Lucy Linder (Catlett) Aguirre.

[3] Family anecdotes (oral)

[4] Memorial notice - R.N. Leatherwood (1844-1920) Committee of Resolutions, Masonic Lodge, Arizona Historical Society L438-3-4.

[5] C. L. Sonnichsen, *Tucson, the Life and Times of an American City,* (Norman: University of Oklahoma Press, 1982), pp. 102-112.

[6] *Arizona State Records*, U. S. Court of Private Land Claims, 1900, Plaintiff, Arizona Land and Cattle Co.

[7] Homer Croy, *Cole Younger-Last of the Great Outlaws*, (Lincoln: University of

Nebraska Press, 1999), pp. 159-176.

[8] Ibid., p. 169.

[9] Aguirre ms. Note the controversial spelling of Mamie's nickname "Mame."

[10] This is the same amount Elkins sent Cole Younger to help rehabilitate Cole after a lengthy jail term

[11] C.L. Sonnichsen, *Pioneer Heritage* (Tucson: The Arizona Historical Society, 1884), p. 58. ("Teacher, Mary Aguirre, was elected vice-president of the Auxiliary.")

[12] Aguirre ms.

[13] *Personal files*, also found in the Aguirre files Arizona Historical Society, Tucson.

[14] *Arizona Daily Star*, May 3, 1906, Tucson, Arizona.

Chapter 21—A Painful Death

[1] Aguirre ms.

[2] Reconstructed from oral accounts told by family.

Sources

Interviews with author

Ongoing interviews with great-granddaughters in Arizona and New Mexico.
Yginio F. Aguirre. Casa Grande, Arizona, 1996-2004.
Eleanor Bernard. Tucson, Arizona, March 1997, November 1999, April 2000.
Bruce and Karen Buchanan. Arivaca, November 2000-2001.
Delores Cannon. Tucson, April 1999.
Caco Elias. Interview with author, Arivaca, October 1999.
Mary Kasulaitis. Librarian/historian. Undated interviews with author 1997-2004.
Peggy Smith. Undated phone conversations 1998-2002, Kansas City.

Letters

William McPherson, St. Louis, Missouri, to Joab Bernard, Washington, DC,
February 4, 1844.
　　　　Photocopy in author's files.
Arabella Bier Bernard, Westport, Missouri, to husband Joab Bernard, Las Ve-
gas, New Mexico, October
　　　25, 1864. Photocopy in author's files.
　　　　　　　　to Mary Aguirre, Las Vegas, New Mexico, October 26, 1864.
　　　　Photocopy in author's files.
Annie (Bernard) Rice, Westport, Missouri, to husband Phidelah Rice, La Veta,
Colorado, July 27, 1871.
　　　　Photocopy in author's file.
　　　　　　　　to husband Phidelah Rice, Canon City, Colorado, July 30, 1871.
　　　　Photocopy in author's files.
Phidehlah Rice, Canon City, Colorado, to Annie (Nan Bernard) Rice, Westport,
Missouri, July 1871.
　　　　Photocopy in author's files.
Pedro Aguirre, Buenos Aires Ranch, Arizona, to mother Mary Aguirre, Tucson,
Arizona, September 11,
　　　1886. Photocopy in author's files.
Mary Bier Aguirre, Tucson, Arizona, to son Pedro Aguirre, Nogales, Arizona,
May 5, 1902.
　　　　Photocopy in author's files.
Senator Stephen Elkins, West Virginia, to Mary Bier Aguirre, Tucson, Arizona,
July 3, 1903.
　　　　Photocopy in author's files.
Pedro Joab Aguirre, Cerro Prieto, Mexico, to Miss Hattie Aguirre, Tucson, Ari-
zona, April 5, 1906.
　　　　Photocopy in author's files.
Mary Aguirre, San Jose, California to daughter-in-law, Lucy Aguirre, Tucson,
May 20, 1906.
　　　　Photocopy in author's file.

Newspapers

Arizona Citizen (Tucson).
Arivaca Connections (Arivaca, Arizona).
Arizona Daily Star (variation, Weekly Star) (Tucson).
Arizona Miner (variations, Prescott Miner, Weekly Arizona Miner) (Prescott).
Arizona Republican, (Phoenix).
Border Star (Westport, Missouri).
Kansas City Times (Missouri).
New Mexican (Las Cruces, New Mexico).
*Tombstone Epitaph (*Tombstone, Arizona).
Tombstone Nugget (Tombstone, Arizona).
Weekly Arizonian and Weekly Arizonan (Tucson).

Manuscripts, journals and archival material

Aguirre, Mary Bier: Unpublished journals, photo album and scrapbook. Photocopies in author's collection.

Aguirre, Yginio, taped interviews, copies in author's collection, 1997.

Church of the Latter-day Saints, Family History Library Catalog, March 1997, microfilm records of the San Albino Church, Mesilla, New Mexico: #0016827-Baptisms, 1852-1912; #0016829 Marriages 1852-1956; Deaths 1852-1956

Daab, Frederick, Daab files, letters and manuscripts: copies at WHMC - Kansas City, Missouri.

Johnson, M. W., *History of the Arivaca Ranch* 1701-1856. Arizona History, B. Fireman, May 12, 1974

Pima County, Arizona Territory, Probate Court. dated July 21, 1891, *Estate of Epifanio Aguirre*, deceased, January 16, 1870.

_____ . Probate Court. filed February 25, 1907, *Estate of Pedro Aguirre* deceased, Feb. 21, 1907.

_____ . Probate Court. filed March 30, 1907, *Estate of N. W. Bernard* deceased March 23, 1907.

Pima County, Arizona. *Mining Claims* "Aribaca," Bernard, Rice and Wood May 10, 1879.

_____ . Court of Private Land Claims, Feb. 1900, Tucson, Arizona Aribaca Land and Cattle Company plaintiff versa United States et. al. Defendants.

Rice, M. M. *Bob Leatherwood Reminiscences*, copy in Arizona Historical Society, Library/Archives.

University of Arizona Library: Map, Territory of Arizona, General Land Office 1881, 1897.

U. S. Government Federal Census 1860, Dona Anna County, New Mexico.

_____ . 1880, Pima County, Arizona.

U. S. Government Federal Historic American Building Survey Arivaca Ranch, Photo file. Dec. 1937.

_____ . Dept. of Agriculture Forest Service. Ora Blanco, Aug. 10. 1908. Heirs of N. W. Bernard

Books and Articles—primary sources

Aguirre, Yginio F., *Echoes of The Conquistadores.* Casa Grande: privately
    printed, 1994.
_____. "The Last of the Dons." *Journal of Arizona History*, vol. 10
    (winter 1969) pp. 239-55.
_____. *Memories of Rancheros & Vaqueros of the Southwest.* Casa
    Grande: privately printed, 2000.
Barnes, Will C. *Arizona Place Names.* 2nd ed. Tucson: The University of Ari-
    zona Press, 1988.
Bolton, Herbert Eugene. *The Padre on Horseback.* Chicago: Loyola University
    Press, 1986.
Boyer, Glenn G. *I Married Wyatt Earp.* Tucson: The University of Arizona
    Press, 1998.
Brownell, Elizabeth R. *They Lived In Tubac.* Tucson: Westernlore Press, 1986.
Cady, John H. *Arizona Yesterday.* Tucson: Adobe Corral, Westerners Interna-
    tional, 1995.
Caldwell, Martha B. *Annals of Shawnee Methodist Mission and Indian Manual
    Labor School.* 2nd ed. Topeka, Kansas: The Kansas State Historical
    Society, 1977.
Christopher, Adrienne. "The Life of Stephen Elkins." *Westport Historic Quar-
    terly.* undated copy in Westport Historical Archives, Kansas City.
    p. 30.
Coyer, Vincent. *Peace With The Apaches of New Mexico and Arizona.* Tucson:
    Territorial Press, 1964. Washington, DC: Washington Government
    Printing Office, (first edition 1872.)
Coolidge, Dane. *California Cowboys.* Tucson: The University of Arizona Press,
    1985.
Cordley, Richard. *A History of Lawrence.* Lawrence, Kansas: E. F. Caldwell,
    1895.
Crowe, Rosalie and Tod, Diane. *Arizona Women's Hall of Fame.* Phoenix: The
    Phoenix Gazette, 1985, pp. 12-14.
Croy, Homer. *Cole Younger, Last of the Great Outlaws.* Nebraska: University of
    Nebraska Press, 1999.
_____. *Jesse James Was My Neighbor.* Lincoln: University of Nebraska
    Press, 1997.
Giese, Dr. Dale. *Forts Of New Mexico.* Giese.
Goff, William A. *Old Westport.* Kansas City, Mo: Westport Historical Society,
    1977.
Grant, Ulysses S. "The Civil War." *The National Geographic Magazine*, vol.
    119 (April 1961) pp. 437-491.
Harris, Linda. *Las Cruces and Illustrated History.* Las Cruces, New Mexico:
    Arroyo Press, 1993.
Kasulaitis, Mary. "Arivaca Ranch." *The Connection.* Arivaca, Arizona (January-
    April 1999)
_____. "The Village of Arivaca, A Short History" *The Smoke Signal*, vol.
    75 (Fall 2002) pp. 1-124.

La Tourrette, Genevieve. "Fort Union Memories." *New Mexico.* Las Cruces: National Park Service.

Martin, Douglas D. *An Arizona Chronology 1846—1912.* Tucson: The University of Arizona Press, 1963.

Moore, Kathleen Jones. *An Everlasting Possession.* Kansas City: Moore, 1965.

_____. "The Odyssey of James Hamilton." *The Westport Historic Quarterly* vol. 5 (December 1969) pp. 3-35.

_____. "Westport Building Recalls Merchants Who Served the Westbound Pioneers," *Kansas City Star* (Oct 10, 1959)

Mulligan, R. A. , "Apache Pass and Old Fort Bowie," *Smoke Signal*, #11(1979)

Murbarger, Nell. *Ghosts of the Adobe Walls.* Tucson: Treasure Chest Publications, Inc., 1964.

Noble, David Grant. *Pecos Ruins.* Santa Fe, New Mexico: Ancient City Press, undated.

Noble, David Grant. *Santa Fe, History of an Ancient City.* Santa Fe: School of American Research Press, undated.

Noon, Fred, "Arivaca, Arizona," *Arizona Cattlelog.*

_____. "Arivaca Valley History," *Arivaca Visitors' Guide.* Copy at Arivaca Museum, Arizona.

Ready, Alma. *Open Range and Hidden Silver, Arizona's Santa Cruz County.* Nogales, Arizona: ALTO Press, 1973, p. 22-25.

Roberta, Virginia Culin. *With Their Own Blood, a Saga of Southern Pioneers.* Texas: Texas Christian University Press, 1992.

Russell, Mrs. Hal. *Land of Enchantment*, Memoirs *of Marian Russell Along the Santa Fe Trail.* Preface writer Marc Simmons. Albuquerque: University Press 1981.

Simmons, Marc: *The Old Trail To Santa Fe.* Albuquerque: University of New Mexico Press, 1996.

_____. *Following The Santa Fe Trail.* Santa Fe: Ancient City Press, 1986.

_____. *Ranchers, Ramblers and Renegades.* Santa Fe: Ancient City Press, 1984.

Sonnichsen, C.L. *Tucson—The Life and Times of an American City.* Norman: University of Oklahoma Press, 1982.

Theobald, John and Lillian. *Arizona Territory Post Offices & Postmasters.* Phoenix: Arizona Historical Foundation, 1961.

Utley, Robert M. *A Clash of Cultures.* Washington, D.C.: National Park Service, 1977.

Varney, Phillip. *Arizona Ghost Towns and Mining Camps.* 3rd ed. Phoenix: Arizona Highways, 1995.

Walker, Henry. "Wagon Freighting In Arizona" *The Smoke Signal* vol. 28 (Fall 1973) pp. 1-104.

Whitney, Carrie Westlake. *History of Kansas City, Missouri 1808—1908*, vol. I, Chicago: The S. J. Clarke Publishing Company, 1908.

Suggested Reading and Resources

Aguirre-Bernard files copies in Tucson: Arizona Pioneers Historical Society Archives/Library.

Brown, Dee. *The Gentle Tamers*. Lincoln: University of Nebraska Press, 1981.

Barnes, Will C. *Gunfight In Apache County, 1887*, edited by Neil B. Carmony, Tucson: Trails of Yesterday Books , 1997.

Banks, Leo W. *Stalwart Women*. Phoenix: Arizona Highways, 1999.

Dutton & Bunting. *Arizona Then And Now*, Phoenix: Ag2 Press, 1981.

Gardner, Mark L. *The Mexican Road, Trade, Travel and Confrontation on the Santa Fe Trail*. Manhattan, Kansas: Sunflower Press, 1999.

Hand, George O. *Next Stop: Tombstone, George Hand's Contention City Diary, 1882*. Tucson: Trails to Yesterday Books, 1995.

_____ . *Whiskey, Six Guns & Red-light Ladies* George O Hand's Saloon Diary. Silver City, New Mexico: High Lonesome Books, 1994.

_____ .Civil War In Apache Land Hand, Sergeant George Hand's Diary, Silver City, New Mexico: High Lonesome Books, 1996.

James, Harold L. *The Santa Fe Trail*. James, 1989.

Kansas City, MO. *A History of Kansas City, Missouri*. http://www.kcmo.nsf/web/history?opendocument

Macoffin, Susan. *Down the Santa Fe Trail and Into Mexico—The Diary of Susan Shelby Macoffin, 1846-1847*. Lincoln, Nebraska: University of Nebraska Press, 1982.

McGraw, William C.: Southwest Saga—the way it really was!: Golden West Publishers, Phoenix, Arizona.

Macpherson, M. A. and MacLaren, Eli. Outlaws and Lawmen of the West. Edmonton, Alberta: Lone Pine Publishing, 2000.

Murphy, Dan. *Santa Fe Trail, Voyage of Discovery, The Story Behind The Scenery*. Las Vegas, Nevada: KC Publications, Inc., 1994.

Noble, David Grant. *History of an Ancient City—Santa Fe*, New Mexico. Santa Fe: School of American Research Press, 1989.

_____ . Pecos Ruins—Geology, Archaeology, History and Prehistory. Santa Fe: Ancient City Press.

O'Brien, Mary Barmeyer. *Heart of The Trail, The Stories of Eight Wagon Train Women* Helena, Montana: Falcon® Publishing Co., Inc., 1997.

Scadron, Arlene. *On Their Own, Widows and Widowhood in the American Southwest 1848-1939.* Chicago: University of Illinois Press, 1988.

Simmons, Marc. "Pecos Pueblo On the Santa Fe Trail." *Pecos Ruins,* undated.

Stephenson, Patricia and Kimmelman, Alex J. *Tom Marshall's Tucson*. Tucson: Print Expressions, Inc. 1996.

Trimble, Marshall. *Arizona Cavalcade of History*. Tucson: Treasure Chest Publications, 1990.

Trimble, Marshall. *In Old Arizona.* Phoenix: Golden West Publishers, 1993.

White, William W. *The Santa Fe Trail by Air*. Logan, Utah: Western Airtrails, 1996.

Index